Implementing and Administering Microsoft Windows 2000 Directory Services

Implementing and Administering Microsoft Windows 2000 Directory Services

iUniverse.com, Inc.

San Jose   New York   Lincoln   Shanghai

Implementing and Administering Microsoft Windows 2000 Directory Services

Published by iUniverse.com, Inc.

For information address:
iUniverse.com, Inc.
5220 S 16th, Ste. 200
Lincoln, NE 68512
www.iuniverse.com

Cover Creation by Shay Jones

Graphic Production by Matt Bromley, Associate Consultant
Domhnall CGN Adams, Corporation Sole - http://www.dcgna.com
5721-10405 Jasper Avenue
Edmonton, Alberta Canada T5J 3S2
(780) 416-2967 - dcgna@yahoo.com

ISBN: 0-595-14820-4

Printed in the United States of America

Acknowledgments

We are pleased to acknowledge the following people for their important contributions in the creation of this study guide.

Technical Writer—Barb Kowalik

Editors—Grace Clark and Nina Gettler

Indexer—Loral Pritchett

Proofreaders—Kerry Holland and Steve Reed

Cover Creation, Text Conversion and Proofing—Shay Jones, AA, MCSE, MCP

Technical Reviewer—Jay Graham, MCSE+I

Graphic Designer—Matt Bromley

V.P., Publishing and Courseware Development— Candace Sinclair

Course Prerequisites

The Implementing and Administering Microsoft Windows 2000 Directory Services study guide targets individuals with the knowledge and skills necessary to install, configure, and administer Microsoft Windows 2000 Active Directory directory services. In addition, you must understand how to implement group policy to centrally manage users and computers.

Prerequisites include the completion of the following courses:

- Microsoft Windows 2000 Network and Operating System Essentials

- Implementing Microsoft Windows 2000 P{professional and Server

- Implementing a Microsoft Windows 2000 Network Infrastructure

In addition, you should have a thorough understanding of DNS, which includes hands-on experience configuring DNS and setting up forward and reverse lookup zones.

Furthermore, we recommend that you have a working knowledge of the English language so that you can understand the technical words and concepts presented in this study guide.

To feel confident about using this study guide, you should have the following knowledge or ability:

- The desire and drive to become a certified MCSE through our instructions, terminology, activities, quizzes, and study guide content

- Basic computer skills, which include using a mouse, keyboard, and viewing a monitor

- Basic networking knowledge including the fundamentals of working with Internet browsers, e-mail functionality, and search engines

- IP, remote connectivity and security

Hardware and Software Requirements

To apply the knowledge presented in this study guide, you will need the following minimum hardware:

- For Windows 2000 Professional, we recommend 64 megabytes of RAM (32 megabytes as a minimum) and a 1-gigabyte (GB) hard disk space.

- For Windows 2000 Server, we recommend a Pentium II or better processor, 128 megabytes of RAM (64 megabytes minimum), and a 2-GB hard drive. If you want to install Remote Installation Server with Windows 2000 Server, you should have at least two additional gigabytes of hard disk space available.

- CD-ROM drive

- Mouse

- VGA monitor and graphics card

- Internet connectivity

To apply the knowledge presented in this study guide, you will need the following minimum software installed on your computer:

- Microsoft Windows 2000 Advanced Server

- Microsoft Windows 2000 Professional

Symbols Used in This Study Guide

To call your attention to various facts within our study guide content, we've included the following three symbols to help you prepare for the Implementing and Administering Microsoft Windows 2000 Directory Services.

 Tip: The Tip identifies important information that you might see referenced in the certification exam.

 Note: The Note enhances your understanding of the topic content.

 Warning: The Warning describes circumstances that could be harmful to you and your computer system or network.

How to Use This Study Guide

Although you will develop and implement your own personal style of studying and preparing for the MCSE exam, we've taken the strategy of presenting the exam information in an easy-to-follow, ten-lesson format. Each lesson conforms to Microsoft's model for exam content preparation.

At the beginning of each lesson, we summarize the information that will be covered. At the end of each lesson we round out your studying experience by providing the following four ways to test and challenge what you've learned.

Vocabulary—Helps you review all the important terms discussed in the lesson.

In Brief—Reinforces your knowledge by presenting you with a problem and a possible solution.

Activities—Further tests what you have learned in the lesson by presenting ten activities that often require you to do more reading or research to understand the activity. In addition, we have provided the answers to each activity.

Lesson Quiz—To round out the knowledge you will gain after completing each lesson in this study guide, we have included ten sample exam questions and answers. This allows you to test your knowledge, and it gives you the reasons why the "answers" were either correct or incorrect. This, in itself, enhances your power to pass the exam.

You can also refer to the Glossary at the back of the book to review terminology. Furthermore, you can view the Index to find more content for individual terms and concepts.

Introduction to MCSE Certification

The Microsoft Certified Systems Engineer (MCSE) credential is the highest-ranked certification for professionals who analyze business requirements for system architecture, design solutions, deployment, installation, and configuration of architecture components, as well as troubleshooting system problems.

When you receive your MCSE certification, it proves your competence by having earned a nationally-recognized credential as an information technology professional who works in a typically complex computing environment of medium to large organizations. It is recommended that a Windows 2000 MCSE candidate should have at least one year of experience implementing and administering a network operating system environment.

The MCSE exams cover a vast range of vendor-independent hardware and software technologies, as well as basic Internet and Windows 2000 design knowledge, technical skills and best practice scenarios.

To help you bridge the gap between needing the knowledge and knowing the facts, this study guide presents Implementing and Administering Microsoft Windows 2000 Directory Services knowledge that will help you pass this exam.

 Note: This study guide presents technical content that should enable you to pass Implementing and Administering Microsoft Windows 2000 Directory Services certification exam on the first try.

Audience Profile

This exam is targeted at the MCSE professional who will work in medium to very large computing environments which use the Windows 2000 network operating system.

It is suggested that each student has a minimum of one year's experience implementing and administering network operating systems in environments with the following requirements:

- Support for 200 to 26,000 users

- Physical network locations range from 5 to over 150

- Network services and applications include file and print sharing, database, messaging, proxy server or firewall, dial-in server, desktop management, and Web hosting

- Connectivity for individual offices and users at remote locations to the corporate network and the Internet

Skills Measurements

The Implementing and Administering Microsoft Windows 2000 Directory Services Infrastructure study guide prepares you for the certification exam, which measures the following skills:

- Installing, configuring and troubleshooting the Windows 2000 Active Directory components

- DNS for Active Directory

- Active Directory security solutions

- Managing, monitoring and optimizing the desktop environment by using Group Policy

Figures

Tables

Table of Contents

Lesson 4: User Account and Group Resource Implementation . . 155

Lesson 5: Administrative Control of Active Directory Objects . . 226

Logical and Physical Structure of Active Directory

Directory services are used to identify users and resources on a network. Active Directory is the Windows 2000 version of directory services. You use it as a management tool for the organization of network objects, such as users, printers, and computers. Simply described, Active Directory is a database of all your network objects, and it lets you locate these objects with very precise queries.

Active Directory represents both a physical and a logical structure. The physical structure takes in your network's configuration, devices, and bandwidth. The logical structure is intangible—it equates your business processes to the Active Directory configuration. Its logical resources are structured according to how the people in the organization work.

Once you have organized and defined the components in Active Directory, the physical structure of the network will disappear for your users. For example, if Jill Hill wants to print to the color printer down the hall instead of to the laser printer in the next room, she no longer has to know which domain the server resides in or which server hosts the printer. She simply pulls up a list of available printers and chooses the one she wants.

After completing this lesson, you should have a better understanding of the following topics:

- Active Directory Overview

- Logical Components of Active Directory

- Physical Components of Active Directory

Active Directory Overview

By using Active Directory you can design a directory structure that matches the needs of your organization. Besides using Active Directory as an administrative service, administrators and users can use the directory service as a source of information. Table 1.1 describes the Active Directory directory service features.

Table 1.1 Service Features

Feature	Description
Data stores	Active Directory is also known as the directory that stores information about objects.
Schema	A set of rules that defines the classes of objects and attributes in the directory, the constraints and limits on instances of these objects, and the format of their names.
Global Catalog	It contains information about every object in the directory, allowing users and administrators to find directory information, no matter which domain in the directory contains the data.
Query and index mechanism	Objects and their properties can be published and found by network users or applications.
Replication service	It distributes directory data across a network. Any change to directory data is replicated to all domain controllers in the domain.
Integration with the security subsystem	It provides a secure logon to the network and access control on both directory data queries and data modifications.

In the best structures, Active Directory resources are ordered according to the way the employees work and not to simplify the construction of networks. You must first design the logical structure of your Active Directory and match its structure to how employees interact with the organization. This logical, top-down design, which moves from the smallest to the largest units, is a hierarchical structure (Figure 1.1).

Figure 1.1 Hierarchical Structure Diagram

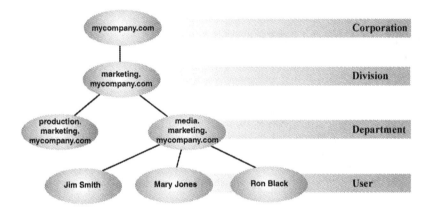

Tip: To gain the full benefits of Active Directory, the computer accessing the Active Directory over the network must be running the correct client software. To computers not running Active Directory client software, the directory will appear just like a Microsoft Windows NT 4.0 directory.

Logical Components of Active Directory

In Active Directory, you can organize the network resources into a configuration that reflects the logical structure in your organization. Pulling together these resources lets users find resources by their names, instead of by their actual position. Since you group resources logically, Active Directory makes the network's physical structure transparent to the user. Figure 1.2 illustrates the relationship of the Active Directory components.

Figure 1.2 Resources in a Hierarchical Structure

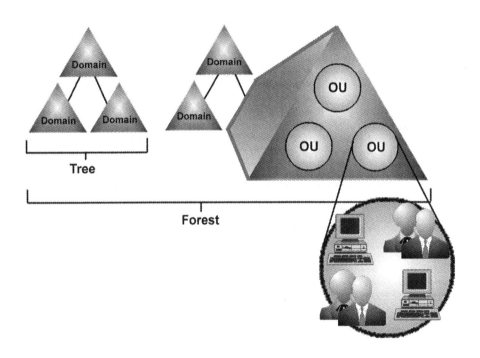

Organizing Logical Structure Objects

The components that comprise networks built with Active Directory include the following:

- Objects

- Organizational Units (OUs)

- Domains

- Trees

- Forests

Active Directory Objects

The basic building block of the Active Directory directory service is the object. Active Directory stores information about network resources and the services that make information accessible by using objects. An object is an element—a distinct, named set of attributes representing something concrete, such as a user, a printer, or an application. The attributes hold information describing the thing that the directory object identifies. Attributes of a user could include the user's given name, surname, and e-mail address (Figure 1.3).

Figure 1.3 Active Directory Objects and Attributes

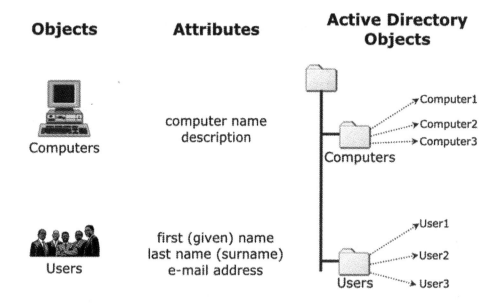

To define these objects in the logical structure of Active Directory, you should understand the following characteristics of objects:

Object Classes—These define the types of objects that can be created in Active Directory. They do not contain data but are a format for creating data.

Object Class Attributes—These define the characteristics of object classes. They have structure in an object class but not value. For example, an employee class could consist of the following attributes:

• Employee identity number

• Department

• First name

- Last name

- Phone number

Instances of Objects—These take the template and put the values into the attributes. For example, our employee, Jill Hill has the following values:

- 65432   (Employee identity number)

- Communications   (Department)

- Jill   (First name)

- Hill   (Last name)

- (555) 555-1234   (Phone number)

You create objects by right-clicking on a container object in the Active Directory and choosing New from the pop-up menu. From the New menu, you select the type of object you want to create. You can see the choices available in Figure 1.4. A wizard guides you through the creation of the object type you select.

Figure 1.4 New Object Creation

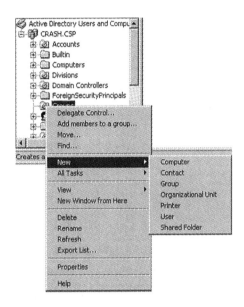

In Active Directory, you can create the types of objects listed in Table 1.2.

Table 1.2 Object Types

Object	Description
Computer	An object that represents a computer on the network.
Contact	An object that is an account without any security permissions. You cannot log on to the network as a contact. Typically, you use contacts to represent external users for e-mail.
Group	A container object that can hold users, computers, and other groups. You can use groups to simplify the management of a large number of objects.
Organizational Unit	A container object you use to logically organize other containers and objects, such as users, groups, and computers. These are used in a similar manner as you use folders to organize files on your hard drive.
Printer	An object that signifies a shared printer on your network.
User	An object that is a security principal. Your users can log on to the network with these credentials. You can assign access permissions based on this object.
Shared Folder	An object that represents a shared folder on your network.

Organizational Units

In Windows 2000, an Organizational Unit (OU) is the smallest division inside a domain. It is a logical container used to store similar objects so that they are in a convenient location for access and administration. You can store the following objects in an OU:

- Printers

- Shared files

- Users

- Groups

- Applications

When you create a domain, Active Directory automatically creates some standard OUs. When you open the administrative tool Active Directory Users and Computers, you will see the OUs that are created by default (Figure 1.5). You can identify OUs since they are those folders that have a book icon under the folder. Plain folders are specialized containers.

Figure 1.5 Active Directory Users and Computers

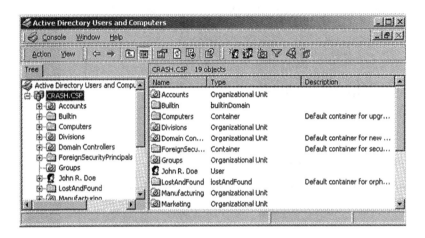

You create OUs to further define the domain namespace. By doing this, you can arrange users, groups, files, and other information into a usable hierarchy. Additionally, you can delegate administration by assigning permissions for the OUs to other users within your company.

An OU model needs to reflect the administrative model of an organization. You can organize and nest OUs to create a logical structure that maps to the way you work and organize your business (Figure 1.6).

Figure 1.6 Organizational Structure and Network Administrative Model

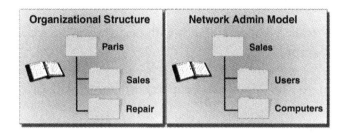

When you organize user accounts and resources into hierarchical OUs, you can create a much clearer representation of the actual business structure in the domain. With the delegation features of Active Directory, users and user groups can perform very specific administrative tasks, such as resetting passwords or clearing print queues. The OU hierarchy inside a domain is independent of the structure of other domains.

You can create OUs for any of the following reasons:

• To assign administrative rights that are limited to a specific OU and the objects it contains

• To simplify Group Policy

• To create a logical and significant organization for administrators

Major benefits are gained through configured OUs when you delegate administrative tasks in domains. This can be illustrated in the following example. The mycompany.com domain in Figure 1.7 has three OUs: ACCTG, MKTG, and SALES. Users are added to the SALES OU each November for the Christmas season. Each new user needs to access the company's sales material and permission to use the shared printers. The manager, Jill Hill, will create the users and provide them with the access they require. Management wants you to set up security to stop Jill Hill from managing any resources in the ACCTG and MKTG OUs. In Microsoft Windows NT 4.0 networks, you would need to create a number of domains to provide this level of administrative authority.

This can be done easily using Windows 2000. To give Jill Hill the authority she requires, follow these steps:

1. Assign Jill Hill the Create User Objects permission in the SALES OU.

2. Create a new group in the SALES OU (called SALESUSERS) with permissions to access the sales material and to use the shared printers.

3. Grant Jill Hill the Write permission to the Members property of the new SALE-SUSERS group.

Figure 1.7 Define Security with Organizational Units

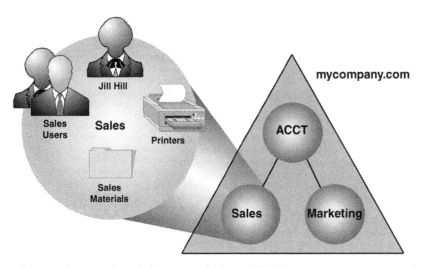

After you have assigned these permissions, Jill Hill can create new users in the SALES OU and add them to the SALESUSERS group. Since you have assigned her a limited set of permissions, these will be the full extent of her capabilities in the domain. She will not be able to perform administration tasks in the ACCTG or MKTG OUs, and if she tries, she is denied.

When you set permissions on an OU, you can specify to which objects they apply:

• To this object only

• To this object and all sub-objects

- To objects and/or containers within this container only

- To sub-objects only

Domains

The term domain has a different meaning in Windows 2000 than it had in Microsoft Windows NT 4.0. In Windows 2000, a domain is a group of resources that shares common security and administrative boundaries. The geographic location of resources does not have primary importance. In Microsoft Windows NT 4.0, domains usually consist of either resources that are grouped geographically or user accounts that are not necessarily grouped geographically.

Following are several distinct characteristics of a Windows 2000 domain:

Domain controller—A Windows 2000 domain has at least one domain controller.

Database replication—A domain's directory database replicates between all domain controllers in the domain.

Tree—A tree is a hierarchy of Windows 2000 domains, each representing a partition in Active Directory.

Triangle in database design—In the design process for the logical structure of an Active Directory database, you use a triangle in the design flowchart to represent a domain (Figure 1.8).

Figure 1.8 Domain Represented as a Triangle

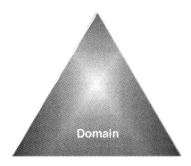

Following are some of the similarities between a Windows 2000 domain and a Microsoft Windows NT 4.0 domain:

Domains organize your network—Instead of having all of users, groups, computers, etc. in one large store, domains allow you to make logical divisions for your network. You use domains to separate a network based on geographic regions or by departments.

Domains are security boundaries—This means that while an administrator in one domain may have full control over that domain, he does not have the ability to administer other domains. This can be especially important in large distributed networks with decentralized administration. In addition, you define certain security policies, such as password policies, at the domain level. If your network requires different password guidelines for different users, your only option would be to implement several domains.

Windows 2000 domains are partitions of the database. Unless you have a single-domain network, Active Directory is not a single database. It is a database that is split up between the various domains in your network. Each domain controller contains all of the information for objects only in its domain. Changes made to the objects will only be replicated to domain controllers within a domain. For example, if mycompany has 6 domains with 4 million objects each, there is a total of 24 million objects, but each domain controller will only store and be accountable for the 4 million objects within its own domain.

Domains that are built with Active Directory can store millions of objects. The types of objects that can be stored in Active Directory domains are those considered interesting to the networked community, such as a user, a group, a printer, and so on (Figure 1.9).

Figure 1.9 Windows 2000 Domain Example

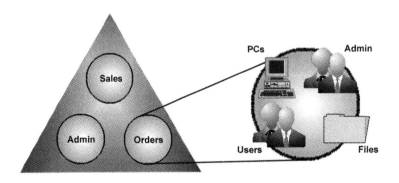

You may need more than one Windows 2000 domain under the following conditions:

- To support decentralized administration

- To limit domain replication traffic

- To balance domain replication traffic

- To support multiple domain policies

- To address international differences

- To comply with internal political pressures

Trees

Just like OUs, you use trees to further define the Active Directory namespace. A tree is a hierarchy of Windows 2000 domains, each representing a partition in Active Directory (Figure 1.10). The first Windows 2000 domain you create forms the root of your organization's tree. Each domain you create after it becomes its child. Those children in turn, may have child domains of their own, creating a parent-child relationship. One advantage of this parent-child relationship is that child domains inherit some of the attributes of their parent. For example, when a new domain joins the tree, it is automatically configured with its parents' common configuration, Global Catalog, and Schema.

Figure 1.10 Tree Structure

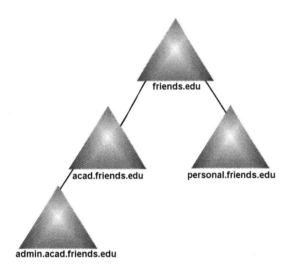

A simple tree is shown in Figure 1.11. The tree forms a contiguous namespace. Using Domain Name System (DNS) standards by appending the name of the parent domain to the relative name of the child domain. For example, the child domain of mycompany.com in Figure 1.11 is retail.sales.mycompany.com.

Figure 1.11 Tree Example

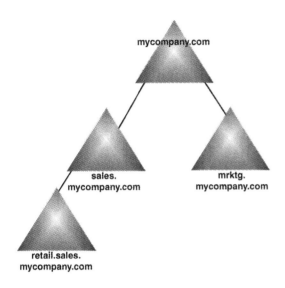

DNS is an Internet standard that easily converts readable host names to numeric IP addresses. This enables identification and connection to processes running on computers on Transmission Control Protocol/Internet Protocol (TCP/IP) networks.

Domain names for DNS are based on the DNS hierarchical naming structure, which is an inverted tree structure: a single root domain. The Active Directory domain namespace in Windows 2000 mirrors the DNS namespace.

Each computer in a DNS domain is uniquely identified by its DNS Fully Qualified Domain Name (FQDN). Active Directory is integrated with DNS in the following ways:

Hierarchical structure—Active Directory and DNS have the same hierarchical structure. Although separate and implemented differently for different purposes, an organization's namespace for DNS and Active Directory have an identical structure. DNS zones can be stored in Active Directory.

Domain controllers—Active Directory clients use DNS to locate domain controllers. To locate a domain controller for a specified domain, Active Directory clients query their configured DNS server for specific resource records.

Forests

When you have more than one tree in a network, you have formed a forest. A forest is a collection of two or more trees, each having its own distinct namespace. A transitive trust relationship is established between the root domains in each tree when you create a forest. Because this trust is transitive, every domain in the forest can share its resources with every other domain. In Figure 1.12, mycompany.com and YourCompany.com form a forest. The namespace is contiguous only within each tree.

Figure 1.12 Forest Structure

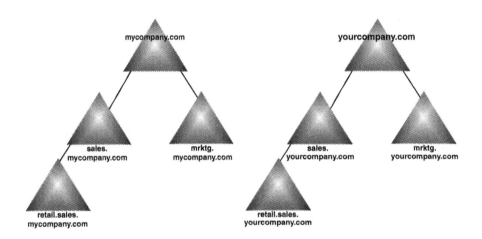

Each tree in a forest has the following characteristics:

- All trees in a forest have a common schema

- Trees in a forest have different naming structures, according to their domains

- All the domains in the forest share the same Global Catalog

- Domains in a forest operate independently, but implicit two-way transitive trusts exist between domains and domain trees enable communication across the whole organization

Note: A contiguous namespace is formed only in each tree.

Comparing Trees and Forests

Some companies only need a single tree to support their enterprises, while others need a forest of trees. Trees and forests both form a structure where every domain shares the same configuration, Global Catalog, and Schema. When one of your domains is joined to this hierarchy, it establishes a two-way transitive Kerberos trust relationship with its immediate parent. Therefore, all domains forming a tree or forest can share their resources globally.

There are more differences than similarities between trees and forests. Therefore, to decide if you should organize your company's Windows 2000 domains into a tree or forest, you should consider the differences listed in Table 1.3.

Table 1.3 Distinctions between Trees and Forests

Trees	Forests
Form a single contiguous namespace	Made of several different namespaces
Useful for companies that operate as a single entity	Useful for companies that operate as separate entities or joint partnerships.
Simpler for administrators and users to navigate and understand.	More difficult for users and administrators to navigate and understand.
Lightweight Directory Access Protocol (LDAP) searches in a tree can always be resolved by LDAP referrals	LDAP searches in a forest will not always be resolved. Forest searches are limited to replicated attributes in the Global Catalog and objects in the tree from which a search is initiated.

Physical Components of Active Directory

You use the physical components to build a directory structure that matches the physical structure of your organization. When determining the structure, you will need to review both the functional and geographic divisions within your organization to determine the best network design for your organization (Figure 1.13).

Figure 1.13 Functional and Geographic Divisions

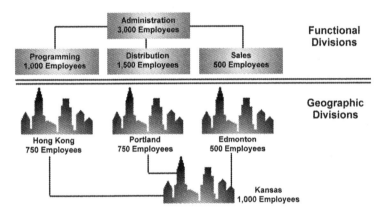

The physical components of Active Directory are:

• Sites

• Domain controllers

Understanding Sites

A site is a combination of one or more Internet Protocol (IP) subnets connected by a link to concentrate network traffic. The typical site often has the same boundaries as a Local Area Network (LAN) as shown in Figure 1.14. Sites are part of your physical network topology, and each site can contain domain controllers from one or more domains.

Figure 1.14 Planning Sites

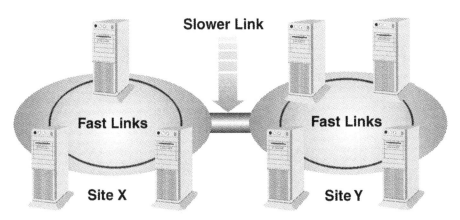

During the planning stage for Active Directory, you define the site topology for your organization. When you group subnets on your network, you should combine only those subnets that have fast, cheap, and reliable network connections with one another. At this time, fast network connections are at least 512 kilobits (Kbps) per second. Usually, a bandwidth of 128 Kbps and higher is sufficient, depending on the network's available bandwidth.

 Warning: Do not confuse sites with namespace. Sites are not part of the namespace!

Active Directory is primarily a collection of namespaces. A namespace is a logical container to which an object can be resolved. When you browse the logical namespace, you see computers and users grouped into domains and OUs, not sites. Table 1.4 shows you how to distinguish between a namespace and a site.

Table 1.4 Namespace and Sites Comparison

Namespace	Sites
Computers	Computer objects
Domains	Container objects
OUs	Container objects used to organize objects into logical administrative groups

Sites may span multiple domains. Likewise, domains may span multiple sites. Sites are used to control replication. Figure 1.15 graphically shows how site topology works.

Figure 1.15 Site Topology

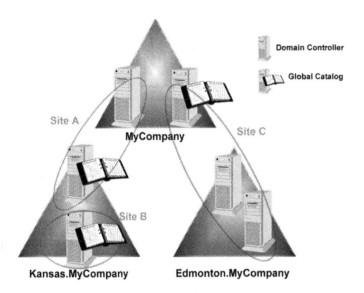

The following describes how the site domains in Figure 1.15 relate to one another:

- Site A contains a domain controller from the root domain mycompany and a domain controller from the child domain edmonton.mycompany

- Site B contains a domain controller only from kansas.mycompany

- Site C contains domain controllers from edmonton.mycompany and the root mycompany

Sites serve the following three main purposes:

- Sites are used to locate services (such as logon and Distributed File System (DFS) services)

- Sites are also used to control replication throughout a forest; the Active Directory automatically creates more replication connections between domain controllers in the same site than between domain controllers in different sites.

- Replication between domain controllers in different sites is compressed by 10-15%, resulting in less network bandwidth utilization over the slower links between sites

 Tip: Domains are logical structures and sites are physical structures.

Domain Controllers

Domain controllers are the Windows 2000 servers that have been configured to provide Active Directory services to network users and computers. Domain controllers manage and store domain-wide information. They also manage user-to-domain interactions, including user logon, authentication to the directory, and searches through the directory. A domain can contain one or more domain controllers, and each domain controller in a domain has a complete replica of the domain's portion of the directory. This replication provides the robust fault tolerance that is characteristic of this environment.

 Tip: A single domain can span multiple sites located in different geographical areas, and a single site can include user accounts and computers that belong to multiple domains.

Domain controllers perform the following services:

- Store a complete copy of all Active Directory information for the domain

- Manage changes to that information

- Replicate those changes to other domain controllers in the same domain

- Automatically replicate all changes to objects

- Immediately replicate certain important updates, such as the disabling of a user account

- Use multimaster replication, in which no one domain controller is the master domain controller

- Provide fault tolerance because if one domain controller is offline, another domain controller can provide all required functions

- Manage all aspects of users' domain interactions, such as locating Active Directory objects and validating user logon attempts

Managing Active Directory Components

Along with the standard logical and physical components, you also need to understand the Schema and the Global Catalog.

Active Directory Schema

The Schema is a blueprint of all objects in the domain. The Schema contains definitions of all the object classes and attributes that you can store in the directory. Active Directory can manage the Schema objects with the same object management functions it uses for the rest of the objects in Active Directory.

 Tip: All of the objects that can be stored in the directory are defined in the Schema. When first created, a default Schema exists, which contains definitions for users, computers, domains etc. This is why you can only have one Schema per domain, since you cannot have multiple definitions of the same object.

For each object class, the Schema defines what attributes an instance of the class must have, what additional attributes it may have, and what object class can be a parent of the current object base. A Schema consists attributes and classes.

Note: Attributes and classes are also referred to as Schema objects or metadata.

Attributes—These are defined separately from classes. Each attribute is defined only once and can be used in multiple classes. This enforces consistency in naming standards and aids resolution.

Classes—Object classes describe the possible Active Directory objects that can be created. Each class is a collection of attributes.

The Schema is extensible, which means that new object classes and their attributes can be added at any time. Applications then have immediate access to the new classes. For development and testing purposes, you can also view and modify the Active Directory Schema with the Active Directory Schema snap-in, which is included with the Windows 2000 Administration Tools on the Windows 2000 Server compact disc.

 Warning: Be sure to plan and prepare before extending the Schema because it cannot be deleted, only deactivated. It is automatically replicated.

When you install Active Directory, you install a default base Schema. This Schema contains the object-class definitions and attributes of the components in Windows 2000. As you add to your directory, you can extend or modify the Schema by adding or altering classes and attributes in the following ways:

- Create a new object class

- Create a new object attribute

- Modify an object class

- Modify an attribute

- Disable an object class

- Disable an attribute

The default Schema definition is defined in the SCHEMA.INI file that also contains the initial structure for the NTDS.DIT (storage for the Directory data). This file is located in the %systemroot%\ntds directory, and is a plain ASCII format file.

 Note: Before you can use the Active Directory Schema snap-in, it must be installed. From the I386 directory of the Windows 2000 Server CD-ROM, run ADMINPAK.MSI to install this snap-in and several other administrative tools.

The Schema is extensible which means it can be changed but modifying the Schema is a dangerous task as it will affect the entire domain forest (since a forest shares a common Schema). You can modify the schema by starting the Schema Manager through the Resource Kit Tools console or by you can create a custom Microsoft Management Console (MMC) and add the Active Directory Schema snap-in to it.

To modify the schema, follow these steps:

1. From the **Start** menu, choose Run, type **MMC**, and then select OK.

2. From the menu bar, choose **Console**, and then select **Add/Remove Snap-in**.

3. From the Add/Remove Snap-in page, select **Add**.

4. From the list of available snap-ins, select **Active Directory Schema**, select **Add**, and then select **Close**.

5. Select OK to close the Add/Remove Snap-in page.

6. In the Tree (left-hand) pane, right-click **Active Directory Schema**, and then choose **Operations Master**.

Figure 1.16 Change Operations Manager Screen

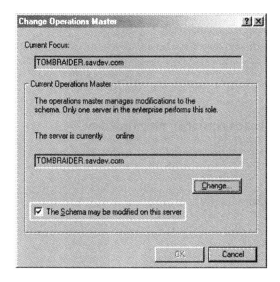

7. The Change Schema Master window displays the current computer holding the domain name space FSMO role (Figure 1.16).

8. Select **The schema may be modified on this server**, and then select OK to save your changes and close the window.

Alternately, to directly edit the registry, follow these steps:

1. Start the **registry editor** (REGEDIT.EXE).

2. Select the registry key: **HKEY_LOCAL_MACHINE\SYSTEM\CurrentControlSet\Services\ NTDS\Parameters**.

3. Double-click **Schema Update Allowed**.

4. Set to **1**.

5. Click **OK** and close the registry editor.

The Global Catalog

The Global Catalog is a searchable index that enables the users to locate objects without having to know their locations. By default, a Global Catalog is created automatically on the initial domain controller in the forest. It contains a replica of all the objects in the directory for its host domain and a partial replica of all objects contained in the directory of every other domain in the forest (Figure 1.17).

Figure 1.17 Global Catalog as a Central Information Repository

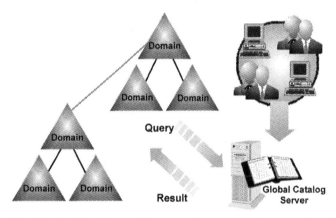

The Global Catalog enables searches among the trees in a forest. Since it stores some, but not all, of the property values for every object in the forest, it only holds those attributes you are most likely to use for a search. The default Schema settings determine which attributes appear in the Global Catalog. To add attributes to the Global Catalog, you have to modify the Schema.

The Global Catalog runs on domain controllers. You manage the service using the MMC. The MMC is a Windows 2000 Server system file.

To access the MMC, follow these steps:

1. From the **Start** menu, choose **Run**, type MMC, and then click **OK** (Figure 1.18).

Figure 1.18 The Run Command

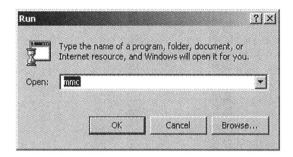

2. From the Menu bar, choose **Console**, and then select **Add/Remove Snap-in**.

3. From the Add/Remove Snap-in page, select **Add**.

4. From the list of available snap-ins, select **Active Directory Sites and Services**, select **Add**, and then select **Close** (Figure 1.19).

Figure 1.19 MMC Display

5.   Click OK to close the Add/Remove Snap-in page.

Vocabulary

Review the following terms in preparation for the certification exam.

Term	Description
Active Directory	The directory service included with Windows 2000 Server. Active Directory stores information about objects on a network and makes this information available to users and network administrators. Active Directory gives network users access to permitted resources anywhere on the network using a single logon process. It provides network administrators with an intuitive hierarchical view of the network and a single point of administration for all network objects.
attribute	A single property of an object. An object is described by the values of its attributes. Attributes of a user might include the user's first and last names and e-mail address. Attributes are also the data items describing the objects represented by the classes defined in the Schema. Attributes are defined in the Schema separately from the classes, allowing a single attribute description to be applied to many classes.
class	In Active Directory, a class is used to organize objects into a logical group. Examples of object classes are those representing user accounts, groups, computers, domains, or OUs.
containers	Objects that can contain other objects. For example, a domain is a container that can contain users, computers, and other objects. Unlike other objects, it does not usually represent something concrete.
domain	In Windows 2000 Active Directory, a collection of computers defined by the administrator of a Windows 2000 Server network that shares a common directory database. A domain has a unique name, security policy, and security relationships with other domains and represents a security boundary for a Windows 2000 Network. On a standalone computer, the domain is the single computer. When multiple domains are connected together, they constitute a domain tree. Multiple domain trees make up a forest.

Term	Description
Domain Controller	In a Windows 2000 Server domain, a computer running Windows 2000 Server that authenticates domain logons and maintains the security policy and the master database for a domain.
extensible	Administrators can add new classes of objects to the Schema and new attributes to existing classes of objects. The Schema contains a definition of each object class and of the attributes of each object class that can be stored in the directory.
DFS	Distributed File System is a file management system where files can be located on numerous computers connected over a local or wide area network, and logically represented from a single share point.
DNS	Domain Name System is a hierarchical distributed database that is employed for name/address translation. DNS is the namespace used on the Internet to translate computer and service names into TCP/IP addresses. Active Directory uses DNS as its location service.
FQDN	The Fully Qualified Domain Name is a DNS name that uniquely identifies the computer on the network. By default, it is a concatenation of the host name, the primary DNS suffix, and a period. For example, an FQDN might be sales.mycompany.com.
LAN	A Local Area Network is a group of computers and other devices connected by a communications link that allows one device to interact with any other on the network over a relatively limited area.
physical components	Active Directory uses the logical and physical components to build a directory structure to match the needs of your organization. The Active Directory physical components are sites and domain controllers.

Term	Description
LDAP	Lightweight Directory Access Protocol version 3 is the primary access protocol for Active Directory. LDAP is defined by a set of Proposed Standard documents in Internet Engineering Task Force (IETF) RFC 2251.
MMC	The Microsoft Management Console is a framework for administrative consoles. A console has one or more windows that can provide views of the console tree and the administrative properties, services, and events that are acted on by the items in the console tree. The main MMC window provides commands and tools for authoring consoles.
TCP/IP	Transmission Control Protocol/Internet Protocol is a set of software networking protocols used on the Internet. It provides communication across interconnected networks of computers with diverse hardware architectures and operating systems. TCP/IP includes standards for how computers communicate and conventions for connecting networks and routing traffic.
OU	Organizational Unit is a container object that is an Active Directory administrative partition. OUs hold users, groups, resources, and other OUs. You can use OUs to delegate administration to distinct subtrees of the directory.
replication	Replication is the exchange of updated database information among domain controllers so that all the domain controllers contain identical database information. There are several different methods of replication. Active Directory uses multimaster replication.
schema	A description of the object classes and attributes stored in Active Directory. For each object class, the Schema defines what attributes an object class must have, what additional attributes it may have, and what object class can be its parent.

Term	Description
trees	A set of domains connected to each other through transitive bi-directional trusts.
site	A location in a network that holds Active Directory servers. A site is defined as one or more well-connected TCP/IP subnets. (Well-connected means that network connectivity is highly reliable and fast.) Defining a site as a set of subnets allows administrators to configure Active Directory access and replication topology to take advantage of the physical network.

In Brief

If you want to...	Then do this...
Start MMC Active Directory Schema snap-in	1. From the **Start** menu, and choose **Run**. 2. Type **MMC**, and then press **Enter**. 3. From the **Console** menu, choose **Add/Remove Snap-in**, select **Add**, then **Close**, and then click **Ok**. 4. From the console tree, right-click **Active Directory Schema** and choose **Operations Master**.
Use the Container Shortcut menu to create a new object	1. Right-click on any **container,** choose **New,** and then select the type of object you wish to create. 2. Follow the steps in the resulting wizard to create the object.
Gain the full benefits of Active Directory	The computer accessing the Active Directory over the network must be running the correct client software.
See the default OUs created by Active Directory	Open the administrative tool Active Directory Users and Computers

Lesson 1 Activities

Complete the following activities to better prepare you for the certification exam.

1. List the reasons why you would create OUs.

2. Your organization will be hiring a number of temporary workers for a short period of time. They will need to be able to use the special promotions materials in the Admin department and the color printers. Your employer has asked that the Junior Admin manager, Jim Smith, be able to create the users and provide them with the access they require. They do not want Jim Smith to have access to any other department's resources. Explain what you would do to set up the scenario.

3. Define the distinct characteristics of a Windows 2000 domain.

4. Define an object and the kinds of objects you can create in Active Directory.

5. Explain the business conditions that would predicate the need for more than one domain for your organization.

6. Describe what a tree is.

7. Give an explanation of what the Schema is and does.

8. Define the purpose of Active Directory.

9. Describe the differences between sites and domains.

10. List the common characteristics that the trees in a forest share.

Answers to Lesson 1 Activities

1. You can create OUs for any of the following reasons:

   • To assign administrative rights that are limited to a specific OU and the objects it contains

   • To simplify Group Policy

   •To create a logical and significant organization for administrators

2. • Assign Jim Smith the Create User Objects permission in the Admin OU.

   • Create a new group in the Admin OU called TEMPUSERS, with permissions to access the special promotions materials and the color printers.

   • Grant Jim Smith the Write permission to the Members property of the new TEMPUSERS group.

   • After you have assigned these permissions, Jim Smith will be able to create new users in the TEMPUSERS OU and add them to the Admin group. Since he has limited permissions, this will be the full extent of his abilities in the domain.

   • If Jim Smith tries to perform administrative tasks in any other domain, he will be denied.

3. Following are some distinct characteristics of a Windows 2000 domain:

   • A Windows 2000 domain has at least one domain controller

   • A domain's directory database replicates between all domain controllers in the domain

   • A single domain can form a tree

   • In the design process for the logical structure of an Active Directory database, you use a triangle in the design flowchart to represent a domain

4. An object is a distinct, named set of attributes that represents something concrete, such as a user, a printer, or an application.

   The types of objects you can create are: Computer, Contact, Group, Printer, User, and Shared Folder.

5.   You may need more than one Windows 2000 domain under the following conditions:

• To support decentralized administration

• To isolate domain replication traffic

• To balance domain replication traffic

• To support multiple domain policies

• To address international differences

• To comply with internal political pressures

6.   Multiple domains can form a domain tree. As the name implies, a tree is hierarchical. The root domain is always created first. It becomes the parent domain to child domains that are added directly below it, forming a hierarchy. Child domains can also be parents to other domains.

7.   The Schema is a blueprint of all objects in the domain. The Schema contains definitions of all the object classes and attributes that you can store in the directory. Active Directory can manage the Schema objects with the same object management functions it uses for the rest of the objects in Active Directory. For each object class, the Schema defines what attributes an instance of the class must have, what additional attributes it may have, and what object class can be a parent of the current object base. A Schema consists of two types of definitions:

• Attributes

• Classes

8.   Active Directory is the directory service included with Windows 2000 Server. It stores information about objects on the network and makes this information available to users and administrators. Active Directory gives network users access to permitted resources anywhere on the network using a single logon process.

9.   A site is a combination of one or more IP subnets that should be connected by a high speed link. A domain is a logical grouping of servers and other network resources organized under a single name. A site is a component of the physical structure, while a domain is part of the logical structure.

10.   Each tree has the following characteristics:

• All trees in a forest have a common Schema

• Trees in a forest have different naming structures, according to their domains

• All the domains in the forest share the same Global Catalog

• Domains in a forest operate independently, but forests enable communication across the whole organization

• Implicit two-way transitive trusts exist between domains and domain trees

Lesson 1 Quiz

These questions test your knowledge of features, vocabulary, procedures, and syntax.

1.   What is the basic unit of organization and security in Active Directory?
      A.   OU
      B.   Domain
      C.   Site
      D.   Global Catalog

2.   Which of the following are similarities between Microsoft Windows NT 4.0 domains and Windows 2000 domains?
      A.   Domains organize your network.
      B.   Domains are security boundaries.
      C.   Domains address international differences.
      D.   Domains partition your database.

3.   Which of the following statements best describes trust relationships between Windows 2000 domains?
      A.   The parent domain has a two-way trust relationship with each child domain, but you must manually establish trust relationships between the child domains.
      B.   Inter-domain trust relationships are defined by explicit one-way trust relationships between domain controllers.
      C.   When a domain is joined to a Windows 2000 domain tree, a transitive trust relationship is automatically established between the new domain and its parent domain.
      D.   The trust relationship between each domain and its parent domain must be established and managed individually.

4.   How is Active Directory integrated with DNS?
      A.   Object classes
      B.   Hierarchical structure
      C.   Instances of objects
      D.   Domain controllers

5.   What are the logical components of Active Directory?
      A.   Network configuration, devices and bandwidth
      B.   It equates your business processes to the Active Directory configuration.
      C.   Objects, OUs, domains, trees and forests
      D.   Sites, domain controllers

6.   What does extensible mean?
      A.   Contains a partial replica of every Windows 2000 domain in the directory.
      B.   The definition of an entire database; the universe of objects that can be stored
            in the directory is defined in the Schema
      C.   Administrators can add new classes of objects to the Schema and new
            attributes to existing classes of objects.
      D.   The properties of an object.

7.   What are the logical structure elements in Active Directory and their definitions?
      A.   An object is a concrete item that can be organized by classes and shares
            common sets of attributes.
      B.   Attributes are categories of information that define the characteristics of all
            objects.
      C.   The Schema is the set of definitions for the Active Directory objects.
      D.   All objects in Active Directory are protected by a security descriptor.

8.   How are the logical structures organized and what relationships do they form?
      A.   Elements are organized into OUs within a domain.
      B.   Objects are listed in the Global Catalog.
      C.   Domains link together to form trees.
      D.   Trees join together to create a forest.

9.   When you set permissions on an OU, you can specify to which objects they apply.
      What are they?
      A.   To this object only
      B.   To this object and all sub-objects
      C.   To objects and/or containers within this container only
      D.   To sub-objects only

10.   To define objects in the logical structure of Active Directory, you should understand
      the characteristics of objects. What are they?
      A.   Object classes and object class attributes.
      B.   Object names cannot use the following characters: /\[];:|=,+?< > .
      C.   Defined in the Schema separately from the classes.
      D.   Instances of objects.

Answers to Lesson 1 Quiz

1.   Answer B is correct. A domain is the basic unit for security and organization.

      Answer A is incorrect. OUs are containers for Active Directory objects.

      Answer C is incorrect. A site in Active Directory is defined as one or more well-connected Internet Protocol (IP) subnets.

      Answer D is incorrect. The Global Catalog is a server that centralizes directory information about Active Directory objects.

2.   Answers A and B are correct. Domains organize your network and are security boundaries

      Answer C is incorrect. You would want to create more than one Windows 2000 domain to address international differences.

      Answer D is incorrect. Domains are partitions of your database. Unless you have a single domain network, Active Directory is not a single database.

3.   Answer C is correct. When a domain is joined to a Windows 2000 domain tree, a transitive trust relationship is automatically established between the new domain and its parent domain.

      Answer A is incorrect. With Windows 2000 transitive trust relationships, all domains implicitly trust other domains in the tree.

      Answer B is incorrect. Windows 2000 domains have transitive trust relationships.

      Answer D is incorrect. When you join a Windows 2000 domain to a domain tree, the transitive trust relationship is established automatically.

4.   Answers B and D are correct. Active Directory and DNS have the same hierarchical structure. Although separate and implemented differently for different purposes, an organization's namespace for DNS and Active Directory have an identical structure. DNS zones can be stored in Active Directory. Active Directory clients use DNS to locate domain controllers. To locate a domain controller for a specified domain, Active Directory clients query their configured DNS server for specific resource records.

      Answer A is incorrect. Object classes define the type of objects that can be created in Active Directory.

      Answer C is incorrect. Instances of objects take the template defined by object class attributes and put the values into the attributes.

5.   Answers B and C are correct. The logical structure of Active Directory equates your business processes to the configuration and can be defined as the objects, OUs, domains, trees and forests.

Answers A and D are incorrect. The physical structure of Active Directory is the network configuration, devices, and bandwidth and can be defined in the sites and domain controllers.

6.   Answer C is correct. Extensible means administrators can add new classes of objects to the Schema and new attributes to existing classes of objects.

Answer A is incorrect. The Global Catalog contains a partial replica of every Windows 2000 domain in the directory.

Answer B is incorrect. The Schema is the definition of an entire database; the universe of objects that can be stored in the directory is defined in the Schema.

Answer D is incorrect. Attributes are the properties of an object.

7.   Answers A, B and C are correct. Objects, attributes and the Schema are all part of the logical elements in Active Directory.

Answer D is incorrect. The security descriptor is part of Active Directory security.

8.   Answers A, C and D are correct. Each of these make up the logical structure.

Answer B is incorrect. The Global Catalog is used by Active Directory to find objects.

9.   All answers are correct. When you set permissions on an OU, you can specify to which objects they apply: to this object only, to this object and all sub-objects, to objects and/or containers within this container only, and to sub-objects only.

10.   Answers A and D are correct. Object classes, object class attributes, and instances of objects are the characteristics of objects.

Answer B is incorrect. The characters listed are excluded from object names but this is not considered to be a characteristic of objects.

Answer C is incorrect. Attributes are defined in the Schema separately from the classes.

Domain Name System Server Service

Active Directory uses the Domain Name System (DNS), the Internet standard for name resolution, as its location service. In order for Active Directory to function correctly, a number of Active Directory-related DNS records must exist in DNS. The majority of these records are of the Service Location (SRV) type. Active Directory queries the SRV records to find the Internet Protocol (IP) addresses of the Active Directory services being hosted on different domain controllers. The domain controllers may include the Global Catalog service, Lightweight Directory Access Protocol (LDAP) service and Kerberos service.

After completing this lesson, you should have a better understanding of the following topics:

- DNS and Active Directory Overview

- DNS Configuration

- DNS Troubleshooting

- Active Directory DNS Zones Configuration

- Zone for Dynamic Updates Configuration

- DNS Management

- DNS Monitoring

- DNS Data Replication Management

DNS and Active Directory Overview

Active Directory is the Windows 2000 directory service. A directory service consists of the following components:

• An information repository used to store information about objects

• The services that make that information available to users and applications

Active Directory uses the Domain Name System (DNS) as a means of locating and identifying the specified domain. When looking for a specific domain controller in a domain, a client questions DNS for SRV, the address resource records that provide the names and IP addresses of LDAP, the protocol used to query and update servers.

Since Active Directory uses DNS for its location service, you cannot install Active Directory without having DNS on your network. However, you can install DNS without Active Directory. When you install DNS on a Windows 2000 domain controller, you choose whether you want to use Active Directory for replication and storage for DNS.

For DNS to work as a location service for Active Directory, it is essential that you have a DNS server to host the following locator records:

A—An Address resource record is used to map a DNS domain name to a host IP address on the network.

SRV—A Service resource record is used in a zone to register and locate well-known Transmission Control Protocol/Internet Protocol (TCP/IP) services. The SRV resource record is specified in RFC 2052 and is used in Windows 2000 to locate domain controllers for Active Directory Service.

CNAME—A Canonical Name is a resource record used to map an alternate alias name to a primary canonical DNS domain name used in the zone.

You can configure your Windows 2000 DNS server automatically by using the Active Directory Installation Wizard. It will do all the installation and configuration for DNS. You do not need to manually configure DNS to support Active Directory unless you use a DNS server other than Windows 2000, or you want a particular configuration. You manually configure DNS using the DNS console (Figure 2.1).

Figure 2.1 DNS Console

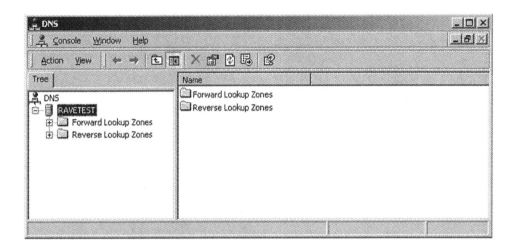

Incorporating DNS Into Active Directory

Active Directory and DNS are both namespaces. A namespace is a set of distinct names for the resources in a network. The names in a namespace can be resolved to the objects they represent. For DNS, namespace is the hierarchical structure of the domain name tree. For example, each domain label, such as acctg or sales used in a Fully Qualified Domain Name (FQDN), such as acctg.ibidpub.com, points to a branch in the domain namespace tree. For Active Directory, namespace corresponds to the DNS namespace in structure but resolves Active Directory object names (Figure 2.2).

Figure 2.2 How DNS Finds the IP Address of a Computer Based on its Name

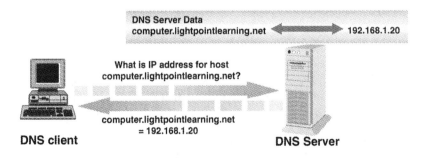

DNS and the Internet

Every computing device on the Internet has a unique 32-bit Internet Protocol (IP) address, such as 154.23.17.8. When you are looking for a site on the Internet, you can refer to these devices by their IP addresses. For example, you might point your Web browser to http://206.xxx.xxx.200 to access a specific Web site. However, most users prefer to point their Web browser to a more user-friendly name such as http://www.ibidpub.com. The ability to use user-friendly names requires a database that can convert www.ibidpub.com to an IP address, such as 206.xxx.xxx.200. Converting names to addresses is called name resolution.

 Note: Country names can be part of the top-level domains. For example, .ca for Canada, .uk for the United Kingdom.

The management of IP addresses on the Internet is handled by using the globally distributed DNS database, but DNS can also be implemented locally to manage addresses within private TCP/IP) networks. DNS is organized into a hierarchy of domains. DNS has several top-level domains further subdivided into second-level domains. The root of the Internet domain namespace is managed by an Internet authority (currently, the Internet Network Information Center (InterNIC)). This organization is responsible for delegating administrative responsibility for the top-level domains of the DNS namespace as described in Table 2.1 and for registering second-level domain names.

Table 2.1 Examples of Top Level Domains

Top Level Domain	Description
.gov	Government organizations
.com	Commercial organizations
.edu	Educational institutions
.org	Non-commercial organizations
.net	Commercial sites or networks

Second-level domains represent namespaces that are formally registered to institutions (and to individuals) to provide them with an Internet presence. Figure 2.3 shows how a company's network connects.

Figure 2.3 How a Company Fits into the DNS Namespace

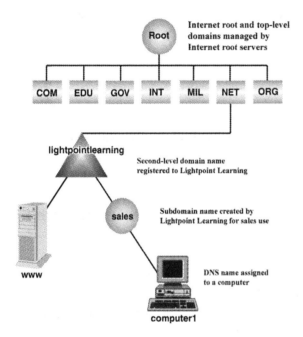

Host names refer to specific computers on a network or on the Internet. For example, in the following Fully Qualified Domain Name (FQDN) Computer1.acctg.ibidpub.com, the host name is Computer1.

Note: The host name does not have to be the same as the computer name, Network Basic Input/Output System (NetBIOS) name, or any other naming protocol.

Active Directory and the Global DNS Namespace

Active Directory is designed to exist within the scope of the global Internet DNS namespace. When an organization using Windows 2000 Server for its network operating system needs an Internet presence, the Active Directory namespace is kept as one or more hierarchical Windows 2000 domains beneath a root domain registered as a DNS namespace. You can choose not to be part of the global Internet DNS namespace, but DNS service is still necessary to find Windows 2000-based computers.

According to the DNS naming conventions, each part of a DNS name separated by a period (.), which stands for a node in the DNS hierarchical tree structure and could be an Active Directory domain name in the Windows 2000 tree structure. Shown in Figure 2.4, the root of the DNS hierarchy is a node with a null label (" "). This root of the Active Directory namespace (the forest root) has no parent. It provides the LDAP entry point to Active Directory. LDAP is the primary access protocol for Active Directory.

Figure 2.4 Comparing DNS and Active Directory Namespace Roots

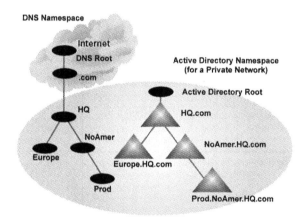

In operating systems prior to Windows 2000, a computer is identified on the network by a NetBIOS name. NetBIOS is an Application Programming Interface (API) that can be used by programs on a Local Area Network (LAN). NetBIOS offers programs similar instructions for asking for the lower-level services necessary to manage names, conduct sessions, and send information between nodes on a network. In Windows 2000, a computer is recognized by its full computer name, which is a DNS FQDN, that is a concatenation of the host name and the main DNS suffix. For example, in Figure 2.4, sales.ibidpub.com is a concatenation of the domain sales and the root domain ibidpub.

Tip: You can establish and view the FQDN from the Network Identification property page of the System Properties dialog box by right-clicking My Computer and selecting Properties.

To change the host name, choose Properties, and to change the primary DNS suffix, select More.

Different DNS implementations call for different character and length restrictions. Table 2.2 shows the limitations for each implementation.

Table 2.2 Name Restrictions

Restriction	Standard DNS (Including Microsoft Windows NT 4.0)	DNS in Windows 2000	NetBIOS
Characters	Supports RFC 1123 A—Z a—z 0—9 and the hyphen (-)	Several different configurations are possible	Unicode characters, numbers, white space, symbols: ! @ # $ % ^ & (. - _ { } ~
FQDN length	63 bytes per label and 255 bytes for an FQDN	63 bytes per label and 255 bytes for an FQDN Domain controllers limited to 155 bytes for an FQDN	15 bytes

Tip: Although you can create complex DNS names, create shorter, user-friendly names to avoid unnecessary administrative work.

Table 2.3 summarizes the differences between each kind of name using the example FQDN acctg.ibidpub.com.

Table 2.3 DNS and NetBIOS Names

Name Type	Description
NetBIOS name	Used to uniquely distinguish the NetBIOS services on the first IP address bound to an adapter. This unique NetBIOS name is connected to the IP address of the server through broadcast, Windows Internet Name Service (WINS), or the LMHosts file. By default, it is the same as the host name up to 15 bytes, and if not 15 bytes long, any additional spaces necessary to make the name 15 bytes long, plus the service identifier. The NetBIOS name is also known as a NetBIOS computer name. For example, a NetBIOS name might be acctg.
Host name	Either the FQDN or the first label of an FQDN. In this lesson, host name refers to the first label of an FQDN. For example, the first label of the FQDN acctg.ibidpub.com is acctg.
Primary DNS suffix	Every Windows 2000 computer can be given a primary DNS suffix to be used for name resolution and registration. You specify the primary DNS suffix on the Network Identification property page within My Computer. The primary DNS suffix is also known as the primary domain name and the domain name. For example, the FQDN acctg.ibidpub.com has the primary DNS suffix ibidpub.com.

Name Type	Description
NetBIOS name	Used to uniquely distinguish the NetBIOS services on the first IP address bound to an adapter. This unique NetBIOS name is connected to the IP address of the server through broadcast, Windows Internet Name Service (WINS), or the LMHosts file. By default, it is the same as the host name up to 15 bytes, and if not 15 bytes long, any additional spaces necessary to make the name 15 bytes long, plus the service identifier. The NetBIOS name is also known as a NetBIOS computer name. For example, a NetBIOS name might be acctg.
Host name	Either the FQDN or the first label of an FQDN. In this lesson, host name refers to the first label of an FQDN. For example, the first label of the FQDN acctg.ibidpub.com is acctg.
Primary DNS suffix	Every Windows 2000 computer can be given a primary DNS suffix to be used for name resolution and registration. You specify the primary DNS suffix on the Network Identification property page within My Computer. The primary DNS suffix is also known as the primary domain name and the domain name. For example, the FQDN acctg.ibidpub.com has the primary DNS suffix ibidpub.com.
Connection-specific DNS suffix	The connection-specific DNS suffix is assigned to an adapter. The connection-specific DNS suffix is also known as an adapter-specific DNS suffix. For example, a connection-specific DNS suffix might be acquired01-ext.com
Full computer name	A full computer name is a form of FQDN. A single computer can be identified by more than one FQDN. Only the FQDN that is a concatenation of the host name and the primary DNS suffix is the full computer name. In this example, it would be acctg.ibidpub.com.
Fully Qualified Domain Name	The FQDN is a DNS name that uniquely identifies the computer on the network. It is a concatenation of the host name, the primary DNS suffix, and a period. In this example, it would be acctg.ibidpub.com.

DNS Configuration

Active Directory uses DNS as its location service, making it possible for computers to find the location of domain controllers and particular services via the SRV records. To find a domain controller in a particular domain, a client queries DNS for resource records that provide the names and the IP addresses of the LDAP servers for the domain.

When you start the Active Directory Installation Wizard and choose to create a new domain, the wizard finds the DNS server that is authoritative for the name of the new Active Directory domain. It then checks if the selected server will accept dynamic updates. If the test is positive, the wizard will not install and configure a local DNS server.

If the Active Directory Installation wizard cannot find the DNS server that is authoritative for the name, or if the server it finds does not support dynamic updates or is not configured to accept dynamic updates, the Active Directory Installation wizard will ask if you want the wizard to automatically install and configure a local DNS server. If you choose yes, the wizard automatically installs and configures the DNS Server service.

During an automatic configuration, the Active Directory Installation Wizard will add the forward lookup zone, which will host the locator records, to the DNS server. It also configures the DNS server to accept dynamic updates. A forward lookup zone is a zone that holds the information needed to resolve names within the DNS domain.

After the Active Directory Installation Wizard finishes, you are prompted to restart the computer. When the computer restarts, Netlogon will try to add the locator resource records to the DNS server by sending a dynamic update request to the authoritative DNS server. Locator resource records are essential to allow other computers to find the domain controller.

If you are creating an Active Directory domain, you must do some further configuration. To configure the DNS server to support Active Directory, you must ensure that the following tasks have been accomplished:

- Ensure that you have a forward lookup zone that is authoritative for the resource records registered by Netlogon

- Configure the forward lookup zone to allow dynamic updates

• Unless the selected DNS server is a root DNS server, from the parent server, delegate the forward lookup zone to this server

Installing DNS for Active Directory

You must install the DNS server before configuring the server. To install and configure the DNS server, follow these steps:

1. From the **Start** menu, choose **Settings** and then select **Control Panel.**

2. Double-click **Add/Remove Programs**, and then choose **Add/Remove Windows Components**.

3. From the Windows Components list, select **Networking Services**, and then select **Details**.

4. Select the box to the left of Domain Name System (DNS) to select it, and then click **OK**.

5. Choose **Next**, and Windows 2000 installs DNS.

6. When the installation completes, choose **Finish**.

Figure 2.5 Networking Services Selection

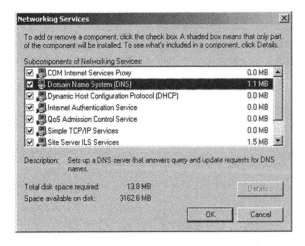

Configuring DNS for Active Directory

Before you can configure DNS and Active Directory, check the TCP/IP settings of your computer to ensure it is configured to use a DNS server. If your computer is the first DNS server on the network, you can configure your computer to use itself as a DNS server.

To configure DNS and Active Directory, follow these steps:

1. From the **Start** menu, choose **Programs**, **Administrative Tools**, and then select **Configure Your Server** (Figure 2.6).

Figure 2.6 Configure Your Server Wizard

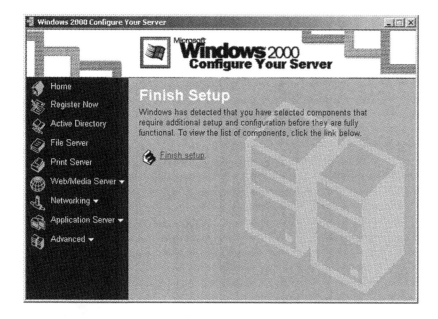

2. The **Configure Your Server** wizard installs and configures Active Directory (Figure 2.7) and prompts you with an option to configure the DNS server component.

Figure 2.7 Installation Wizard

3. When prompted to do so, restart your computer.

Using the Configure DNS Server Wizard

In most cases, you do not need to manually configure DNS to support Active Directory. You let the Installation Wizard automatically configure DNS. You use the Configure DNS Server Wizard to set up DNS if you want a configuration different from the default one the wizard defines for you. For example, you might want your DNS server to be different from your domain controller.

If you plan to use the Configure DNS Server Wizard, you must perform the following tasks before running the wizard:

• If the DNS server is not installed, you must install it

- If this server is not the root DNS server, configure its network connections to point to the other DNS servers in your network

While you are running the wizard, or after you have finished using the wizard, you must create a forward lookup zone that is authoritative for the locator records that Netlogon will add.

After you have configured your DNS server by using the wizard, you must perform the following tasks:

- Enable dynamic updates on that zone

- Add a delegation to the new forward lookup zone in its parent zone

- Make sure the server that will be a domain controller has network connectivity to this server

Before configuring DNS, verify that your DNS client settings are correct.

To verify DNS client setting, follow these steps:

1. From the Desktop, right-click **My Network Places**, and choose **Properties**.

2. Right-click the connection for which you want to configure the DNS server, and then choose **Properties** (Figure 2.8).

Figure 2.8 DNS Server Properties Page

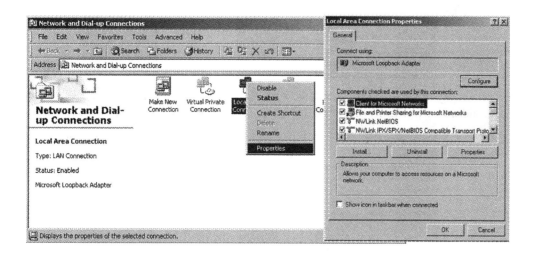

3. Choose **Internet Protocol (TCP/IP)** and then select **Properties**.

4. From the **Internet Protocol (TCP/IP) Properties** page, type the **IP address** of the existing DNS server in the **Preferred DNS server** field (Figure 2.9).

 Note: You can also add the IP address of an alternate DNS server in the Alternate DNS server field.

Figure 2.9 TCP/IP Properties Page

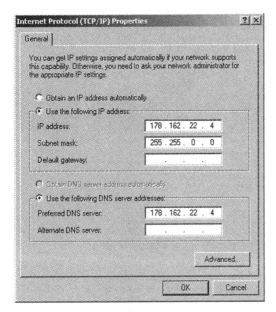

5. If you need to identify more than one alternate DNS server, choose **Advanced**, select the **DNS** property page, and then type the servers in the DNS server addresses box, as shown in Figure 2.10.

Figure 2.10 Advanced TCP/IP Settings Page

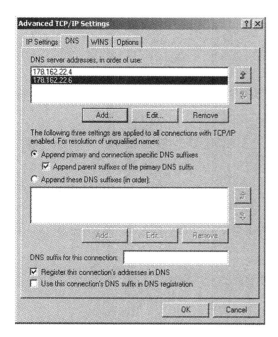

The Configure DNS Server Wizard uses the DNS client information to determine if there are any root DNS servers on the network. For more information about setting the DNS server IP address, see Windows 2000 Server Help.

To configure the DNS server, follow these steps:

1. From the **Start** menu, choose **Programs**, choose **Administrative Tools**, and then select **DNS**.

2. In the Tree pane, select the DNS server.

3. Right-click the server and choose **Configure the Server**.

4. The Configure DNS Server Wizard (Figure 2.11) begins and prompts you through the process of setting up DNS.

Note: In some situations, setting up DNS includes creating a reverse lookup zone. The Configure DNS Server Wizard prompts you for all the information needed to create the appropriate forward and reverse lookup zones.

Figure 2.11 DNS Server Configuration Wizard

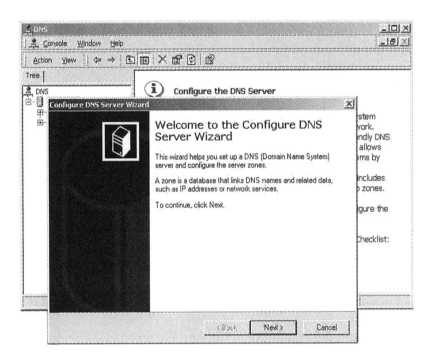

DNS Troubleshooting

There are a number of useful troubleshooting tools to help you avoid common errors. These procedures will help you verify that you have correctly configured your name servers. They also explain how to diagnose and solve common DNS problems. Table 2.4 contains a listing of the tools and their descriptions.

Table 2.4 DNS Troubleshooting Tools

Tool	Description
Nslookup	Used to perform DNS queries and to examine the contents of zone files on local and remote servers
Ipconfig	Used to view DNS client settings, display, and flush the resolver cache, as well as to force a dynamic update client to register its DNS records
Event Viewer	Used to view DNS client and server error messages
DNS Log	Used to monitor certain events, which you can configure the DNS server to do, and log them in the DNS log for your examination
Network Redirector Command	Used to stop DNS client caching and to flush the cache by using the network redirector commands net start and net stop
Monitoring in the DNS Console	Used to perform test queries by using options on the Monitoring property page in the DNS console
Network Monitor	Used to examine the packets that the DNS servers on your network send and receive
Netdiag	Used to identify problems with your DNS configuration

Event Viewer

The Event Viewer logs errors with the Windows 2000 operating system and services such as the DNS server. If you are having problems with DNS, you can check Event Viewer for DNS-related events.

To open the event viewer, follow these steps:

1. From the **Start** menu, choose **Programs**, **Administrative Tools**, and then select **Event Viewer** (Figure 2.12).

Figure 2.12 Event Viewer

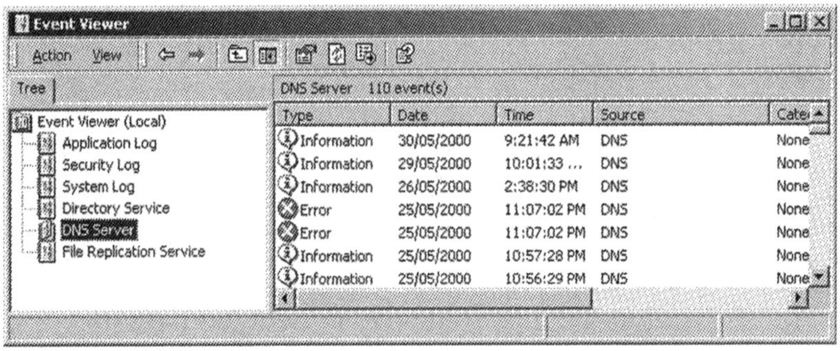

2. Choose **DNS Server** to view messages about the DNS server.

3. Select **System Log** to view messages about the DNS client.

Active Directory DNS Zones Configuration

Windows 2000 DNS is RFC-compliant and will operate with other DNS implementations. It has been tested to work with Microsoft Windows NT 4.0, BIND 8.2, BIND 8.1.2, and BIND 4.9.7. BIND stands for Berkeley Internet Name Domain. It is an implementation of DNS written and ported to most available versions of the UNIX operating system. The Internet Software Consortium maintains the BIND software. However, Windows 2000 supports some features that other implementations of DNS do not support. Table 2.5 compares Windows 2000 to Microsoft Windows NT 4.0, BIND 8.2, BIND 8.1.2, and BIND 4.9.7.

Table 2.5 Comparison of Features

Feature	Windows 2000	Microsoft Windows NT 4.0	BIND 8.2	BIND 8.1.2	BIND 4.9.7
Support for the Internet Engineering Task Force (IETF) Internet-Draft	Yes	Yes (with Service Pack 4)	Yes	Yes	Yes
Support for dynamic update	Yes	No	Yes	Yes	No
Support for secure dynamic update based on the GSS-TSIG algorithm	Yes	No	No	No	No
Support for Windows Internet Name Service (WINS) and Windows-Specific Resource Records (WINS-R) records	Yes	Yes	No	No	No
Support for fast zone transfer	Yes	Yes	Yes	Yes	Yes
Support for incremental zone transfer	Yes	No	Yes	No	No
Support for Universal Character Set Transformation Format 8-bit (UTF-8) character encoding	Yes	No	No	No	No

WINS Lookup Interoperability Considerations

WINS dynamically maps IP addresses to computer names (NetBIOS names). With WINS, users can access resources by name instead of by IP addresses. WINS servers support clients running Microsoft Windows NT 4.0 and earlier versions of Windows.

A WINS lookup works best if all authoritative servers run Windows 2000 or Microsoft Windows NT 4.0 in zones configured for WINS lookup. WINS lookup needs two special, Windows-specific resource records-WINS or WINS-R resource records. Computers running third-party implementations of DNS do not support WINS and WINS-R records. If you want to use a mix of Microsoft and third-party DNS servers to host a zone, you could have data errors or failed zone transfers if you have not set up your Windows 2000 server to turn off replication of WINS and WINS-R records.

Zone for Dynamic Updates Configuration

A DNS namespace can be divided into zones that store name information about one or more DNS domains. The zone becomes an authoritative source for each DNS domain name included in a zone. The DNS namespace represents the logical structure of your network resources while DNS zones provide the physical storage for these resources.

The DNS service includes a dynamic update capability, called Dynamic DNS (DDNS). When you use DNS, and there are changes to the domain for which a name server has authority, you must manually update the zone database file in the primary name server. With DDNS, nameservers and clients in the network automatically update the zone database files as shown in Figure 2.13.

The DNS service allows client computers to dynamically update their resource records in DNS. This improves DNS administration by reducing the time needed to manage zone records manually. The dynamic update feature can be used in conjunction with Dynamic Host Configuration Protocol (DHCP) to dynamically update resource records when a computer's IP address is released and renewed. Computers that run Windows 2000 can send dynamic updates.

Figure 2.13 DDNS Updates Zone Database

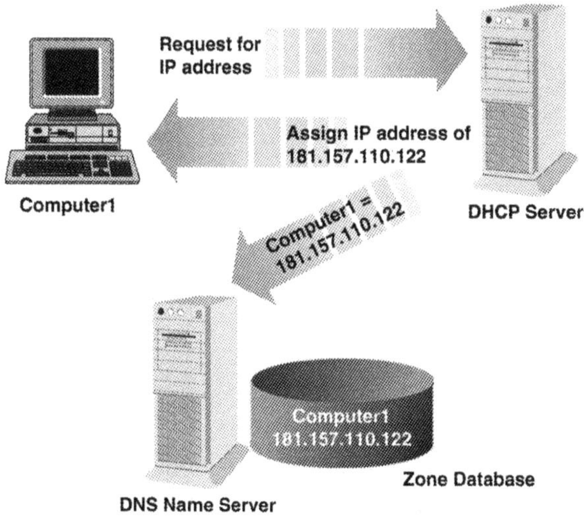

You can amalgamate DNS zones and Active Directory to provide improved fault tolerance and security. Every Active Directory integrated zone is replicated among all domain controllers within the Active Directory domain. All DNS servers running on these domain controllers can act as primary servers for the zone, accepting dynamic updates. In addition, Active Directory propagates only the relevant changes. You can configure Active Directory–integrated zones for secure dynamic update. With secure dynamic update, only authorized users can make changes to a zone or record.

There are two zone types: forward lookup zones and reverse lookup zones.

Creating a Forward Lookup Zone

A forward lookup zone allows you to execute forward lookup queries. On name servers, you must configure at least one forward lookup zone for DNS to work.

To create a forward lookup zone, follow these steps:

1. From the **Start** menu, choose **Programs**, **Administrative Tools**, and then select **DNS** (Figure 2.14).

Figure 2.14 DNS Zones Page

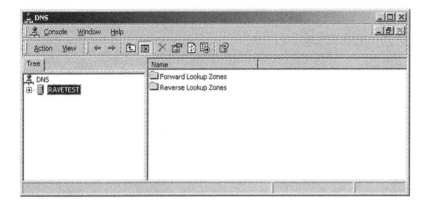

2. Expand the **DNS server**.

3. Right-click **YOURCOMPUTER**, and then choose **New Zone**.

4. The **New Zone Wizard** appears (Figure 2.15) and prompts you to set up a forward lookup zone, where there are four configuration options: zone type, zone name, zone file, and master DNS servers.

Figure 2.15 New Zone Wizard

Zone Type

You can configure the following three zone types:

Active Directory Integrated—The Active Directory Integrated-zone is the master copy of a new zone. The zone uses Active Directory to store and replicate zone files.

Standard Primary—The Standard Primary zone is the master copy of a new zone stored in a standard text file. This is administered and maintained on the computer where you created the zone.

Standard Secondary—The Standard Secondary zone is a replica of an existing zone. These are read-only and stored in text files. When creating a secondary zone, you must specify the DNS server. You create a secondary zone to provide redundancy and reduce the load on the name server containing the primary zone database file.

Zone Name

Usually a zone is named after the highest domain in the hierarchy, including the root domain for the zone.

Zone File

For the standard primary forward lookup zone type, you must specify a zone file. The zone file is the zone database file name, which defaults to the zone name, with a .dns extension. For example, if your zone name is ibidpub.com, the default zone database filename would be IBIDPUB.COM.DNS. When migrating a zone from another server, you can import the existing zone file.

Creating a Reverse Lookup Zone

A reverse lookup zone allows reverse lookup queries. Reverse lookup zones are not required. However, a reverse lookup zone is required to run troubleshooting tools and to record a name instead of an IP address in the Internet Information Services (IIS) file.

To create a new reverse lookup zone, follow these steps:

1. From the **Start** menu, choose **Programs**, **Administrative Tools**, and then selecdt **DNS**.

2. Expand the **DNS server**.

3. Right-click **Reverse Lookup Zone**, and select **New Zone**.

4. The **New Zone Wizard** installs and prompts you through the set up of a reverse lookup zone (Figure 2.16), with four configuration options: zone type, reverse lookup zone, zone file and Master DNS Servers.

Figure 2.16 New Zone Wizard Reverse Lookup

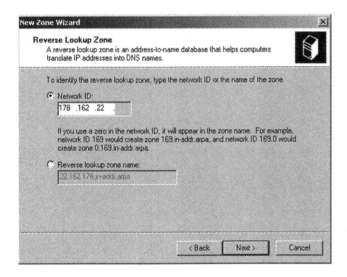

Zone Type

The same three zone types as for forward lookup zones, Active Directory-integrated, Standard Primary, or Standard Secondary, are available.

Reverse Lookup Zone

Enter the network ID or the name of the zone to identify the reverse lookup zone. For example, a network ID with an IP address of 170.365.27.311 would be a network ID of 170.365. All reverse lookup queries within the 170.365 are decided in this new zone.

Zone File

For the standard primary forward lookup zone, you must specify a zone file. The network ID and the subnet mask determine the default zone file name. DNS reverses the IP octets (group of eight) and adds the in-addr.arpa suffix. For example, the reverse lookup zone of 170.365 network is 365.170.in-addr.arpa.dns.

Benefits of Active Directory-Integrated Zones

For networks deploying DNS to support Active Directory, directory-integrated primary zones are recommended and provide the following benefits:

• Multi-master update and enhanced security based on the capabilities of Active Directory

• Zones are replicated and synchronized to new domain controllers automatically whenever a new zone is added to an Active Directory domain

• By integrating storage of your DNS namespace in Active Directory, you simplify planning and administration for both DNS and Active Directory

• Directory replication is faster and more efficient than standard DNS replication

Master DNS Servers

For the standard secondary reverse lookup zone type, you must detail the DNS server from which you want to copy the zone. You enter one or more DNS servers.

DNS Management

Windows 2000 DNS is managed through DNS Manager, which is provided as a Microsoft Management Console (MMC) snap-in. It provides all the functionality necessary to administer DNS server, its zones, and security.

Following are some of the DNS Manager features:

- The New Server Configuration Wizard

- A filtering capability useful for the servers and zones containing a large number of zones and records, respectively

- A security capability, which allows specification of the secondary servers to be notified of any changes on the master zone, and specification of the sets of servers to be sent the updated zone information

Managing DNS with Tools

The primary tool used to manage DNS servers is the DNS console. This can be found in the Administrative Tools folder in Control Panel. The DNS console appears as a Microsoft Management Console (MMC) Snap-in. With it, you can integrate DNS administration into your total network management.

After you install a DNS server, you can use the DNS console to perform these basic administrative server tasks:

- Execute the initial configuration of a new DNS server

- Connect to and manage a local DNS server on the same computer or remote DNS servers on other computers

- Add or remove forward and reverse lookup zones

- Add, remove, or update resource records in zones

- Change how zones are stored and replicated between servers

- Change how servers deal with queries and control dynamic updates

- Change security for specific zones or resource records

You can also use the DNS console to carry out the following tasks:

- Server maintenance

- Check the contents of the server cache and clear it when required

- Tune advanced server options

- Configure and perform aging and scavenging of stale resource records stored by the server

For remote administration of Windows 2000 DNS servers, the DNS console can be operated from non-server computers, if you have installed the DNS Server service on them.

Note: The DNS console can only be used to manage Windows 2000 DNS servers

DNS Console

You can use the DNS console to perform a test query to determine if your server is working properly. To carry out test queries using the DNS console, follow these steps:

1. From the **Start** menu, choose **Programs**, choose **Administrative Tools**, and then select **DNS**.

2. From the Tree pane of the DNS console, select the server.

3. Right-click the server and choose **Properties**.

4. From the Server Properties window, select the **Monitoring** property page (Figure 2.17).

Figure 2.17 DNS Console Monitoring Property Page

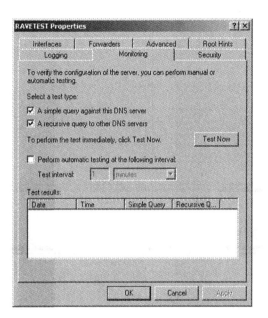

5. From the Monitoring property page, select the tests you wish to perform, and then select **Test Now**.

Command-Line Utilities

There are several command-line utilities. You use these to manage and troubleshoot DNS servers and clients. Table 2.6 describes some of these utilities. They can be run either by typing them at a command prompt or by entering them in batch files for scripted use.

Table 2.6 Command-Line Utilities

Command	Description
Nslookup	Used to perform query testing of the DNS domain namespace
Dnscmd	A command-line interface for managing DNS servers. You use this utility for scripting batch files to automate routine DNS management tasks, or to perform simple unattended setup and configuration of new DNS servers on your network.
Ipconfig	This command is used to view and to modify IP configuration details used by the computer. In Windows 2000, additional command-line options have been included with this utility. They provide help in troubleshooting and supporting DNS clients.

DNS Monitoring

There are two options for monitoring DNS servers:

- Default logging of DNS server event messages to the DNS server log

- Debug options for trace logging saved to a text file on the DNS server computer

DNS Monitoring Tools

In Windows 2000, server event messages are kept in their own system event log. You can view the DNS server log using Event Viewer. The DNS server log holds the events logged by the DNS Server service. For example, when the DNS server starts or stops, a message is written to the log. Other important DNS service events are logged as well, such as when the server starts but cannot locate any initializing data, such as zones or boot information that is kept in the Windows 2000 registry or in Active Directory.

You can also use Event Viewer to view and monitor any client-related DNS events. These are written by the DNS client.

With the DNS console you can selectively enable additional debug logging options for temporary trace logging to a text-containing DNS server activity. The file created and used for this feature, DNS.LOG, is stored in the *systemroot*\System32\Dns folder.

DNS Server Event Logging

For Windows 2000 Server, DNS server event messages are separate from events caused by other applications and services in the DNS server log and can be viewed using the Event Viewer. The DNS server log contains basic predetermined events logged by the DNS server service, such as when the service starts and stops (Figure 2.18).

Figure 2.18 Event Viewer

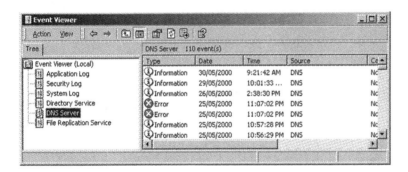

You can also use Event Viewer to view and monitor client-related DNS events. These events appear in the system log and are written by the DNS client service at any computer running Windows 2000.

Debug Options

Using the DNS console, you can set additional logging options to create a temporary trace log of DNS server activity. The text file created and used for this feature, DNS.LOG, is stored in the systemroot\System32\Dns folder. For Windows 2000 DNS servers, the Debug logging options are described in Table 2.7.

Table 2.7 DNS Server Debug Logging Options

Logging Option	Description
Query	Logs queries received by the DNS server service from clients
Notify	Logs notification messages received by the DNS server service from other servers
Update	Logs dynamic updates received by the DNS server service from other computers
Questions	Logs the contents of the question section for each DNS query message processed by the DNS server service
Answers	Logs the contents of the answer section for each message processed by the DNS server section
Send	Logs the number of DNS query messages sent by the DNS server service
Receive	Logs the number of DNS query messages received by the DNS server service
UDP	Logs the number of DNS requests received by the DNS server over a User Datagram Protocol (UDP) port
TCP	Logs the number of DNS requests received by the DNS server over a TCP port
Full Packets	Logs the number of full packets written and sent by the DNS server service
Write Through	Logs the number of packets written through by the DNS server service and back to the zone

By default, all debug logging options are disabled. You can choose which options to carry out for general troubleshooting and debugging of the server.

Debug logs can often be resource intensive. This affects server performance and consumes disk space. They should only be used temporarily, when more detailed information about server performance is needed.

To set the DNS Server debug options, follow these steps:

1. From the **Start** menu, choose Programs, choose Administrative Tools, and then select DNS.

2. From the Tree pane of the DNS console, right-click the server and choose **Properties**.

3. From the Server Properties window, select the **Logging** property page.

4. From the list of debug logging options, select the options you will log, and then choose **OK** (Figure 2.19).

Figure 2.19 Server Properties Logging Property page

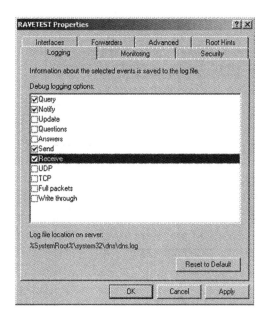

DNS Data Replication Management

Besides storing zone files on DNS servers, you can store a primary zone in Active Directory. When you store a zone in Active Directory, zone data is stored as Active Directory objects and replicated as part of Active Directory replication.

Active Directory replication provides an advantage over standard DNS alone. With standard DNS, only the primary server for a zone can modify the zone. With Active Directory replication, all of the domain controllers for the domain can modify the zone and then replicate the changes to other domain controllers. This replication process is called multi-master replication because multiple domain controllers, or masters, can update the zone.

Replicating DNS Data

Although Active Directory–integrated zones are transferred by using Active Directory replication, you can also perform standard zone transfers to secondary servers as you would with standard DNS zones.

Active Directory—integrated storage provides the following benefits:

Fault Tolerance—Although you can still perform standard zone transfers with Active Directory–integrated zones, Active Directory multi-master replication gives better fault tolerance. Standard zone transfers and updates depend on a single primary DNS server to update all the secondary servers. However, when using Active Directory replication, there is no single point of failure for zone updates.

Security—You can limit access to updates for any zone or record to prevent insecure dynamic updates.

Simpler Management—Since Active Directory does the replication, you do not need to set up and maintain a separate replication topology (zone transfers) for DNS servers.

Effective Replication of Large Zones—Active Directory replication works on a per-property basis and propagates only those changes that you specify as relevant changes. This is more efficient than full zone transfers or incremental transfers which replicate at the object level..

Integrated Storage

When you configure a primary zone to be Active Directory–integrated, the zone is stored in Active Directory. Figure 2.20 shows this arrangement.

Figure 2.20 Active Directory–Integrated Zone

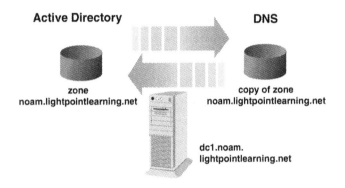

The DNS server module only contains a copy of the zone. When it starts, it reads a copy of the zone from Active Directory. When the DNS server receives a change, it writes the change to Active Directory.

Through Active Directory replication, the zone is replicated to other domain controllers. In addition, the DNS server can send its copy of the zone through standard zone transfers to any secondary DNS server that requests it. The DNS server can perform both incremental and full zone transfers.

DNS servers update Active Directory by using the following process: The DNS server questions Active Directory to ensure the copy of the zone in the memory of the DNS server is up to date when an update occurs. If not, the DNS server asks for any changes and adds these changes to the in-memory copy. Then the server confirms that all the prerequisites are satisfied. Prerequisites are conditions that must be satisfied before records can be updated. Finally, to accept the change, the DNS server updates the primary zone data in Active Directory.

Storage Location

The Active Directory directory service is an object-oriented database that organizes network resources in a hierarchical structure. An object represents every resource. Each object has attributes that define its characteristics.

The classes of objects and the attributes of each object are defined in the Active Directory Schema. Table 2.8 shows the DNS objects in Active Directory.

Table 2.8 DNS Objects in Active Directory

Object	Description
dnsZone	Container created when a zone is stored in Active Directory
dnsNode	Leaf object used to map and associate a name in the zone to resource data
dnsRecord	Multi-valued attribute of a dnsNode object used to store the resource records associated with the named node object
dnsProperty	Multi-valued attribute of a dnsZone object used to store zone configuration information

Figure 2.21 shows DNS objects that are represented in Active Directory.

Figure 2.21 DNS Objects in Active Directory

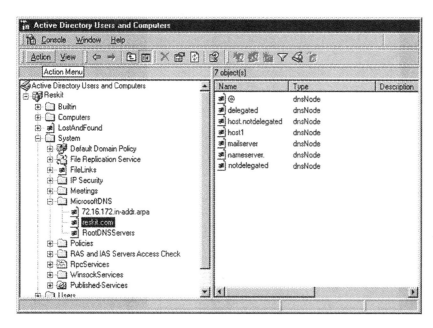

In the above example, within the Microsoft DNS container object are the dnsZone container objects. In Figure 2.21, Microsoft DNS contains the following dnsZone objects:

- The reverse lookup zone, 72.16.172.in-addr.arpa

- The forward lookup zone, reskit.com

- The root hints, RootDNSServers

You can view the DNS objects from within the Active Directory Users and Computers console. To view zones stored in Active Directory, follow these steps:

1. From the **Start** menu, choose **Programs**, choose **Administrative Tools**, and then select **Active Directory Users and Computers**.

2. From the menu bar, choose **View**, and then select **Advanced Features**.

3. Expand the server, expand **System**, and then expand **MicrosoftDNS**.

4. Select the folder associated with the DNS server. The dnsZone objects display in the Details (right) pane.

5. Double-click any dnsZone object to display its properties (Figure 2.22).

Figure 2.22 DNSZone Objects

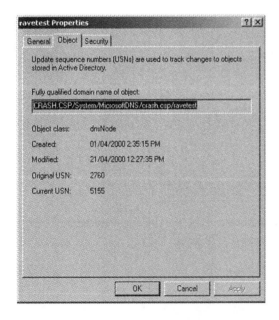

Vocabulary

Review the following terms in preparation for the certification exam.

Term	Description
A	Address resource record is a resource record used to map a DNS domain name to a host IP address on the network.
API	An Application Programming Interface is a set of routines used by an application program to direct the performance of procedures by the computer's operating system.
BIND	BIND stands for Berkeley Internet Name Domain, and is an implementation of DNS that is written and ported to the UNIX operating system.
CNAME	Canonical Name is a canonical resource record used to map an alternate alias name to a primary canonical DNS domain name used in the zone.
DDNS	Dynamic Domain Name System is a DNS service that includes a dynamic update capability. With DDNS, nameservers and clients in the network automatically update the zone database files.
DHCP	Dynamic Host Configuration Protocol is a TCP/IP service protocol that offers dynamic leased configuration of host IP addresses and distributes other configuration parameters to eligible network clients.
DNS	The Domain Name System is a hierarchical distributed database employed for name/address translation. DNS is the namespace used on the Internet to translate computer and service names into TCP/IP addresses. Active Directory uses DNS as its location service.
forward lookup zone	A forward lookup zone holds the information needed to resolve names within the DNS domain.
FQDN	A Fully Qualified Domain Name is a DNS name that uniquely identifies the computer on the network. It is a concatenation of the host name, the primary DNS suffix, and a period. For example, an FQDN might be sales.ibidpub.com.

Term	Description
full computer name	The full computer name is a type of FQDN. A computer can be identified by more than one FQDN. However, only the FQDN that is a concatenation of the host name and the primary DNS suffix is the full computer name.
IETF	The Intnernet Engineering Task Force is a group that maintains Internet standards through the use of vendors and researchers.
IIS	Internet Information Server is a Microsoft Web server which operates on Microsoft Windows NT 4.0 platforms.
InterNIC	The InterNIC is a database managed by AT&T that allows the public to search for and register a domain name and IP address for the purpose of setting up a Web site. The database provides search capabilities to discover if a name is already in use.
IP	The Internet Protocol is a routable protocol in charge of IP addressing, routing, and the fragmentation and reassembly of IP packets. It is used widely on the Internet for the exchange of information.
LAN	A Local Area Network is made up of computers and other devices connected by a communications link that allows one device to interact with any other in a limited area.
LDAP	Lightweight Directory Access Protocol v3 is the primary access protocol for Active Directory. It is defined by a set of Proposed Standard documents in Internet Engineering Task Force (IETF) RFC 2251.
LMHosts	A LM Hosts file displays computer names (NetBIOS) and IP addresses of accessible computers on your network. It is a plain text file that maps IP addresses to computer friendly names.
MMC	The Microsoft Management Console is a framework for hosting the consoles (administrative tools). Consoles contain tools, folders or other containers, Web pages, and other administrative items. The main MMC window provides commands and tools for authoring consoles.
namespace	Active Directory and DNS are both namespaces. A namespace is a set of distinct names for the resources in a network. The names in a namespace can be resolved to the objects they represent.

Term	Description
NetBIOSs	Network Basic Input/Output System (NetBIOS) is an Application Programming Interface (API) that can be used by programs on a Local Area Network (LAN). NetBIOS offers applications a similar set of instructions for asking for the lower-level services necessary to manage names, conduct sessions, and send information between nodes on a network.
NetBIOS name	The NetBIOS name is used to uniquely identify the NetBIOS services listening on the first IP address that is bound to an adapter. This unique NetBIOS name is resolved to the IP address of the server through broadcast, WINS, or the LMHosts file.
RFC	Request for Comments pertains to an Internet standard whereby anyone can receive information about the Internet by submitting a request.
SRV	A Service resource record used in a zone to register and locate well-known TCP/IP services. The SRV resource record is specified in RFC 2052 and is used in Windows 2000 to locate domain controllers for Active Directory Service.
TCP/IP	Transmission Control Protocol/Internet Protocol is the Internet's standard communication protocol.
UDP	User Datagram Protocol is a TCP component offering connectionless packet delivery. While it is direct, it does not guarantee delivery or correct sequencing of packets.
WINS	Windows Internet Name Service is a Microsoft software service that dynamically maps IP addresses to computer names (NetBIOS names). This lets users access resources by name instead of forcing them to use difficult to remember and hard to recognize IP addresses. WINS servers support clients running Microsoft Windows NT 4.0 and earlier Windows operating systems.

In Brief

If you want to...	Then do this...
Configure a zone for DDNS	1. From the **DNS console**, right-click the **forward or reverse lookup zone** that you want to configure, and choose **Properties**. 2. From **General** property page, select one of the three options from the **Allow dynamic updates** menu, according to the following descriptions: • No—does not allow dynamic updates for this zone • Yes—allows dynamic updates for this zone • Only Secure Updates—allows only dynamic DNS updates that use secure DNS for this zone (this is the preferred option)
Configure DNS and Active Directory	1. From the **Start** menu, choose **Programs**, **Administrative Tools**, and then **Configure Your Server**. 2. From the **Windows 2000 Configure Your Server Wizard** choose **Active Directory**. 3. Choose **Start** to begin the Active Directory wizard, and then follow the promps in the wizard.
Configure the DNS server to support Active Directory	• Ensure you have a forward lookup zone that is authoritative for the resource records registered by Netlogon • Configure the forward lookup zone to allow dynamic update • Unless the selected DNS server is a root DNS server, from the parent server, delegate the forward lookup zone to this server

If you want to...	Then do this...
Create a forward lookup zone	1. From the **Start menu**, choose **Programs, Administrative Tools**, and then select **DNS**.
	2. From the console tree, expand your server, right-click **Forward Lookup Zones**, and then choose **New Zone**.
	3. Follow the prompts in the New Zone Wizard.
Create a new reverse lookup zone	1. From the **Start menu**, choose **Programs, Administrative Tools**, and then select **DNS**.
	2. From the console tree, expand your server, right-click **Reverse Lookup Zones**, and then choose **New Zone**.
	3. Follow the prompts in the New Zone Wizard.
Install and configure the DNS server:	1. From the **Start menu**, choose **Settings**, and then select **Control Panel**.
	2. Double-click **Add/Remove Programs**, and then select **Add/Remove Windows Components**.
	3. Select Networking Services, and then select Details.
	4. From the list of networking services, select **Domain Name System (DNS)**, and then choose OK.
	5. Choose **Next**, and then select **Finish** when the installation finishes.
Set the DNS Server debug options	1. From the **Start** menu, choose Programs, Administrative Tools, and then select **DNS**.
	2. From the console tree, right-click the DNS name server, and then choose **Properties**.
	3. Select the **Logging** property page.
	4. Select the debugging options you want to log, and then choose **OK**.

If you want to...	Then do this...
Use the DNS Console to perform a test query to determine if your server is working properly	1. From the DNS console, right-click the DNS name server, and then choose **Properties**. 2. Select the **Monitoring** property page. 3. Select the tests you want to perform, and then choose **Test Now**.
Verify DNS client setting	1. Right-click **My Network Places**, and then choose **Properties**. 2. Right-click the **connection** for which you want to configure the DNS server, and then select **Properties**. 3. Select **Internet Protocol (TCP/IP)** and then **Properties**. 4. On the **Internet Protocol (TCP/IP) Properties** page, type the IP address of the existing DNS server in the **Preferred DNS server** field, or add the IP address of an alternate DNS server in the **Alternate DNS server** field. 5. If you need to identify more than one alternate DNS server, select **Advanced**, the **DNS** property page, and type the servers in the DNS server addresses box.
View zones stored in Active Directory	1. From the **Start** menu, choose **Programs**, **Administrative Tools**, and then **Active Directory Users and Computers**. 2. From the **View** menu, select **Advanced Features**. 3. Expand the domain, expand **System**, expand **MicrosoftDNS**, and then select the container with your domain name. 4. Double-click the **zone** that you want to view.

Lesson 2 Activities

Complete the following activities to better prepare you for the certification exam.

1. Describe the advantages of using the Active Directory integrated zone type.

2. Explain how you use the DNS Console to perform a test query to determine if your server is working properly.

3. Describe what FQDNs are and how DNS uses them.

4. Explain why the DNS is integral to Active Directory.

5. List the benefits of Active Directory integrated zones.

6. Describe the benefits that Active Directory–integrated storage provides.

7. Clarify how Active Directory and the Global DNS Namespace are integrated.

8. You can have DNS without Active Directory, but you cannot have Active Directory without DNS. If you are creating an Active Directory domain, you must add some further configuration. Describe the steps to configure the DNS server to support Active Directory.

9. Describe the tasks you must perform before running the Configure DNS Server Wizard.

10. The New Zone Wizard prompts you through the set up of a forward lookup zone. There are four configuration options and three zone types. Explain how they work together.

Answers to Lesson 2 Activities

1. Multi-master update and enhanced security are based on the capabilities of Active Directory. Zones are replicated and synchronized to new domain controllers automatically when a new zone is added to an Active Directory domain. When you integrate the storage of your DNS namespace in Active Directory, you simplify planning and administration for both DNS and Active Directory. Directory replication is faster and more efficient than standard DNS replication.

2. To use the DNS Console to perform a test query to determine if your server is working properly, follow these steps:

    1. Within the **DNS console**, double-click the **server name** to expand the server information.

    2. Right-click the **server**, and then select **Properties**.

    3. Select the **Monitoring** property page.

    4. Select the tests you want to perform, and then select **Test Now**.

3. A Fully Qualified Domain name (FQDN) is a Domain Name System (DNS) domain name that has been stated clearly and unambiguously to indicate its location in the domain name space tree. Fully qualified names differ from relative names in that they are stated with a period (.). For example retail.sales.ibidpub.com, qualifies retail in its position to the root of the namespace.

4. For Windows 2000, the DNS service has been integrated into the design and implementation of Active Directory. DNS name resolution is needed to locate Windows 2000 domain controllers. The Netlogon service uses DNS server support for the Service (SRV) resource record to provide registration of domain controllers in your DNS namespace. Active Directory can be used to store, integrate, and replicate zones.

5. The benefits of Active Directory-integrated zones are as follows:

    • Multi-master update and enhanced security based on the capabilities of Active Directory

    • Zones are replicated and synchronized to new domain controllers automatically whenever a new zone is added to an Active Directory domain

    • By integrating storage of your DNS namespace in Active Directory, you simplify planning and administration for both DNS and Active Directory

    • Directory replication is faster and more efficient than standard DNS replication

6.   Active Directory–integrated storage provides the following benefits:

Fault Tolerance—Although you can still perform standard zone transfers with Active Directory–integrated zones, Active Directory multi-master replication gives better fault tolerance. Standard zone transfers and updates depend on a single primary DNS server to update all the secondary servers. However, using Active Directory replication, there is no single point of failure for zone updates.

Security—You can limit access to updates for any zone or record to prevent insecure dynamic updates.

Simpler Management—Since Active Directory does the replication, you do not need to set up and maintain a separate replication topology (that is, zone transfers) for DNS servers.

Effective Replication of Large Zones—Active Directory replication works on a per-property basis and propagates only those changes that you specify as relevant changes. This is more efficient than full zone transfers.

7.   Active Directory is designed to exist within the Internet DNS namespace. When an organization using Windows 2000 Server for its network operating system needs an Internet presence, the Active Directory namespace is kept as one or more hierarchical Windows 2000 domains beneath a root domain registered as a DNS namespace. You can choose not to be part of the global Internet DNS namespace, but DNS service is still necessary to find Windows 2000 based computers.

8.   If you are creating an Active Directory domain, you must do some further configuration. To configure the DNS server to support Active Directory, you would perform the following steps:

• Ensure that you have a forward lookup zone that is authoritative for the resource records registered by Netlogon

• Configure the forward lookup zone to allow dynamic update

• Unless the selected DNS server is a root DNS server, from the parent server, delegate the forward lookup zone to this server

9.   If the DNS server is not installed, you must install it. If this server is not the root DNS server, configure its network connections to point to the other DNS servers in your network.

10.   The New Zone Wizard guides you through the process of setting up a forward lookup
       zone. There are four configuration options:

       • Zone types

       • Zone name

       • Zone file

       • Master DNS Servers

       You can configure the following three zone types:

       Active Directory Integrated—The Active Directory Integrated zone is the master
       copy of a new zone. The zone uses Active Directory to store and replicate zone files.

       Standard Primary—The Standard Primary zone is the master copy of a new zone
       stored in a standard text file. This is administered and maintained on the computer
       where you created the zone.

       Standard Secondary—The Standard Secondary zone is a replica of an existing zone.
       These are read-only and stored in text files. When creating a secondary zone you must
       specify the DNS server. You create a secondary zone to provide redundancy and
       reduce the load on the name server containing the primary zone database file.

Lesson 2 Quiz

1.   What is the function of a forward lookup query?
      A.   Resolving an IP address to a name
      B.   Reducing the DNS traffic on the network
      C.   Resolving a name to an IP address
      D.   Converting the IP address to a dotted decimal notation

2.   What is the function of a reverse lookup query?
      A.   Resolving an IP address to a name
      B.   Reducing the DNS traffic on the network
      C.   Resolving a name to an IP address
      D.   Converting the IP address to a dotted decimal notation

3.   What is the definition of Domain Name System (DNS)?
      A.   A static, hierarchical name service for TCP/IP hosts
      B.   Allows users to specify a user-friendly name instead of a numeric IP address
      C.   Maps DNS domain names to IP addresses, and vice versa
      D.   Active Directory uses DNS as its location service

4.   Why are debug logs disabled by default?
      A.   Debug logs can often be resource intensive. This affects server performance and consumes disk space.
      B.   The functions to carry out additional trace-level logging of selected types of events or messages for general troubleshooting and debugging of the server are always turned on.
      C.   DNS server event messages are separate from events caused by other applications and services.
      D.   They should only be used temporarily, when more detailed information about server performance is needed.

5.   What are the benefits of directory-integrated primary zones?
      A.   Multi-master update and enhanced security from Active Directory
      B.   Allows users, computers, and applications to query the DNS to specify remote systems by Fully Qualified Domain Names rather than by IP addresses
      C.   The process of resolving a NetBIOS name to its IP address
      D.   The set of connections that domain controllers use to replicate information among themselves

6.   You can use the DNS Console to perform a number of tasks. Which of the
      following is NOT a task for which you can use the DNS Console?
      A.   Performing initial configuration of a new DNS server
      B.   Modifying security for specific zones or resource records
      C.   Viewing and modifying IP configuration details used by the computer
      D.   Tuning advanced server options

7.   Which of the following are ways Active Directory is integrated with DNS?
      A.   It is an optional software component and appears under Networking
            Services in the component list.
      B.   Active Directory and DNS have the same hierarchical structure.
      C.   DNS zones can be stored in Active Directory.
      D.   Active Directory clients use DNS to locate domain controllers.

8.   What is Domain Name Service (DNS)?
      A.   The DNS database is a tree structure called domain name space. Each
            domain (node in the tree structure) is named and can contain sub-domains.
            The domain name identifies the domain's position in the database in
            relation to its parent domain. A period separates each part of the name for
            each network node in the DNS domain.
      B.   It maintains consistent hierarchical naming scheme across your
            organization.
      C.   It allows Internet connection using Internet naming conventions.
      D.   It is used to ultimately resolve FQDN into an IP address that is then used
            by the networks that connect LANs together.

9.   What is the difference between a zone and a namespace?
      A.   A domain name server stores information about part of the domain namespace
            called a zone. The name server is authoritative for a particular zone.
      B.   A zone is a portion of a domain.
      C.   If there are no sub-domains, then the zone and domain are the same—the zone
            contains all data for the domain.
      D.   A single name server can be authoritative for many zones.

10.   In the DNS name, computer1.acctg.ibidpub.com., what denotes the root node?
      A.   It is the .com.
      B.   It is the ibidpub.com.
      C.   It is the period after the com.
      D.   It is the whole name.

Answers to Lesson 2 Quiz

1. Answer C is correct. A forward lookup query resolves a name to an IP address.

    Answer A is incorrect. It is a reverse lookup query.

    Answer B is incorrect. The name server caches the query results to reduce the DNS traffic on the network.

    Answer D is incorrect. IP addresses are expressed in dotted decimal notation to make IP addressing easier.

2. Answer A is correct. A reverse lookup query resolves an IP address to a name.

    Answer B is incorrect. The name server caches the query results to reduce the DNS traffic on the network.

    Answer C is incorrect. It is a forward lookup query.

    Answer D is incorrect. IP addresses are expressed in dotted decimal notation to make IP addressing easier.

3. Answers A, B, C and D are correct. A Domain Name System is a hierarchical distributed database that is employed for name/address translation. DNS is the namespace used on the Internet to translate computer and service names into TCP/IP addresses. Active Directory uses DNS as its location service, and clients find domain controllers using DNS queries.

4. Answers A and D are correct. Debug logs are often resource intensive, affecting server performance and consuming disk space.

    Answer B is incorrect. However, you can choose which options to enable for additional trace-level logging of selected types of events or messages for general troubleshooting and debugging of the server.

    Answer C is incorrect. DNS server event messages are separate from events caused by other applications and services.

5.   Answer A is correct. The benefits of Active Directory-integrated zones for networks are: multi-master update and enhanced security based on the capabilities of Active Directory; zones are replicated and synchronized to new domain controllers automatically whenever a new zone is added to an Active Directory domain; by integrating storage of your DNS namespace in Active Directory, you simplify planning and administration for both DNS and Active Directory; and directory replication is faster and more efficient than standard DNS replication.

Answer B is incorrect. It is part of the definition of DNS.

Answer C is incorrect. It is NetBIOS name resolution.

Answer D is incorrect. Topology is the set of connections that domain controllers use to replicate information among themselves.

6.   Answer C is correct. This is what the Ipconfig command-line utility does.

Answers A, B and D are incorrect. They are all functions of the DNS Console.

7.   Answer B is correct. Although separate and implemented differently for different purposes, an organization's namespace for DNS and Active Directory have an identical structure.

Answer C is correct. Primary zone files can be stored in Active Directory for replication to other Active Directory domain controllers.

Answer D is correct. To locate a domain controller for a specified domain, Active Directory clients query their configured DNS server for specific resource records.

Answer A is incorrect. If you provide support for clients running Microsoft Windows NT 4.0, you will need to install Windows Internet Name Service (WINS) on one or more servers in the domain. It is an option on the component list.

8.   Answer A is correct. It is the definition of DNS.

Answer B and C are incorrect. They are benefits of DNS.
Answer D is incorrect. It is a description of how DNS resolves FQDNs into IP addresses.

9.   Answers A, B, C and D are correct. Domain name servers store information about the domain name space called a zone. The name server is authoritative for a particular zone. A single name server can be authoritative for many zones. A zone is a portion of a domain.

10.   Answer C is correct. A period separates each part of the name for each network node in the DNS domain. The root node in a DNS database is unnamed. The root node is referenced in DNS names with a trailing period (.). For example: Computer1.acctg.ibidpub.com. It is the period after com that stands for the DNS root node.

Answer A is incorrect. .com is a first-level domain.

Answer B is incorrect. ibidpub.com is the second-level domain.

Answer D is incorrect. It denotes the Computer1 position in the hierarchical tree.

Domains and Active Directory Installation

The physical network structural foundation of Active Directory is built on the site. By designing sites, the administrator's role is to maximize network performance. A site comprises of one or more Internet Protocol (IP) subnets tied together by high-speed and reliable connections. The administrator determines the speed that ensures maximum network performance with minimum loss due to network traffic.

The most important function of sites is to make certain that data transmission is both fast and economical, particularly as it relates to effective replication of the directory services. The Active Directory physical structure manages how and when replication happens both between different sites and within the same site.

After completing this lesson, you should have a better understanding of the following topics:

- Domains and Sites

- Domain Creation

- Active Directory Installation

- Site Creation

- Subnet Creation

- Site Links

- Site Link Bridge Creation

- Connection Object Creation

Domains and Sites

There is no formal association between the limits of a domain or a site. A domain can contain multiple sites (Figure 3.1) and a site can have multiple domains (Figure 3.2). Additionally, domains and sites and domains do not have to maintain the same namespace.

A domain controller is a server containing a copy of the Active Directory. All domain controllers are peers and maintain replicated versions of the Active Directory for the domain. The domain controller plays an important role in both the logical and physical structure of Active Directory. It organizes all the domain's object data in a logical and hierarchical data store. It is also operates to authenticate users, provide responses to queries about network objects, and perform replication of directory services. The physical structure provides the means to transmit this data through well-connected sites.

Figure 3.1 Multiple Sites within a Domain

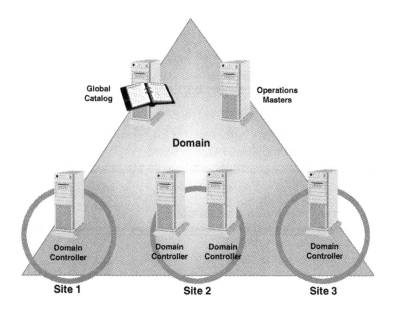

Figure 3.2 Multiple Domains within a Site

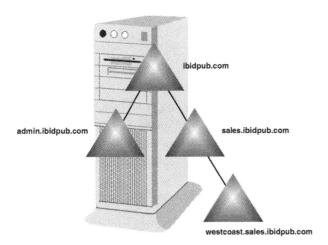

An Active Directory site is a set of Transmission Control Protocol/Internet Protocol (TCP/IP) sub-nets that are well-connected.

 Tip: Well-connected implies high-bandwidth Local Area Network (LAN) (10MB minimum) connectivity, possibly involving several hops through routers.

Sites (physical units) are not part of the Active Directory namespace (a logical construct). Sites may span multiple domains. Likewise, domains may span multiple sites.

 Note: Domains are logical structures and sites are physical structures.

Domain Creation

An Active Directory consists of one or more forests, where a forest has one or more domains. When you create the first domain controller in the network, you create the first domain in a forest. A domain cannot exist without at least one domain controller. A domain is a directory partition.

You use domains to achieve your network management goals. These goals can include defining security, applying Group Policy, structuring the network, and replicating information.

Active Directory lets your Windows 2000 domain controllers function as peers. Clients can update Active Directory on any Windows 2000 domain controller in the domain. Windows 2000 uses the multimaster replication model v5 instead of the single master model that Windows NT 4.0 uses. This is different from the read-write/read-only duties of Microsoft Windows NT 4.0 Server Primary Domain Controllers (PDCs) and Backup Domain Controllers (BDCs). Also, the Microsoft Windows NT 4.0 Server domain system supports single master replication—all changes must be made on the PDC.

The Windows 2000 operating system supports multimaster replication, in which all of a domain's domain controllers can get the changes made to objects and then replicate these changes to all of the other domain controllers in that domain. The first domain controller created in a forest is a Global Catalog server, by default. This Global Catalog holds a complete copy of all the objects in the directory for its domain and a partial replica of all objects stored in the directory of every other domain in the forest.

Each Active Directory domain can have one or more domain controllers providing replication for the directory partition (Figure 3.3). Following are several reasons for having multiple domain controllers in a domain:

* Physical site reasons that give your network better user-connectivity

* If you have a large volume of user activity, it can influence the creation of multiple-domain controller servers

* You need a lower fail rate and redundancy of information

Figure 3.3 Domains and Controllers

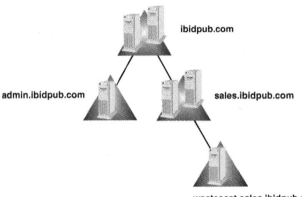

During Active Directory installation, a domain controller is assigned to a site. The site to which it is assigned will remain the same unless you manually relocate the domain controller to different site. The site location of a domain controller is part of the Active Directory replication topology and other system requests.

Creating Windows 2000 Domains

It is important to understand the role of domains within Active Directory. There are similarities between Windows 2000 and Microsoft Windows NT 4.0 domains. Instead of having all users, groups, and computers in one large group, domains let you make logical divisions. You can choose to divide your network by geographic regions or by departments. You can use domains to organize your network.

Another parallel is that Windows 2000 domains are security boundaries. An administrator in one domain may have full control over that domain; however, that administrator cannot administer other domains. This control of administrators is mainly important in large distributed networks with decentralized administration. Additionally, you can only define certain security policies, such as password policies at the domain level. If your network requires different password policies for different users, your only option would be to implement multiple domains.

Another significant feature of domains is that they are partitions of the database. Active Directory is not a single database, unless you have a single-domain network. It is divided between the different domains in a network. Each domain controller contains all the information for objects only in its domain.

Changes made to objects are only replicated to the domain controllers within its domain. For example, if an organization has six domains with 5 million objects each, for a total of 30 million objects, each domain controller would only be responsible for the 5 million objects within its own domain.

Configuring Your Server as a Domain Controller

Dynamic Host Configuration Protocol (DHCP), Domain Name Service (DNS), and DCPROMO (the command-line tool that creates DNS and Active Directory) can be installed manually. To use the Configure Your Server Wizard for installation, follow these steps:

1. Press **Ctrl-Alt-Del** to log on to the server as administrator, and leave the password blank.

2. From **Configure Your Server**, choose **This is the only server in my network** and then select **Next**.

3. Choose **Next** again to configure the server as a domain controller and set up Active Directory, DHCP, and DNS.

4. From within **What do you want to name your domain**, type the name of your domain.

5. From within **Domain name**, type **net**, choose the screen outside the textbox to view the **Preview of the Active Directory domain name**, and then select **Next**.

Note: As shown in Figure 3.4, the combined name appears as LightPointLearning.net within the Preview of Active Directory domain name box. The wizard puts the dot (.) into the name.

Figure 3.4 Configure Your Server Wizard

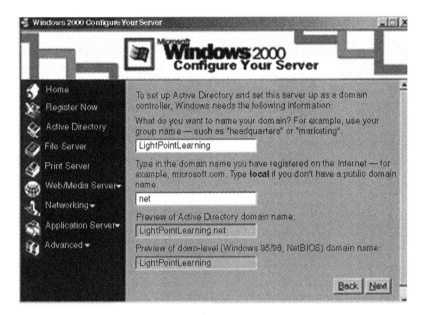

6. Choose **Next** to run the wizard and, when prompted, insert the Windows 2000 Server CD-ROM.

7. When the wizard has completed its tasks, the computer will reboot.

The Configure Your Server Wizard installs DNS and DHCP and configures them and Active Directory. The default values set by the wizard are described in Table 3.1.

Table 3.1 Default Wizard Values

Selection	Value
DHCP Scope	10.0.0.3-10.0.0.254
Preferred DNS Server	127.0.0.1
IP address	10.10.1.1
Subnet mask	255.0.0.0

LightPointLearning.net is the Active Directory domain and DNS name, and LightPointLearning is the down-level domain name.

Active Directory Installation

Active Directory offers a variety of services to organizations. These include authenticating users, managing domain security, enforcing domain policies, and publishing resources such as files, printers, and applications. In an Active Directory domain, you use a hierarchical structure to group resources into Organizational Units (OUs)—objects that contain other objects, such as users or groups. In order to use Active Directory, you must have a Windows 2000 server as a domain controller.

The server can be installed as a standalone server in a workgroup or as a member of a domain. Every domain controller in a domain stores a master copy of the Active Directory database for that domain's naming context. At pre-determined times, any changes to a domain controller in that domain are replicated to other domain controllers in that domain.

Creating Domains, Trees and Forests

The Active Directory Installation Wizard prompts you for information about your organization's domains, trees, and forests. Active Directory can define a single domain. It can also combine multiple domains into trees or forests. The following are short definitions of these terms:

Domain—Domains are administrative and security boundaries. Active Directory data is replicated between domain controllers within a domain.

Tree—A tree is a group of Active Directory domains that share a common schema and a contiguous namespace.

Forest—A forest is a group of Active Directory domain trees that share a common schema but do not have a contiguous namespace.

The first domain you create will always function as the root in a new tree of a domain. When you create a child domain, you link it to the parent domain. When you link a domain to a tree, you create a two-way trust relationship between the new domain and its parent.

Creating DNS names and NetBIOS Domain Names

Active Directory uses the Domain Name System (DNS) to identify and locate all Active Directory objects. Active Directory domains and the objects they contain must conform to DNS naming rules and must use the TCP/IP network protocol.

A DNS server must be present to be able to install Active Directory. If a DNS server is not found, the Installation Wizard will let you install and configure DNS before it proceeds.

After the installation is complete, you can administer your domain using Active Directory (Figure 3.5).

Figure 3.5 Active Directory

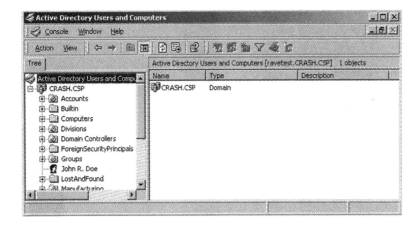

Installing Active Directory on a Windows 2000 Server

After you have installed your Windows 2000 server, you can install Active Directory using the Installation Wizard. To start the wizard, follow these steps:

1. From the **Start** menu, choose **Run**.

2. Type **DCPROMO.EXE**, and click **OK**.

3. From the Installation Wizard (Figure 3.6), choose **Next**.

Figure 3.6 Installation Wizard

4. Within the Active Directory Installation Wizard, choose the server type, if it is to be a new domain controller or a replica domain controller in an existing domain, and select **Next**. (Figure 3.7)

Figure 3.7 Domain Controller Type

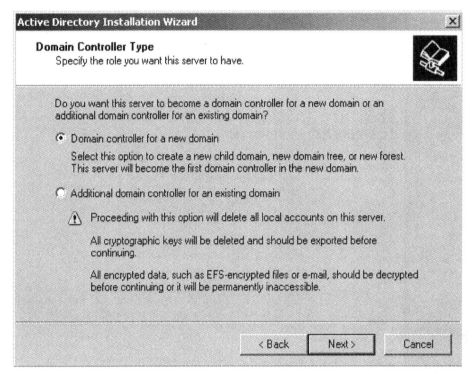

5. Choose the option to create a new domain tree or a new child domain (Figure 3.8), and select **Next**.

Figure 3.8 Create Tree or Child Domain

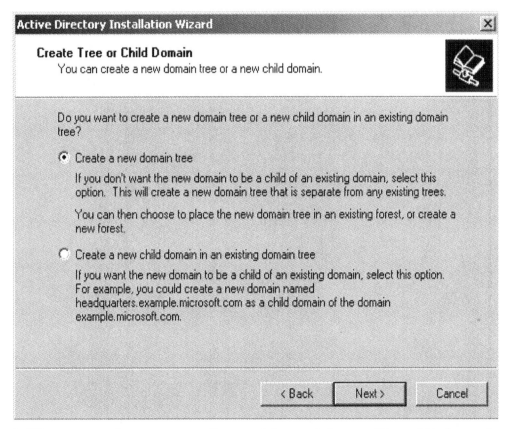

6. When prompted to create a new forest or join an existing one (Figure 3.9) choose the appropriate one for your organization, and then select **Next**.

Figure 3.9 Create or Join Forest

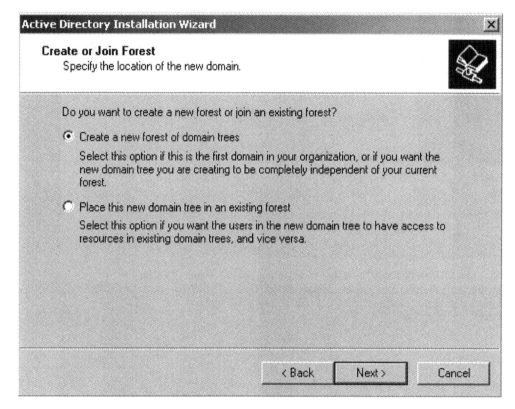

7. Type a name for the new domain (Figure 3.10), and then choose **Next**.

Figure 3.10 New Domain Name

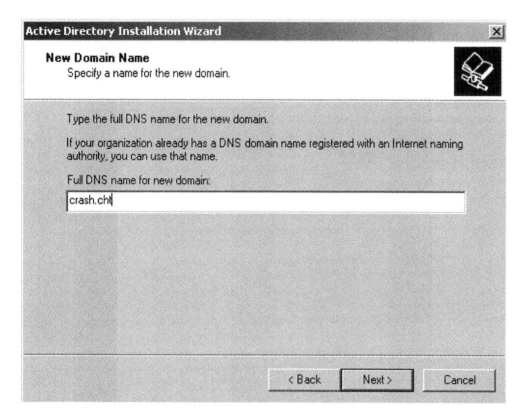

8. The Network Basic Imput/Output System (NetBIOS) equivalent of the DNS name you typed (Figure 3.11) allows computers running earlier versions of Windows to recognize the new domain; accept the suggested name or change it to meet your needs, and then select **Next**.

Figure 3.11 NetBIOS Domain Name

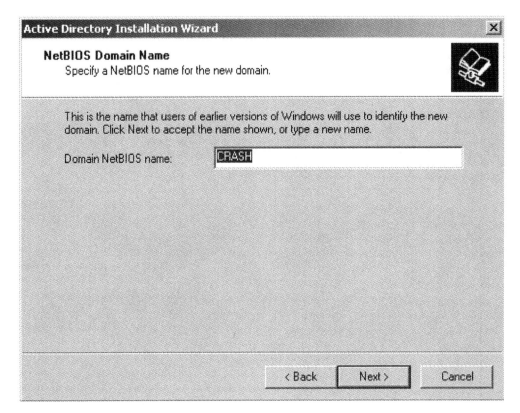

9. The Installation Wizard prompts you for the location of the Active Directory database; you can accept the default or select **Browse** to choose a different location, as shown in Figure 3.12, and select **Next**.

Figure 3.12 Database and Log Locations

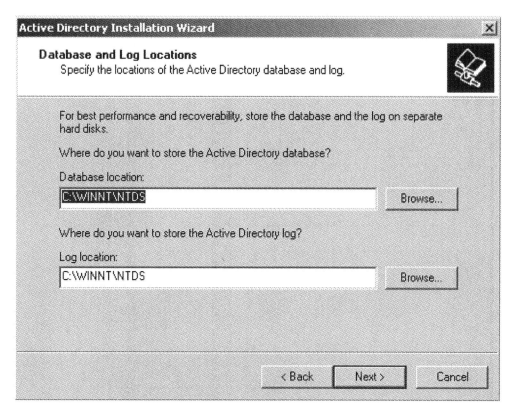

10. You are then prompted for the name of the directory to be shared as the system volume, as shown in Figure 3.13; accept the default values or select **Browse** for a different directory, and then select **Next**.

Figure 3.13 Shared System Volume

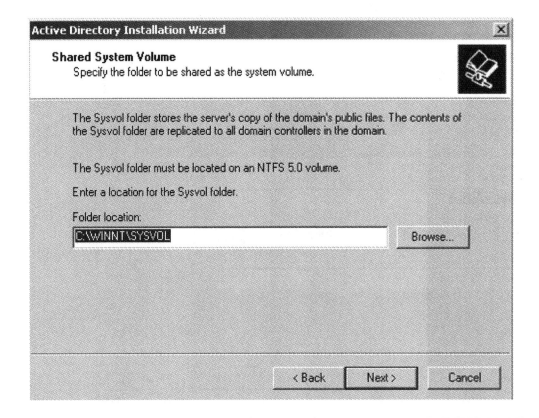

Note: The system volume directory holds the server's copy of the domain's public files. The contents will be replicated among all domain controllers in the domain.

11. Within the summary window of the Installation Wizard (Figure 3.14), confirm the creation of the domain controller, the DNS and NetBIOS name you specified, and the locations for the database, log, and system volume (remember that these values cannot be changed once accepted) by selecting **Back** to make changes or **Next** to accept the values.

Figure 3.14 Installation Summary

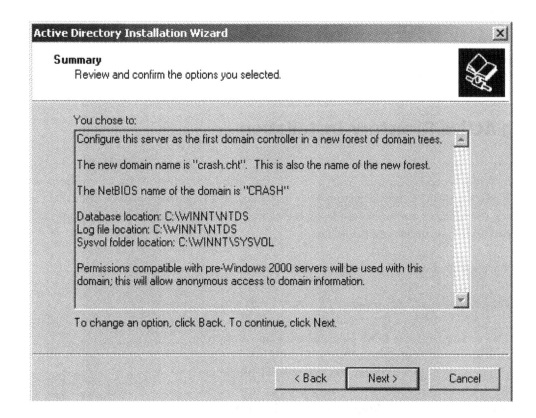

Active Directory Installation Wizard

Summary
Review and confirm the options you selected.

You chose to:

Configure this server as the first domain controller in a new forest of domain trees.

The new domain name is "crash.cht". This is also the name of the new forest.

The NetBIOS name of the domain is "CRASH"

Database location: C:\WINNT\NTDS
Log file location: C:\WINNT\NTDS
Sysvol folder location: C:\WINNT\SYSVOL

Permissions compatible with pre-Windows 2000 servers will be used with this domain; this will allow anonymous access to domain information.

To change an option, click Back. To continue, click Next.

< Back   Next >   Cancel

 Note: When the installation continues, it can take a few minutes, depending on the speed of the server's processor and hard disks.

12. When you see a confirmation of the installation of Active Directory, select **Finish** and restart the server.

Tip: To configure the Active Directory to meet your particular needs, log on as Administrator and use the Active Directory snap-in tool.

Verifying Active Directory Installation

Active Directory has several administrative tools to simplify directory service administration that are included with Windows 2000 Server. You can use the standard tools or use the Microsoft Management Console (MMC) to create custom tools that focus on a single management task. You can also amalgamate several tools into one console, or you can assign custom tools to individual administrators with specific administrative responsibilities.

To verify you have installed Active Directory, you can use one of the following methods:

• Log on as Administrator, and open Active Directory Users and Computers

• View the DNS service from the DNS Management Console snap-in

To verify your Active Directory installation, follow these steps:

1. From the **Start menu**, choose **Programs**, **Administrative Tools**, and then select **Users and Computers** (Figure 3.15).

Figure 3.15 Users and Computers

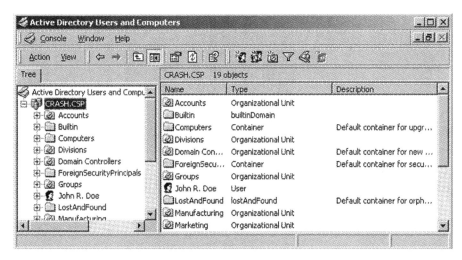

2. To view the DNS service from the DNS console, from the **Start** menu, choose **Programs**, **Administrative** tools, and select **DNS** (Figure 3.16)

Figure 3.16 DNS MMC

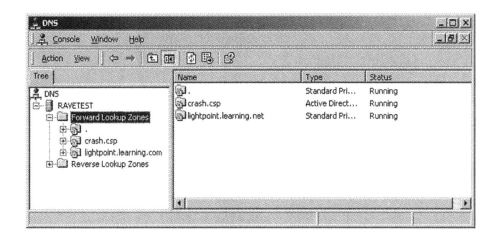

Once Active Directory installation has been verified, it is possible to configure sites. To configure site settings you must complete the following tasks:

• Create a site

• Associate a subnet with the site

• Connect the site using site links

• Select a licensing computer for the site.

Tip: As part of the site setup, you can ensure your organization's legal compliance with Microsoft BackOffice software license agreements. This information is collected on a server by License Logging service in Windows 2000 server and can be configured using the Active Directory Sites and Services.

Site Creation

Since network consistency and cost can vary radically between physical locations, use sites as IP subnets to ensure effective intra-site connectivity. You create a site because rapid and reliable network communication can be established inside that unit. Create links between sites and set the communication to best utilize available bandwidth and control costs.

Sites facilitate the replication of directory data both inside and between sites. Active Directory replicates information inside a site more frequently than across sites. This means the best-connected domain controllers receive updates first.

The domain controllers in other sites receive all the changes to the directory but less often, reducing network bandwidth consumption. A site is delimited by the subnet. It is usually in a specific geographic area and serves three main purposes; locate services, cost assignment, and replication control. Figure 3.17 shows a tree that consists of three domains and sites that cross domain boundaries.

Figure 3.17 Sites and Domains

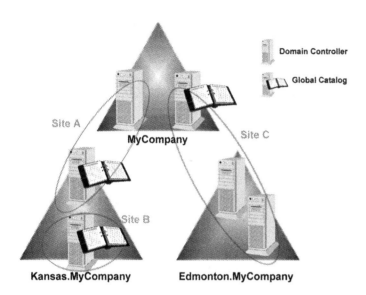

Sites are used to locate services, such as logon and Distributed File System (DFS) services. DFS is a file management system in which files can be located on different computers connected over a Local or Wide Area Network (LAN or WAN). When a client requests a connection to a domain, sites are used so that the client can connect to a domain controller within the same site. If there are no domain controllers in a site with users, then another site that does have domain controllers can provide coverage for the client site.

Site links each have a logical cost assigned to them. If a client is searching for the closest domain controller to log on, they first look for a domain controller (and Global Catalog) in their site. If none exists, they will search for a domain controller in the site with the lowest logical cost assigned to the site link. When a client requests a connection to a service, sites are used to locate and connect to a replica within the same site.

Sites are also used to control replication throughout a forest. The Active Directory automatically creates more replication connections between domain controllers in the same site than between domain controllers in different sites. This results in lower replication latency within a site and lower replication bandwidth between sites. Replication between domain controllers in different sites is compressed 10-15%, resulting in less network bandwidth utilization over the slower links between sites.

Finally, policy objects can be applied to sites (or, more specifically, to computer objects that reside in sites) as a group.

Creating Sites

With Active Directory you can use sites to group servers into containers, which mirror the physical topology of your network and allow you to configure replication between domain controllers. A number of TCP/IP subnets can also be mapped to sites. These subnets allow new servers to automatically join the correct site, depending on their IP address, and for clients to easily find a domain controller closest to them.

When you create the first domain controller at a default site, Default-First-Site-Name is created and the domain controller is assigned to it. Subsequent domain controllers are also added to this site, but they can be moved or renamed.

Sites are administered and created using the Active Directory Sites and Services in the Microsoft Management Console (MMC). To create a new site, follow these steps:

1. From the **Start menu**, choose **Programs**, choose **Administrative Tools**, and then select **Active Directory Sites and Services** (Figure 3.18).

2. From the Tree pane, right-click **Sites**, and then select **New Site**.

Figure 3.18 Sites and Services

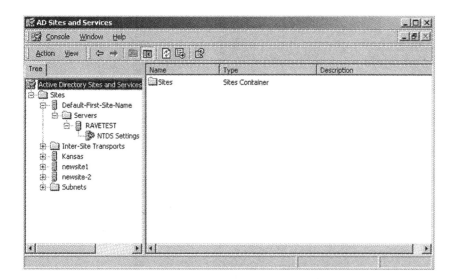

3. From the New Object-Site window, type a name for the site, such as Human Resources.

 Warning: The name must be 63 characters or less and cannot contain (.) or space characters.

4. From the list of link names, select a site link object, and then choose OK.

To rename a site, follow these steps:

1. From the **Start** menu, choose **Programs**, **Administrative Tools**, and then select **Active Directory Sites and Services**.

2. From the Tree pane, select the **Sites** folder.

3. From the Details pane, right-click the site you want to rename, and then select **Rename**.

4. Type a new name for the site and press **ENTER**.

Subnet Creation

Computers on TCP/IP networks are assigned to sites based on their location in a subnet or set of subnets. Subnets group computers in a way that identifies their feasible physical proximity on the network. Subnet information is used to find a domain controller in the same site as the computer, which is authenticating during logon, and also during Active Directory replication to determine the best routes between controllers.

IP addressing

Each TCP/IP host is recognized by a unique logical IP address and each 32-bit IP address identifies the location of a host system on the network. This is similar to how a street address can identify a business. An IP address is separated internally into two parts—a network ID and a host ID.

In an IP address, the network ID, distinguishes a single network segment within a larger TCP/IP network. All of the systems that attach and share access to the same network have the common network ID inside their full IP address. This ID also identifies each network within a larger network.

The host ID distinguishes a TCP/IP node, such as a server or other TCP/IP device, inside each network. The host ID for each device uniquely identifies each single system inside its own network.

A 32-bit address would look like the following:

10000011 01101011 00010000 11001000

To make IP addressing simpler, IP addresses are written in dotted decimal notation. The 32-bit IP address is divided into four 8-bit octets that are converted to decimal (base-10 numbering system) and separated by periods.

The previous IP address expressed in dotted decimal notation would look like the following:

131.107.16.200

Figure 3.19 shows how the IP address (131.107.16.200) is divided into network and host ID sections. The network ID segment (131.107) is shown by the first two numbers of the IP address. The host ID portion (16.200) is shown by the last two numbers of the IP address.

Figure 3.19 IP Address

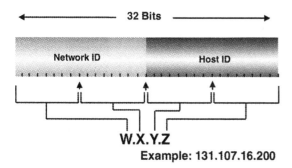

W.X.Y.Z
Example: 131.107.16.200

 Tip: Since IP addresses identify devices on a network, a unique IP address must be assigned to each device on the network.

Usually computers have a single network adapter installed and need only a single IP address. If you have a computer with multiple network adapters, each adapter needs its own IP address. This address is how you would identify subnets.

Creating Subnets

Sites, site links and subnets are all stored in the configuration container, which is replicated to every domain controller in the forest. Every domain controller in the forest has complete knowledge of the site topology. A change to the site topology causes replication to every domain controller in the forest.

Once you have created the site, you can assign various IP subnets.

To create a subnet using the Active Directory Sites and Services MMC, follow these steps:

1. From the **Start menu**, choose **Programs**, **Administrative Tools**, and then select **Active Directory Sites and Services**.

2. From the Tree pane, expand **Sites**.

Figure 3.20 New Subnet

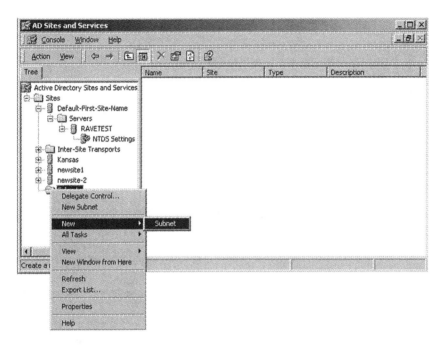

3. Right-click **Subnets**, choose **New**, and then choose **Subnet** (Figure 3.20).

4. Type an IP address and subnet mask for the subnet.

Figure 3.21 New Object Subnet

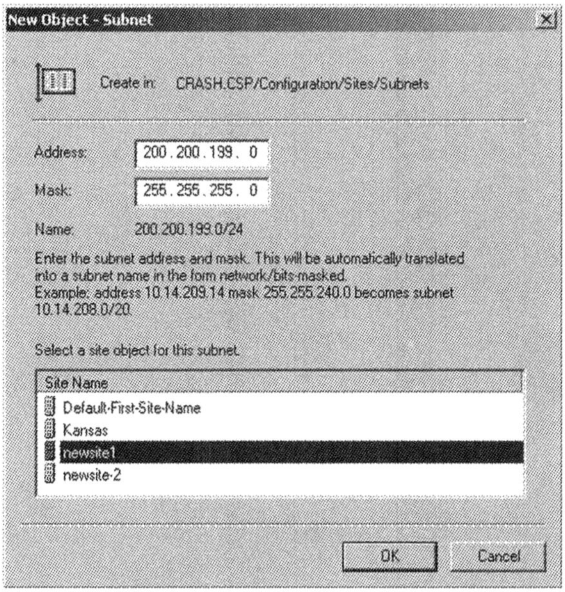

5. From the list of site objects, choose a site, and then choose OK (Figure 3.21).

You now have a subnet linked to a site. You can assign multiple subnets to a site if you wish.

To connect an existing subnet with a site using the Active Directory Sites and Services MMC snap-in, follow these steps:

1. From the **Start menu**, choose **Programs**, **Administrative Tools**, and then select **Active Directory Sites and Services**.

2. From the Tree pane, expand **Sites** and then select **Subnets**.

3. From the Details pane, right-click the, and then choose **Properties**

Figure 3.22 Subnet Property Page

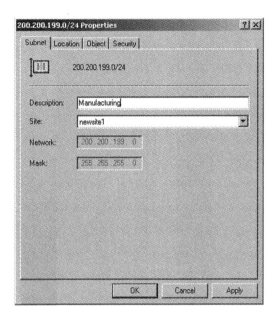

4. From the subnet Properties General property page (Figure 3.22), select a site.

To move a computer into a site, follow these steps:

1. From the **Start** menu, choose Programs, choose Administrative Tools, and then select Active Directory Sites and Services.

2. From the Tree pane, expand **Sites**, expand the name of the site that currently contains the server, and then expand **Servers**.

3. Right-click the server you wish to move and select **Move**.

4. Select the destination site, and then choose **OK**.

Site Links

You must create links between sites before you can replicate the sites. You can enhance site link connectivity by creating site link bridges and designating a specific server, called the bridgehead server, to act as the exchange point for the trading of directory information amongst the sites.

Site link objects describe a collection of sites that can communicate at a similar cost through inter-site transport. For IP transport, a normal site link connects just two sites and corresponds to an actual WAN link. An IP site link connecting more than two sites might correspond to an Asynchronous Transfer Mode (ATM) backbone connecting several buildings or offices in a city through leased lines and IP routers.

To configure inter-site replications you must complete the following tasks:

* Create site links

* Configure site links

* Create site link bridges

The following tasks are optional:

* Configure connection objects

* Designate a bridgehead server

 Warning: You must manually configure site links in a multi-site directory.

Creating Site Links

For scheduled replication to occur between multiple sites, both sites must agree on a transport to communicate. To create a site link using the Active Directory Sites and Services MMC snap-in, follow these steps:

1. From the **Start** menu, choose **Programs**, **Administrative Tools**, and then select **Active Directory Sites and Services**.

2. In the left pane, choose the **plus sign (+)** next to **Inter-Site Transports**.

3. Right-click **IP**, and select **New Site Link** (Figure 3.23).

Figure 3.23 New Site Link

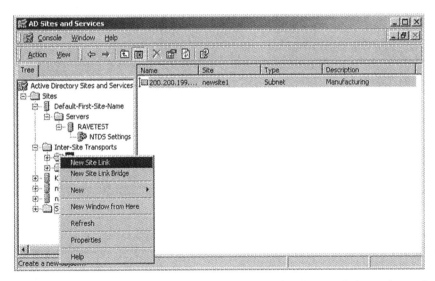

4. Within **New Object–Site Link**, type a name for the site link, as shown in Figure 3.24.

Figure 3.24 New Object Site Link

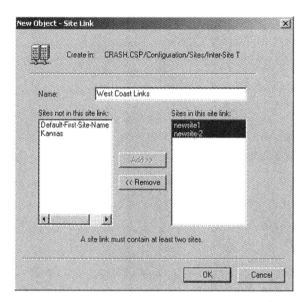

5. In the left pane, choose **Sites**, and then **Add**.

6. When all the sites you want to include in this site link are added to the right pane list, click **OK**.

Replication Protocols

Directory information can be exchanged over site links that use different protocols, such as IP or Simple Mail Transfer Protocol (SMTP).

IP replication is the messenger protocol of TCP/IP and is responsible for addressing and sending IP packets over the network. IP does not guarantee that packets arrive at their destination or arrive in the sequence in which they were sent. Active Directory replication occurs using Remote Procedure Calls (RPC). By default, inter-site IP replication does adhere to replication schedules, although you may choose to configure Active Directory replication to ignore schedules.

Note: IP replication does not require a Certification Authority (CA).

SMTP replication is only used for replication over site links and not for replication within a site. Since SMTP is asynchronous, it ignores all schedules. Do not configure site link replication availability on SMTP site links unless your network's SMTP connections meet the following conditions:

• The site links use scheduled connections

• The SMTP queue is not on a schedule

• Information is being exchanged directly from one server to another

If you decide to use SMTP over site links, you must install and configure an Enterprise Certification Authority. The Certification Authority will sign SMTP messages exchanged between domain controllers to guarantee the validity of directory updates.

 Warning: If you create a SMTP link, you must have an Enterprise Certification Authority (Enterprise CA) available and SMTP must be installed on all domain controllers that will use the site link.

Linking Two Sites

To create a link between two sites, follow these steps:

1. From the **Start menu,** choose **Programs, Administrative Tools,** and then select **Active Directory Sites and Services**.

2. From the Tree pane, expand **Sites,** expand **Inter-site Transports,** and then select one of the transports (either IP or SNMP).

3. From the Details pane, right-click a link and choose **Properties**.

4. Add a site and then choose **OK**.

Note: Creating a site link between two or more sites is a way to influence replication topology. By creating a site link, you provide Active Directory with information about what connections are available, which ones are preferred, and how much bandwidth is available. Active Directory uses this information to choose times and connections for replication that will afford the best performance.

Disabling a Site Link

All site links are bridged together by default. This makes them transitive so that the Knowledge Consistency Checker (KCC) can create the connection objects between domain controllers. To disable this site link transitivity and then manually bridge selected site links to give you more control, follow these steps:

1. From the **Start** menu, choose **Programs**, **Administrative Tools**, and then select **Active Directory Sites and Services**.

2. Expand the **Sites** branch.

3. Expand **Inter-Site Transports**.

4. Right-click the **Protocol** for which you wish to disable transitivity (IP or SMTP), and then choose **Properties**.

5. Deselect **Bridge all Site Links**, and select **Apply** (Figure 3.25).

Note: For more information on Disabling a site link, refer to Microsoft's Technet web page at www.microsoft.com/technet.

Figure 3.25 Deselect Bridge All Site Links

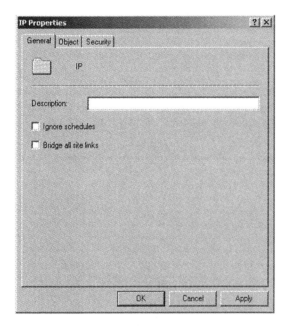

6. Click **OK.**

 Note: You will need to manually create site link bridges to enable connection objects to be created by the KCC.

Site Link Attributes

As part of configuring inter-site replication, you should provide the information described in Table 3.2.

Table 3.2 Configuration Parameters for Inter-Site Replication

Attribute	Descriptions
Site Link Cost	You assign a value for the cost of each connection for inter-site replication. Active Directory always chooses the connection on a per-cost basis. The cheaper connection is used when available. For example, you have a T1 connection and a dial-up connection in case the T1 is unavailable. You would configure a higher cost for the dial-up connection.
Replication Frequency	You assign an integer value that tells Active Directory how many minutes it needs to wait before connecting to check for replication updates. This interval must be more than 15 and less than 10,080 minutes (10,080 minutes = 1 week).
Replication Availability	You define a schedule for the site link to be available for replications. Since STMP is asynchronous, it ignores all schedules, and you do not need to schedule for STMP.

Site Link Bridge Creation

The process for creating a site link bridge is identical to creating a site link, except that, instead of providing site names for the link, you provide site link names for the bridge. A site link bridge object represents a set of site links, all of which can communicate by way of some transport. Normally a site link bridge corresponds with a router (or a set of routers) in an IP network. A site link bridge is useful in networks that are not fully routed.

Any network that you can describe by a combination of site links and site link bridges, you can also describe by site links alone. By using site link bridges, the network description is much smaller and easier for you to maintain because you do not need a site link to describe every possible path between pairs of sites.

You create a site link bridge object for a specific inter-site transport (typically IP transport) by specifying two or more site links for the specified inter-site transport.

A site link bridge object for a specific inter-site transport (most often IP) is created by specifying two or more site links (Figure 3.26). For example:

- Site link AB connects sites A and B through an IP, with a cost of 3

- Site link BC connects sites B and C through an IP, with a cost of 4

- Site link ABC connects AB and BC

- The site link bridge ABC implies that an IP message can be sent from site A to site C with a cost of 7 (3+4)

Figure 3.26 Site Link Bridge

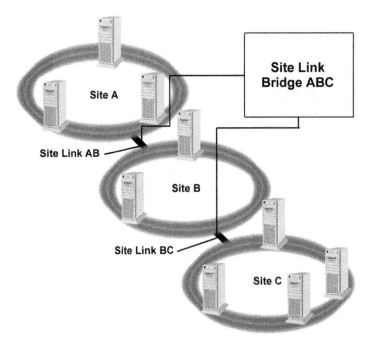

Each site link in a bridge needs to have a site in common with another site link in the bridge. If not, the bridge cannot compute the costs from sites in the link to the sites in other links of the bridge.

Multiple site link bridges for the same transport work together to model multi-hop routing (Figure 3.27). For example:

• Site link CD connects the sites C and D through an IP, with the cost of 2

• Site link bridge BCD connects BC and CD

• The site link bridges ABC and BCD together imply that an IP message can be sent from site D to site A with a cost of 9 (2+3+4)

Figure 3.27 Site Link Bridge Two

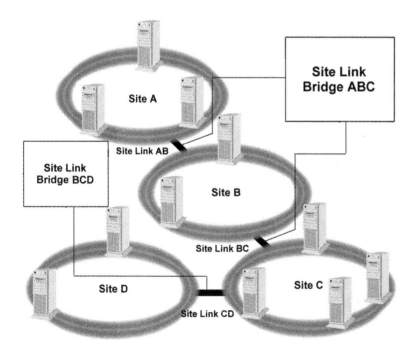

Creating Site Link Bridges

To create a site link bridge using the Active Directory Sites and Services MMC snap-in, follow these steps:

1. From the **Start** menu, choose **Programs**, **Administrative Tools**, and then select **Active Directory Sites and Services**.

2. In the console tree, right-click the **Inter-Site transport folder** for which you want to create a new site link bridge, and then select **New Site Link Bridge**.

3. Within **Name**, type a name for the site link bridge.

4. Select two or more **Site Links** to be bridged, and then select **Add** (Figure 3.28).

Figure 3.28 Bridging Sites

Note: If you have enabled Bridge all Site Links, this procedure will have no effect.

Connection Object Creation

A connection object represents a replication connection from one domain controller to another. The connection object is a child of the replication destination's NT 4.0 Directory Server (NTDS) settings object and points to the replication source.

Connection objects are created in two ways:

• By the KCC running on the destination domain controller

• By an Active Directory administrator

By creating site links and configuring their replication accessibility, relative cost, and replication frequency, you provide Active Directory with information about what connection objects to create to replicate directory data. Active Directory uses site links as indicators for where it should create connection objects, and connection objects use the actual network connections to exchange directory information.

A connection is uni-directional. A bi-directional replication connection is represented as two connection objects under two different NTDS settings objects.

Note: NTDS setting objects represents the Naming Contexts (NCs) held on a particular domain controller.

Replication is performed between Naming Context (NC) replicas. Two domain controllers will often have several NCs in common. They always have at least two—the configuration NC and the schema NC. If a connection exists from one domain controller to another, it will be used for replicating as many NCs as they have in common..

The KCC creates connections to keep your directory connected even in the case of extended failures and outages. Normally, you only create connections manually if the KCC has not connected domain controllers that you think should be connected.

Inside a site, you may decide to add connections to reduce the intra-site replication latency. By default, an update does not take more than three hops from where it begins in a site to any other domain controller. To reduce the hop count to two or one, you add extra links. The cost associated is more Control Processing Unit (CPU)cycles, disk reads, and network messages spent on replication.

Between sites, you may decide to add connections to reduce latency, chiefly in case of failures. The KCC creates new connections to work around failures, but this adds some latency. Here again, the cost is more CPU cycles, disk reads, and network messages spent on replication.

A connection incorporates a replication schedule. You can create a connection manually to achieve a replication schedule that cannot be accomplished by using the KCC. If you create the same connection as the one the KCC would normally create, the KCC will not create an additional connection.

 Note: The KCC will never delete a connection you create.

When you create a site link object, you can specify the replication period. If you do not, a global default replication period (which you can also define) will be created for the site link. When the KCC creates a connection object, its replication period will be the maximum of the time periods along the minimum-cost path of site link objects—from one end of the connection to the other. This means you can control topology and schedule independently.

You control topology by setting the costs on site links. For example, you might set cost=1 for site links that are part of your backbone network and cost=100 for site links with slow connections to branch offices. By setting costs in this manner, you can ensure that a branch office replicates with a domain controller in a site that is part of the backbone and never with a second branch office.

Note: Cost numbers do not have any influence on the replication period.

You control the replication period by setting it on site links. For instance, you could set the global default replication period to 15 minutes and set a longer period for site links corresponding to the slow connections to branch offices.

 Note: The longer default replication period makes more efficient use of a slow link but increases replication latency.

You manage link availability by using the schedule on site links. On most links, you would use 100 percent available—the default on most links, but you may possibly block replication traffic during peak business hours on links to certain branches.

 Note: By blocking replication, you give priority to other traffic but increase replication latency.

You can enable connection objects for change notification. Change notification is automatic within a site. Nevertheless, change notification will occur from a domain controller in one site to a domain controller in another if a connection object, with change notification enabled, connects the two domain controllers in the correct orientation.

 Note: The KCC will not create connections that are enabled for change notification, but an administrator can do so.

Creating Connection Objects

To ensure that the Active Directory service in the Windows 2000 operating system can replicate properly, a service known as the Knowledge Consistency Checker (KCC) runs on all domain controllers and automatically establishes connections between individual computers in the same site. These are known as Active Directory connection objects. An administrator can establish additional connection objects or remove connection objects, but, at any point where replication within a site becomes impossible or has a single point of failure, the KCC steps in and establishes as many new connection objects as necessary to resume Active Directory replication.

To manually configure connections using the Active Directory Sites and Services MMC snap-in, follow these steps:

1. From the **Start** menu, choose Programs, choose Administrative Tools, and then select Active Directory Sites and Services.

2. From the Tree pane, expand **Sites**, expand the site that contains the domain controller, expand **Servers**, and then expand the domain controller.

3. Right-click **NTDS Settings** and then choose **New Active Directory Connection**.

4. From **Find Domain Controllers**, select the domain controller you wish to include in the connection object, and then choose OK (Figure 3.29).

Figure 3.29 Find Domain Controllers

5. From New Object-Connection, type a name for the new connection object, and then choose **OK** (Figure 3.30).

Figure 3.30 New Object Connection

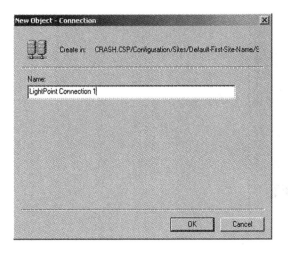

Vocabulary

Review the following terms in preparation for the certification exam.

Term	Description
ATM	Asynchronous Transfer Mode transmits data, voice, and frame relay traffic in real time by breaking data into packets.
BDC	A Backup Domain Controller contains a copy of the directory database and can authenticate users. If the Primary Domain Controller (PDC) fails, then a BDC can be made a PDC. A PDC can be demoted to a BDC if one of the BDC's is promoted to the PDC.
CPU	The Central Processing Unit is the device that processes and transmits data, and where most calculations take place.
DCPROMO.EXE	The utility used to promote a member server to a Windows 2000 domain controller.
DFS	A Distributed File System is a file management system where files can be located on many computers connected over a Local or Wide Area Network.
DHCP	The Dynamic Host Configuration Protocol is a networking protocol that provides safe, reliable, and simple TCP/IP network configuration. It offers dynamic configuration of IP addresses and ensures that address conflicts do not occur. It also conserves the use of IP addresses through centralized management of address allocation.
DNS	The Domain Name System is a hierarchical distributed database employed for name/address translation. DNS is the namespace used on the Internet to translate computer and service names into TCP/IP addresses. Active Directory uses DNS as its location service.
domain	An administrative and security boundary. A domain is also a unit/partion of replication.
Enterprise CA	The Enterprise Certification Authority is responsible for establishing and vouching for the authenticity of public keys belonging to users or other certification authorities.

Term	Description
forest	A group of Active Directory domain trees that share a common schema and configuration NC, but do not have a contiguous namespace.
IP	The Internet Protocol is a routable protocol in charge of IP addressing, routing, and the fragmentation and reassembly of IP packets. It is used widely on the Internet for the exchange of information.
KCC	The Knowledge Consistency Checker is a service that automatically generates a replication topology. It runs on all domain controllers and automatically establishes connections between the machines in a site. When replication within a site becomes impossible or has a single point of failure, the KCC steps in and establishes as many new connection objects as necessary to resume Active Directory replication.
LAN	A Local Area Network is also called LAN. It is made up of computers and other devices connected by a communications link that allows one device to interact with any other in a limited area.
MMC	The Microsoft Management Console is a framework for hosting the consoles (administrative tools). Consoles contain tools, folders or other containers, World Wide Web pages, and other administrative items. The main MMC window provides commands and tools for authoring consoles.
multimaster replication	A replication model in which any domain controller accepts and replicates directory changes to any other domain controller. This differs from other replication models in which the computer stores the single modifiable copy of the directory and other computers store backup copies.
NC	In Active Directory, Naming Context is any contiguous branch, or a subtree within a tree.
NTDS	The Windows New Technology Directory Server is a contiguous subtree of the directory that forms a unit of replication.
OU	Organizational Units are objects that contain other objects, such as users or groups.

Term	Description
PDC	A Primary Domain Controller must be installed before any other domain servers. The Primary Domain Controller maintains the master copy of the directory database and authenticates users. If the PDC fails then a Backup Domain Controller (BDC) can be made a PDC. A PDC can be demoted to a BDC if one of the BDC's is promoted to the PDC.
RPC	Remote Procedure Call is a protocol that allows a program on a server to be executed by another computer. Active Directory replication occurs using Remote Procedure Calls.
site link	A link between two sites that allows replication to occur. Each site contains the schedule that determines when replication can occur between sites that a link connects.
site link bridge	The linking of more than two sites for replication and using the same transport. When site links are bridges, they are transitive (all sites linked for a specific transport implicitly belong to a single site bridge for that transport).
site	A site is a collection of IP subnets. A site object represents a site in Active Directory. Sites are not tied in any way to the Active Directory domain namespace. The name of a directory object does not reflect the site or sites in which the object is stored. A site may contain domain controllers from several domains, and domain controllers from a domain may be present in several sites.
SMTP	Simple Mail Transfer Protocol is a protocol for sending e-mail messages between servers. Most e-mail systems that send mail over the Internet use SMTP to send messages from one server to another.
subnets	Subnets group computers in a way that identifies their feasible physical proximity on the network. Subnet information is used to find a domain controller in the same site as the computer that is authenticating during logon and is used during Active Directory replication to determine the best routes between controllers.

Term	Description
TCP/IP	Transmission Control Protocol/Internet Protocol is a set of software networking protocols used on the Internet. It provides communication across interconnected networks of computers with diverse hardware architectures and operating systems. TCP/IP includes standards for how computers communicate and conventions for connecting networks and routing traffic.
tree	A group of Active Directory domains that share a common schema and a contiguous namespace.
WAN	A Wide Area Network spans a large geographical area and typically consists of two or more LANs.

In Brief

If you want to...	Then do this...
Add a site	1. From the **Start** menu, choose **Programs**, **Administrative Tools**, and then **Active Directory Sites and Services**. 2. In the left pane of the console, right-click **Sites**, and then select **New Site**. 3. Within **New Object–Site**, type a name for the new site. 4. Select a **Site Link Object** that contains the new site; if presented with a Default Site Link, you might associate this site to it at this time, and then click **OK**. 5. When the Active Directory message box appears, click **OK**.
Associate the subnet with a site	1. From the start **Menu**, choose **Programs**, **Administrative** Tools, and then select **Active Directory Sites and Service** 2. From the **Subnets folder**, in the right pane of the console, right-click the subnet, and then select **Properties**. 3. Within **Properties**, select a site you wish to associate with this subnet from the list box. 4. From **Location**, type the site you wish to associate with the subnet, and click **OK**.
Configure your server	1. From the **Start menu**, choose **Programs, Administrative Tools**, and then select **Configure Your Server**. 2. Select the components you wish to configure, and then follow the prompts to install and configure the services.

If you want to...	Then do this...
Create a link between two sites	1. From the **Start menu**, choose **Programs, Administrative Tools**, and then select **Active Directory Sites and Services**. 2. From the console tree, expand **Sites**, expand **Inter-Site Transports**, and then select one of the protocols. 3. From the right pane, right-click the appropriate site and select **Properties**. 4. Select a site, choose **Add**, and then choose **OK**.
Create a new site	1. From the **Start menu**, choose **Programs, Administrative Tools**, and then select **Active Directory Sites and Services**. 2. Right-click **Sites**, and then choose **New Site**. 3. Type a name for the site, select a site link, and then click **Ok**.
Create a site link	1. From the **Start** menu, choose **Programs, Administrative Tools**, and then **Active Directory Sites and Services**. 2. In the console tree, right-click the **Inter-Site transport protocol** you want the site link to use, and select **New Site Link**. 3. In **Name**, type the name to be given to the link. 4. Choose two or more sites to connect, and then select **Add**.
Create a site link bridge	1. From the **Start** menu, choose **Programs, Administrative Tools**, and then **Active Directory Sites and Services**. 2. In the console tree, right-click the **Inter-Site transport** folder for which you want to create a new site link bridge, and then select **New Site Link Bridge.** 3. In **Name**, type a name for the site link bridge. 4. Select two or more site links to be bridged, and then select **Add**.

If you want to...	Then do this...
Create a subnet	1. From the **Start** menu, choose **Programs**, **Administrative Tools**, and then **Active Directory Sites and Services**.
	2. Expand the **Sites** branch, right-click on **Subnets**, and select **New Subnet**.
	3. Type the **Address** and **Mask**, and select the site you wish to associate with the subnet. Click **OK**.
Install Active Directory	1. From the **Start** menu, choose **Run**.
	2. Within **Open**, type **DCPROMO.EXE**, and click **OK**.
	3. Select **Next** to continue.
	4. Choose the server type, and select **Next**.
	5. Choose a new domain tree or a new child domain, and select **Next**.
	6. Type the **DNS** name, and select **Next**.
	7. When the NetBIOS equivalent of the DNS name you typed displays, accept or change the name, and select **Next**.
	8. At the prompt for the name of the directory to be shared as the system volume, accept the default, or select a different directory, and select **Next**.
	9. When a summary window displays your selections, choose **Back** to make changes or **Next** to accept the values.
	10. When a confirmation of the installation of Active Directory displays, select **Finish**.
	11. You will then be prompted to restart the server.

If you want to...	Then do this...
Move computers into a site	1. From the **Start** menu, choose **Programs**, **Administrative Tools**, and then **Active Directory Sites and Services**.
	2. Within the left plane of the **Active Directory Sites and Services** snap-in, right-click the computer you want to move, and select **Move**.
	3. From **Move Server**, select the **Site** to which you want to move the computer, and click **OK**.

Lesson 3 Activities

Complete the following activities to prepare for the certification exam.

1. Explain how to disable site link transitivity.

2. Explain how to create a new site link.

3. Explain how you create a site link bridge.

4. Describe why site link bridges are important for communication.

5. Explain what PDCs and BDCs are.

6. Name the four tasks you need to complete to configure a site.

7. When reviewing the Active Directory replication topology on your network, you notice that your most powerful server is not connected to the domain controller that experiences the most changes as a replication partner. Describe what you should do.

8. Explain what cost and schedule mean in relation to site links.

9. Describe the difference between replication frequency and replication availability.

10. Explain why you would manually configure connections.

Answers to Lesson 3 Activities

1. 1. Within the **Active Directory Sites and Services** MMC snap-in, expand **Sites**.

    2. Expand **Inter-Site Transports**.

    3. Right-click on the protocol for which you wish to disable transitivity (IP or SMTP), and select **Properties**.

    4. Unselect **Bridge all Site Links**, and select **Apply**.

    5. Click **OK**.

    You will need to manually create site link bridges to enable connections made by the KCC.

2. 1. Within the **Active Directory Sites and Services** MMC snap-in, Expand **Sites**.

    2. Expand **Inter-Site Transports**.

    3. Right-click the **IP** or **SMTP protocol** (depending on the type of site link you wish to create), and select **New Site Link**.

    4. Select the sites that should be part of the link, type a name for the link, and click **OK**.

3. 1. Within the **Active Directory Sites and Services** MMC snap-in, expand **Sites**.

    2. Expand **Inter-Site Transports**.

    3. Right-click the protocol for which you wish to create the bridge (IP or SMTP), and select **New Site Link Bridge**.

    4. Type a name for the bridge, and select the site links that will form the bridge.

    5. Click **OK**.

4. Site link bridges are essential for your network. For example, you have 3 sites Kansas, Portland and Edmonton and you have two site links, Kansas to Portland and Edmonton to Portland. If you have turned off site link transitivity, then there is no way for Edmonton and Kansas to talk. The site link bridge lets Portland act as a router for communication between Edmonton and Kansas.

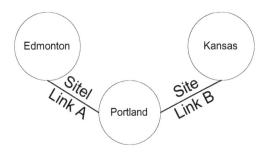

5.   A PDC is a Primary Domain Controller, and a BDC is a Backup Domain
Controller. You must install a PDC before any other domain servers. The Primary
Domain Controller maintains the master copy of the directory database and
authenticates users. A Backup Domain Controller contains a copy of the directory
database and can authenticate users. If the PDC fails then a BDC can be made a
PDC. A PDC can be demoted to a BDC if one of the BDCs is promoted to a PDC.

Lesson 3 Quiz

These questions test your knowledge of features, vocabulary, procedures, and syntax.

1. You want to make a domain controller the domain controller for a new domain. What do you do?
    A. Use DCPROMO.
    B. Use the Active Directory Installation Wizard.
    C. Use DCPROMO and the Active Directory Installation Wizard.
    D. Use the Configure Your Server configuration option.

2. Why do you need a DNS server to run Active Directory?
    A. Active Directory uses DNS to identify and locate all Active Directory objects.
    B. The server contains information about the DNS database that makes computer names available to clients asking for name resolution information across the Internet.
    C. It is a static, hierarchical name service for TCP/IP hosts. You configure the DNS with a list of host names and IP addresses. This allows users to query the DNS to specify remote systems by host names rather than IP addresses.
    D. A number of Active Directory-related DNS records must exist in DNS. The majority of these records are of the type Service location (SRV). Active Directory queries the SRV records to find the Internet Protocol (IP) addresses of the Active Directory services being hosted on different domain controllers

3. What function does the NetBIOS name serve in Active Directory?
    A. NetBIOS provides programs with a uniform set of commands for requesting the lower-level services required to manage names, conduct sessions, and send datagrams between nodes on a network.
    B. NetBIOS names lets those using an earlier version of Windows recognize the new domain.
    C. It enables you to use a Token Ring method of routing.
    D. It provides the means for addressing and sending IP packets over the network. It provides a best-effort, connectionless delivery system that does not guarantee that packets arrive at their destination or in the sequence in which they were sent.

4. What purpose do sites serve?
    A. You create a site because rapid and reliable network communication can be established inside that unit.
    B. Sites are used to locate services.
    C. Sites can be used to control replication.
    D. Sites are logical structures.

5. What are the uses of a subnet?
    A. You must associate one or more subnets with each site. Subnets are derived from the IP address and subnet mask of a computer in the subnet.
    B. They are used to find a domain controller.
    C. They organize all of the domain's object data in a hierarchical store.
    D. Subnets group information and computers in such a way that it identifies their feasible proximity on a network.

6. Why do you create site links?
    A. Site links are created so that replication can happen.
    B. Site links are created automatically by default, and you only need to change them if they are not in the right place.
    C. Site links are created to define a schedule or to cut down on costs.
    D. All site links are bridged together by default. You do not have to create them.

7. Which of the following are the tasks you need to complete to configure inter-site replications?
    A. Create site links.
    B. Add your sites to a zone.
    C. Configure site attributes.
    D. Create site link bridges.

8. What administrative tool do you use to create a site link?
    A. Active Directory Sites and Services
    B. Inter-Site Transports
    C. Active Directory Users and Computers
    D. The MMC

9. To ensure that the Active Directory service in the Windows 2000 operating system can replicate properly, a service known as the KCC runs on all domain controllers and automatically establishes connections between individual computers in the same site. What are these called?
    A. Connection objects
    B. Containers
    C. Hierarchical namespaces
    D. Organizational Units

10. Why would you want to have more than one controller in a domain?
    A. If you have a large volume of user activity, it can influence the creation of multiple domain controller servers.
    B. You need a lower fail rate and redundancy of information.
    C. You wish to simplify administration.
    D. There are physical site reasons to have more than one controller in a domain so that the network has better user connectivity.

Answers to Lesson 3 Quiz

1.   Answers A, B, C and D are correct. DCPROMO runs from the command prompt, or, from the Administrative tools menu, Configure Your Server starts the Active Directory Installation Wizard.

2.   Answers A and D are correct. Active Directory and DNS are both namespaces. The names in a namespace can be resolved to the objects they represent. For DNS, namespace is the hierarchical structure of the domain name tree. For example, each domain label, such as acctg or sales used in a Fully Qualified Domain Name, such as acctg.ibidpub.com, points to a branch in the domain namespace tree. For Active Directory, namespace corresponds to the DNS namespace in structure, but it resolves Active Directory object names.

      Answer B is incorrect. It is the definition of the DNS server, not a reason you must use DNS.

      Answer C is incorrect. It is a definition of DNS names.

3.   Answer B is correct. A NetBIOS name can be read by older versions of Windows.

      Answer A is incorrect. It is the definition of NetBIOS.

      Answer C is incorrect. NetBEUI or NetBIOS Extended User Interface can only use Token Ring source routing as its only method of routing.

      Answer D is incorrect. Internet Protocol is responsible for addressing and sending IP packets over the network. IP provides a best-effort, connectionless delivery system that does not guarantee that packets arrive at their destination or in the sequence in which they were sent.

4.   Answers A, B and C are correct. Sites can be used for all of these purposes.

      Answer D is incorrect. Domains are logical structures and sites are physical structures.

5.   Answer D is correct. Subnets group information and computers in such a way that it identifies their feasible proximity on a network.

      Answer A is incorrect. It is a description of a subnet origin but does not describe a subnet use.

      Answer B is incorrect. Finding Domain Controllers is not a use of subnets.

      Answer C is incorrect. A domain organizes the data.

6. Answers A and C are correct. You create site links for replication and also to define a cost-cutting schedule.

    Answers B and D are incorrect. Site links are not generated automatically and must be created in Active Directory Sites and Services.

7. Answers A, C and D are correct. The tasks needed to configure inter-site replications are to create site links, configure site link attributes (site link cost, replication frequency, and replication availability) and create site link bridges.

    Answer B is incorrect. Zones represent a discrete portion of the domain namespace and do not relate to sites directly.

8. Answer A is correct. The Administrative tool is Active Directory Sites and Services

    Answer B is incorrect. To create a new site, from Active Directory Sites and Services you select Sites folder, open the Inter-Sites Transport folder and right-click either IP or SMTP. Select New Site Link.

    Answer C is incorrect. The Active Directory Users and Computers console allows you to add, modify, delete, and organize user accounts, computer accounts, security and distribution groups, and publish resources in the Active Directory. You can also manage domain controllers and OUs.

    Answer D is incorrect. The MMC is the Microsoft Management console and is used to create, save, and open collections of tools called consoles. When you access the Active Directory administrative tools, you are accessing the MMC for that tool. Sites and Services and Users and Computers are MMC consoles.

9. Answer A is correct. A connection object uses the actual network connections to exchange directory information. Active Directory uses site links as indicators for where it should create connection objects. Without site links, connection objects that use network connections to connect sites will not be created, and domain controllers will be isolated within their sites.

    Answer B is incorrect. A container is like other directory objects in that it has attributes and is part of the Active Directory namespace. However, unlike other objects, it does not usually represent something concrete. It is the container for a group of objects and other containers.

    Answer C is incorrect. A hierarchical namespace, such as DNS namespace and the Active Directory namespace, are hierarchically structured.

    Answer D is incorrect. An Organizational Unit (OU) is a container object that is an Active Directory administrative partition. OUs can contain users, groups, resources, and other OUs.

10.   Answers A, B and D are correct. They are all reasons you would have more than one controller in a domain.

Answer C is incorrect. This what Active Directory offers you as a directory service.

User Account and Group Resource Implementation

Many of the functions in Windows 2000 are best administered using groups. In Windows 2000, a group is a collection of users, computers, contacts, or other groups. Administrators can assign specific rights to group accounts, as well as individual accounts. These rights allow users to perform specific actions, such as logging on to a system interactively or backing up files and directories. Rights are different from permissions because you apply rights to user accounts, and permissions are attached to objects. When you want an application to be available to users managed by the Group policy object, you publish the application. With published applications, each user chooses to install the published application. Another new feature allows an administrator to manage large groups by using Remote Installation Services (RIS). RIS allows you to remotely set up new clients on the server without physically being present at a client's workstation.

After completing this lesson, you should have a better understanding of the following topics:

- Active Directory Objects

- User Account Creation

- Group Creation And Administration

- Resource Publishing

- Organizational Unit (OU) Structure

- Remote Installation Deployment

- Remote Installation Services (RIS) Security Configuration

Active Directory Objects

An object is a file, folder, shared folder, or printer with a specific set of attributes. For example, the attributes of a file object could be its location, size, or the date it was last saved. The attributes of an Active Directory user object could be the user's first name, last name, and e-mail address. Before you can start manipulating objects, it is important to understand which objects are created by Active Directory. The objects described in Table 4.1 are created during the installation of Active Directory.

Table 4.1 Objects Created during Installation

Icon	Folder	Description
	Domain	Snap-ins are located within a domain and the icon represents the domain you are administering.
	Computers	The Computers folder contains all Windows NT 4.0 and Windows 2000 computers in the domain. If you upgrade from a previous version of Windows, Active Directory migrates the computer's account to this folder. You can move these objects.
	System	The System folder contains the Active Directory systems and services information.
	Users	The Users folder contains a list of all users in a domain. Like computers, the user objects can be moved.

You can use Active Directory to create the objects as described in Table 4.2.

Table 4.2 Objects Created with Active Directory

Icon	Object	Description
	User	A user object is a security principle in a directory. A user logs onto the directory with these credentials. Access permissions can be granted to users.
	Contact	A contact object is an account that has no security permissions. Contacts cannot log onto the network. Contacts represent external users for the purpose of e-mail.
	Computer	A computer object on the network is the computer account on Windows 2000 and Windows NT 4.0 workstations and servers.
	Organizational Unit	Organizational units are containers to logically organize directory objects, such as users, groups and computers, in the same manner as you use folders to organize your hard disk.
	Group	A Group can be made up of users, computers and other groups. Groups are used to simplify the management of a large number of objects.
	Shared Folder	A shared Folder is a network share that has been published in the directory.
	Shared Printer	A shared Printer is a network printer that has been published in the directory.

User Account Creation

To log on to a domain or a computer, a user needs an Active Directory user account. Having an account creates an identity for the user. The operating system can then use this identity to authenticate the user and to give authorization to domain resources that are specific to their access.

User accounts are service accounts for some applications. This means you can configure a service for authentication as you would a user account. You can then give the service access to specific network resources through that account. Windows 2000 has the following two predefined user accounts:

- Administrator account

- Guest account

With these accounts, you can log on to a computer running Windows 2000 and access resources on the local computer. The Administrator account is the most powerful as, by default, it is a member of the Administrators group. You must protect this account to avoid a possible security breach to the computer. The Guest account is for initial logon and configuration of a local computer, and by default is disabled. You must enable the Guest account to give it unrestricted access to a computer.

To enable the Windows 2000 user authentication and authorization features, you create an individual user account for each user who will participate on your network. You then add each user account—including the Administrator and Guest accounts—to Window 2000 groups, and assign appropriate rights and permissions to each group.

Creating and Administering Domain User Accounts

A user account is a record of all the information that identifies a user to Windows 2000 and includes the following components:

- Username

- Password required to log on

- Groups in which the user account is a member

- Rights and permissions the user has for accessing the computer, the network, and its resources

You create user accounts using the Microsoft Management Console (MMC) Active Directory Users and Computers. To create a user account, follow these steps:

1. From the **Start** menu, choose **Programs, Administrative Tools** and select **Active Directory Users and Computers**.

2. From the console tree, double-click the domain you wish to use.

3. From the details pane, right-click the organizational unit where you want to add the user, then choose **New**, and select **User**.

4. Within **First name**, type the user's first name.

5. Within **Initials**, type the user's initials.

6. Within **Last name**, type the user's last name.

 Note: The Full Name is automatically displayed after you type a first name and a last name.

7. Within **Full name**, modify the name as desired.

8. Within **User logon name**, type the name the user will use to log on with and then, select the User Principle Name (UPN) suffix to be added on to the user logon name (following the @ symbol), as in Figure 4.1.

9. Choose **Next**.

Figure 4.1 New Object-User

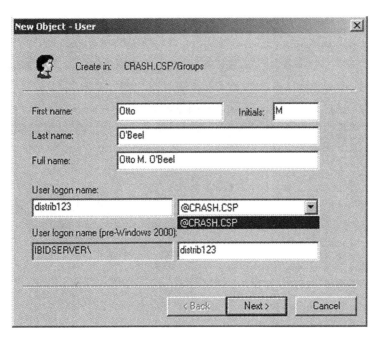

10. Type the user's password in both the **Password** and **Confirm password** sections and then select **Next**.

11. Choose **Finish** to confirm and accept the new entry.

You have now created an account for the user in the specified OU.

Warning: A new user account with the same name as a deleted user account does not automatically take on the permissions and memberships of the deleted account because the security descriptor for each account is unique. To duplicate a deleted user account, all permissions and memberships must be manually recreated.

To add additional information about this user, follow these steps:

1. From the details pane, right-click the organizational unit where you added the user, right-click the user's name, and then choose **Properties**.

2. You can now add more information about the user on the **General** property page as shown in Figure 4.2.

3. Click **OK**.

4. You are provided with a selection of optional entries (Address, Account, Profile, Telephones, and so forth).

Figure 4.2 Additional User Information

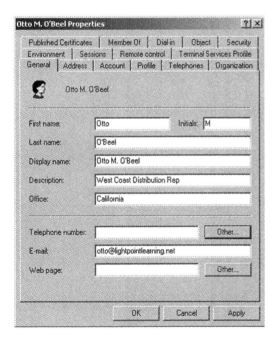

You can move users from one organizational unit to another in the same domain or a different domain. Active Directory Users and Computers cannot move user accounts between domains. To move a user account between domains you must use Movetree, one of the Active Directory support tools. To move a user, follow these steps:

1. Open **Active Directory Users and Computers**.

2. From the console tree, choose **Users** or select a folder that contains the desired user account.

3. From the details pane, right-click the user you want to move, and then choose **Move**.

4. Choose the folder to which you want to move the object to (Figure 4.3).

Figure 4.3 List of Available OUs

5. Select the appropriate OU, and click **OK**.

 Tip: If you have upgraded from an earlier version of Windows NT Server, you may want to move existing users from the Users folder to the newly created OU.

Group Creation and Administration

Groups are Active Directory objects. They can contain users, contacts, computers and other groups. Within Windows 2000, you create groups in domains using Active Directory Users and Computers. Groups can be created in any domain, including the root domain, in any OU or in any container object. Like user and computer accounts, groups are Windows 2000 security principals. Security Identifiers (SIDs) are unique numbers that identify user, group and computer accounts. SIDs are assigned to groups when they are created.

Groups can be nested. This means you can add a group as a member of another group. By nesting groups, it is easier to manage users and reduces network traffic caused by replication of group membership changes. Windows 2000 Server has the following two types of groups:

Distribution Groups—Distribution groups have only one function: to create distribution lists. You use distribution groups with e-mail applications, such as Microsoft Exchange. You can add a contact to a distribution group so that the contact receives e-mail sent to the group. Because you do not assign any permissions to distribution groups, they have no function in security.

Security Groups—security groups are an essential component of the relationship between users and security. Security groups have two roles: to manage user and computer access to shared resources and to filter Group Policy settings. To do this, place users, computers and other groups into a security group. You then assign the appropriate permissions for those specific resources to the security group. Using security groups simplifies administration as you assign permissions once to the group instead of multiple times to each individual user. When you add a new user to an existing group, the user will automatically gain the rights and permissions you have already assigned to that particular group.

 Tip: Remember that you assign permissions only to security groups—not to distribution groups.

Table 4.3 Groups and Contents

Scope	Visibility	May Contain
Domain Local	Domain	Users, Domain Local, Global or Universal Groups
Global	Forest	Users or Global Groups
Universal	Forest	Users, Global or Universal Groups

Creating and Administering Groups

When you create a new group, it is configured as a security group with a global scope. If your network has a number of forests, you can place a user or computer from any trusted domain into a domain local group. To add a group to a domain, follow these steps:

1. From the **Start** menu, choose **Programs**, **Administrative Tools** and select **Active Directory Users and Computers**

2. From the console tree, double-click the domain you want to use.

3. Right-click the folder in which you want to add the group, choose **New**, and then select **Group**.

4. Type the name of the new group.

5. Choose a **Group scope** and **Group type**.

The **Group type** indicates whether the group can be used to assign permissions to other network resources, such as files and printers. Both security and distribution groups can be used for e-mail distribution lists.

The **Group scope** determines the visibility of the group and what type of objects can be contained within the group.

Once users belong to a group, they have all the rights and permissions of that group. If they are members of more than one group, then each user has all the rights and permissions granted to each group to which they belong.

Note: You should only add a new user to the Administrators group if they will only perform administrative duties.

You can add user accounts from the local computer. If the computer participates in a domain, you can add user accounts and global groups to that domain and to trusted domains. To add a user to a group, follow these steps:

1. From the **Start** menu, choose **Settings**, and then select **Control Panel**.

2. From the Control Panel, open **Administrative Tools**, and then open **Computer Management**.

3. In the Tree pane, expand **System Tools**, expand **Local Users and Groups**, and then select **Groups**.

4. In the Details pane, select the group to which you want to add a user.

5. From the menu bar, choose **Action**, and then select **Add to Group**.

6. Choose **Add**.

Figure 4.4 Adding a User to a Group

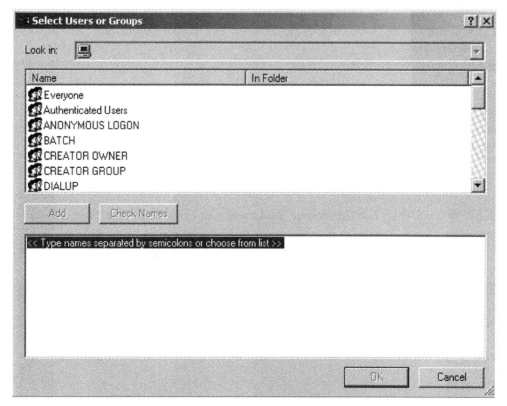

7. From Select Users or Groups (Figure 4.4), type the name of the user account or select it from the list.

 Note: By holding down the CTRL key as you select, you can select several users or groups. You can also type in the user name directly. If the name you type is not clear, an additional list displays and you can verify your selection.

8. If you type in user names, verify them by choosing **Check Names**.

9. Choose OK to save your changes.

By using nesting, you can add one group as a member of another group. Nesting groups consolidates group management and reduces network replication traffic caused by group membership changes. You can only nest groups if you are running the Active Directory in Native Mode. Because nested groups are easier to manage, they reduce your network's administrative overhead.

To create a nested group, follow these steps:

1. Create a new group by right-clicking the group you want to use as the base for the nested group.

2. Choose **New**, and then select **Group**.

3. Type the name of the new group and then click **OK**.

4. Right-click the new Group, and then choose **Properties**.

5. Choose the **Members** property page and then choose **Add**.

6. From the list, choose the group you want to add the new group to, and then select **Add.**

7. Click **OK** to accept your selection.

8. Choose **Apply**, and then click **OK**.

You have now created a nested group.

Resource Publishing

Publishing resources provides a number of features to network users and makes the information about the resources both secure and easy to find. Active Directory stores the information for rapid recovery and adds Windows 2000 security mechanisms to control access. Information needed for published applications is stored in the Group Policy Object (GPO). A GPO is a set of user and computer configuration settings that you store as an object in the Active Directory. When you publish an application, no shortcuts to the application appear on users' desktops, and no local registry entries are made. That is, the application has no presence on the user's desktop.

Understanding Publishing Resources

Publishing information about shared resources such as printers and file folders makes it uncompli-cated for users to find them on the network. Information about Windows NT 4.0 printers and shared folders can be published in the directory using Active Directory Users and Computers.

 Tip: When you install Windows 2000 network printers they are automatically published in the directory.

Shared Folders

When you share a folder, all users can have access to the folder and its contents. Shared folders can hold applications, your organization's data or a user's personal data. Each of these data types will require different permissions for the shared folders. Windows 2000 allows you to specify the folders you want to share with others to centralize administration and facilitate applications upgrading. Any shared network folder, including a Distributed File System (DFS) folder, can be published to the Active Directory.

 Note: Users on the network can use shared folders for centralized access to network files.

You can assign shared folder permissions to user and group accounts, controlling what users can do with the contents of a shared folder. Table 4.4 describes what each of the shared folder permissions allows a client to do.

Table 4.4 Shared Folder Descriptions

Folder Restriction	Shared Folder Permission	Allows the User to...
Most Restrictive	Read	View file and sub-folder names View data in files Navigate to sub-folders Run programs
	Change	All of the above and Add files and sub-folders to the shared folder Change data in files Delete sub-folders and files
Least Restrictive	Full Control	All of the above and Change file permissions Take ownership of files

Creating a shared folder object in Active Directory does not automatically share the folder. You must first share the folder, and then publish it in Active Directory. You provide the following information when you share a folder:

• A share name

• Comments on its content

• Limit the number of users who have access to the folder

• Assign permissions

To share a folder, follow these steps:

1. From within **Windows Explorer**, right-click the folder name that you wish to share and choose **Properties**.

2. Choose the **Sharing** property page, (Figure 4.5) and select **Share this folder**.

Figure 4.5 Sharing Property Page

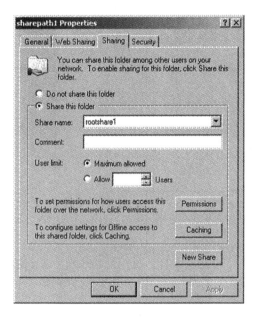

3. Type a name for the share (or accept the default), and type an optional comment about the share.

4. If you wish to limit the number of users accessing the share at any one time, select Allow, and type the maximum number of users that can simultaneously connect.

5. To adjust the share permissions, select **Permissions**.

 Note: By default, the Everyone group is granted the Full Control share permission.

6. When finished, choose OK to save the changes and begin sharing the folder.

Files such as documents, spreadsheets or presentations can now be put into the shared folder. You must publish the shared folder in the Active Directory before other users can access the folder and its contents. To publish the shared folder in the directory, follow these steps:

1. From the **Start** menu, choose **Programs**, **Administrative Tools**, and then select **Active Directory Users and Computers**.

2. From the **Active Directory Users and Computers** snap-in, right-click the OU in which you will publish the folder, choose **New**, and then select **Shared Folder**.

3. Type a name for the shared folder as it will appear in the Active Directory, and then type the Universal Naming Convention (UNC) path of the share. The UNC path is always in the form \\server\share.

4. Click **OK** to save the changes.

Printers and Services

You can publish a printer using the Sharing printer property page. Listed in the directory is enabled by default. The Windows 2000 Server publishes the shared printer by default. The print subsystem automatically propagates any changes made to the printer attributes (location, description, loaded paper, and so forth) to the directory. (Figure 4.6)

To add a new printer, follow these steps:

1. From the **Start** menu, choose **Settings** and then select **Printers.**

2. Double-click **Add Printer**. The **Add Printer Wizard** appears.

3. Choose **Next.**

Figure 4.6 Add Printer Wizard

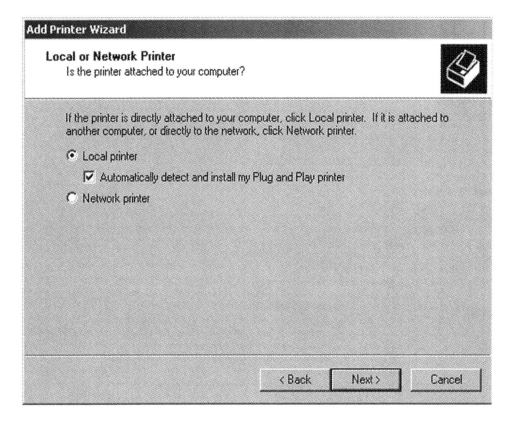

4. Choose **Local Printer**, clear **Automatically detect and install my Plug and Play printer**, and select **Next**.

5. Choose the **Create a new port**, then **Standard TCP/IP Port**, and select **Next**.

6. The **Add Standard TCP/IP Printer Port Wizard** will open, select **Next**.

7. On the **Add Port** page, in the **Printer Name or IP Address,** type the Internet Protocol (IP) address of the printer. Within **Port Name**, type the port name and select **Next**. Choose **Finish**.

8. Choose your printer's manufacturer and model from the list and select **Next**.

9. From within **Printer name** type the name of your printer.

10. From within the **Printer Sharing** page, type a name for the printer.

> Tip: If you have computers running previous versions of Windows, select a printer name that is no more than eight characters long or it will not display correctly on those computers.

11. In the appropriate sections, type in the **Location** and **Comment** information.

12. Print a test page and then choose **Finish.**

After you create the printer, the printer is automatically published in Active Directory and the Listed in the Directory will be enabled.

To locate a printer, follow these steps:

1. From the **Start** menu, choose **Settings, Printers** and then double-click **Add Printer.**

2. Within the **Add Printer Wizard** page, choose **Next.**

3. Choose **Network printer**, and select **Next.**

4. Choose **Find a printer in the Directory**, and select **Next.**

5. The **Find Printers** page will open. If you know the domain where the printer is located, choose **Browse** and select that domain to narrow your search. On the **Printer** page, add the printer **Name, Location**, or **Model** in the appropriate sections and choose **Find Now.**

> Tip: you do not know the name, location or model of the printer, you can select Find Now. All of the printers in the selected domain will be listed.

Printers can be published in the directory that is shared by operating systems other than Windows 2000. The easiest approach is to use PUBPRN script. Located in the \winnt\system32 directory, PUBPRN.VBS will publish all of the shared printers on a selected server.

To publish a printer shared from a non-Windows 2000 server, using the PUBPRN.VBS script, follow these steps:

1. From the **Start** menu, choose **Run,** and type **CMD.**

2. Type **cd\winnt\system32** and choose **Enter**.

3. Type **cscript pubprn.vbs printer server name.** For example:
   <b>LDAP:\\ou=marketing,dc=MyCompany,dc=com

4. Choose **Enter**. The printer will be published to the OU that you have specified.

 Tip: If you already have published printers, rerunning PUBPRN will update instead of overwriting existing printers.

PUBPRN copies only the following subset of the printer's attributes:

• Location

• Model

• Comment

• UNCPath

Other attributes can be added to the computer using the Active Directory Users and Computers snap-in.

 Note: You can also use the Active Directory Users and Computers snap-in to publish printers on non-Windows 2000 servers.

To use the Active Directory Users and Computers snap-in to publish printers, follow these steps:

1. From the **Start** menu, choose **Settings**, **Control Panel** and then select **Administrative Tools**.

2. Choose **Active Directory Users and Computers**.

3. Right-click the slected organizational unit, choose **New**, and select **Printer**.

4. The **New Object-Printer** page will open. Type the path to the printer, such as **\\server\share name**.

5. Click **OK**.

One of the major benefits of publishing printers in the directory is users can browse for a specific printer, send a print job to that printer and install the printer drivers directly from the server.

To browse and use printers in the directory, follow these steps:

1. From the **Start** menu, choose **Search**, and select **For Printers**.

2. **Find Printers** opens. Select the subdirectory where you would like to search for printers. In **Name**, **Location**, or **Model,** type the appropriate information. (Figure 4.7).

3. Choose **Find Now** for a list of published printers.

Figure 4.7 Find Published Printers

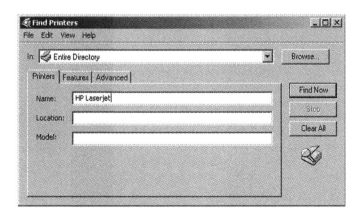

Organizational Unit (OU) Structure

You should build OUs that represent your organization's business or operative structure. Each domain can put into operation it own OU hierarchy. If there are several domains, you can create OU structures inside each domain that are independent from each of the other domains.

Implementing an Organizational Unit (OU) Structure

To create an OU, you use Active Directory Users and Computers MMC. The OUs you make are created on the first available domain controller contacted by the MMC, and then the OU is replicated to all of the other domain controllers.

To create an OU, follow these steps:

1. From the **Start** menu, choose **Settings, Control Panel** and then double-click **Administrative Tools.**

2. Choose **Active Directory Users and Computers**.

3. elect the location where you want to create the OU, either a domain, such as Lightpoint.net or another OU.

4. From within the **Action** menu, choose **New** and then select **Organizational Unit**.

5. The **New Object-Organizational Unit** page will open. Within **Name**, type the name of the OU (Figure 4.8).

6. Click **OK**.

Figure 4.8 New Object OU

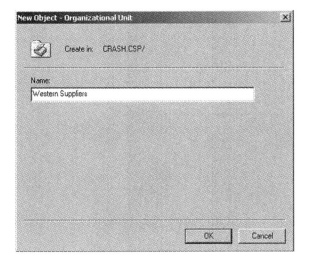

Default properties are connected to each of the OUs you create. These properties associate to the object attributes. When you search for an OU in a directory, you use these properties.

 Tip: It is important that you supply comprehensive property definitions for each OU that you create. For example, when you search, you can use an OU's definitions.

The Organizational Unit Properties page holds the information about each OU. Table 4.5 describes the pages and properties collected on each.

Table 4.5 OU Property Pages

Page	Description
General	Description Street address City State or Province Zip or postal code Country or region
Managed by	Manager's name Office location Street address City State or Province Zip or postal code Country or region Telephone number and fax number
Group Policy	Group policy links

To set the OU properties, follow these steps:

1. From the **Start** menu, choose **Settings**, and then select **Control Panel**.

2. Double-click **Administrative Tools**, and then choose **Active Directory Users and Computers**.

3. Expand the domain, right-click the correct OU, then select **Properties**.

4. Select the page for the properties that you want to include or change for the OU, then type or change the values for each property, such as the General property page (Figure 4.9).

Figure 4.9 General Property Page

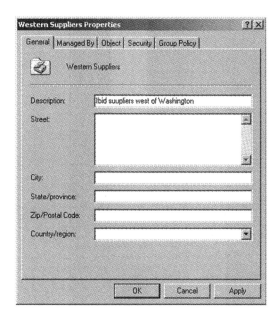

Remote Installation Deployment

You can set up a single or a group of new client computers, without having to be there, by using Windows 2000 Remote Installation Services (RIS). Operating systems on remote boot-enabled computers can be installed by connecting the computer to the network, starting the client computer and logging on with a user account.

Figure 4.10 shows the components and services that are part of RIS.

Figure 4.10 Remote Installation

Remote operating system installation uses some services existing on the client computer and it adds others. Following are some of the added services:

Boot Information Negotiation Layer (BINL)—The BINL service is added during the RIS installation and supplies management of the RIS environment. BINL is responsible for answering client network requests, querying the Active Directory for the client computer and ensuring the correct policy and configuration settings are put on the client computer during installation. If the client computer has not been set up, BINL creates the client computer account in Active Directory.

Trivial File Transfer Protocol Daemon (TFTPD)—The TFTPD service hosts specific file download requests made by the client computer, on the server side. The TFTPD service is used to download the Client Installation Wizard (CIW) and all of the client pages in the CIW during a single session.

Single Instance Storage (SIS)—The SIS service reduces disk space requirements on the volumes used for storing RIS installation images. When you install RIS as an optional component, you are prompted for a drive and directory to install RIS. The SIS service then attaches itself to this RIS volume and looks for any duplicates. If SIS finds duplicates, it creates a link to them, reducing the disk space required.

Deploying Windows 2000 with Remote Installation Services (RIS)

There are two types of remote boot-enabled client computers, those with Pre-boot eXecution Environment (PXE) Dynamic Host Configuration Protocol (DHCP) based remote boot Read Only Memory System (ROMS) and those with network cards supported by the RIS Boot Disk.

Remote operating system installation uses the PXE DHCP-based remote boot technology to start the installation of the operating system from a remote source to the client hard disk. The DHCP is a networking protocol that provides safe, reliable and simple TCP/IP network configuration. It offers dynamic configuration of IP addresses and ensures that address conflicts do not occur. It also conserves the use of IP addresses through centralized management of address allocation. The remote source is a server that supports RIS and provides the same installation as that of a CD or pre-configured Remote Installation Preparation (RIPrep) desktop image.

 Note: Windows 2000 Professional is currently the only installation option supported by RIS.

In the CD-based installation, the files reside across the network on a RIS server; however, it is comparable to setting up a computer from Windows 2000 Professional CD-ROM.

With the RIPrep imaging option, you can completely clone a complete desktop configuration—with the operating system configuration, desktop customizations and locally installed applications. First, you install and configure the Windows 2000 Professional operating system, its services and any standard applications on a computer. You then run a wizard that copies the installation image and replicates it to a RIS server on the network, for installation to other computers on the network.

When the image has been posted to a RIS server, any user with a PXE based remote-boot enabled client computer can request to install those images from any available RIS server on the network. As a user can do the installation without administrative assistance, saves both the time and expense associated with an administrator installation.

Installing an Image on a RIS Client Computer

Installing RIS is a two-step process. First add the RIS component. Then install RIS.

Adding RIS is the first stage of the setup procedure. The files required for installation are copied to the server's hard disk. You can do this during the Windows 2000 installation or by using Add/Remove Programs.

To add the RIS component, you can access Windows Component during the installation process for Windows 2000 Server or you can follow these steps:

1. From the **Start** menu, choose **Settings** and then **Control Panel.**

2. Select **Add/Remove Programs**, then choose **Add/Remove Windows Components**.

3. Within the **Windows Components Wizard** (Figure 4.11) choose **Remote Installation Services**, then select **Next**.

 Note: The RIS image cannot be stored 0on the same physical drive as the Operating System (OS).

Figure 4.11 Windows Components Wizard

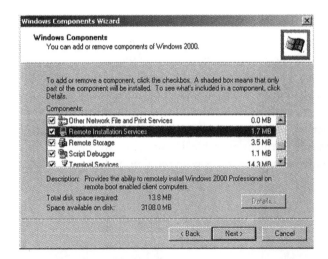

4. When prompted, insert the Windows 2000 CD in the CD-ROM drive.

5. In **Systems Settings Change**, choose **Yes** to restart the server before installing RIS.

The second stage of RIS setup occurs during the RIS installation. To install RIS on the server, follow these steps:

1. From the **Start** menu, choose **Settings**, and **Control Panel**.

2. Double-click **Administrative Tools**, and select **Configure Your Server**.

3. Within the **Confirm Your Server** page, choose **Finish Setup**.

4. Within the **Add/Remove Programs** page, in the **Configure Remote Installation Service** section, choose **Configure** to start the **Remote Installation Services Setup Wizard**.

5. After the **Welcome To The Remote Installation Services Setup Wizard** page opens, choose **Next**.

6. Continue to make the appropriate selections through the prompts:

- The location on the server where the RIS folder will be created

- If the RIS server should start to service client computers right after setup.

- The location of the Windows 2000 Professional CD-ROM or where on the network the files are stored

- The location on the server where the image installation files will be stored

- A user friendly description and help text that describes the operating system image to the CIW users

Depending on the settings you have chosen, when the Remote Installation Services Setup Wizard is finished, RIS may begin to service the client computers or pauses while you set RIS configuration options.

Creating a RIS Boot Disk

With Windows 2000 the administrator has been provided with a tool to create a remote boot disk for computers that do not have a PXE-based remote boot ROM. You can use the RIS remote boot disk with a variety of Peripheral Component Interconnect (PCI) network adapter cards. Using a RIS boot disk does away with the need to retrofit existing client computers with a new network card.

 Note: The RIS boot disk imitates the PXE remote boot sequence and supports commonly used network cards.

You must create a boot disk to support existing client computers that do not have a PXE-based remote boot-enabled ROM but do have a network adapter. The RIS boot disk works like the PXE boot—turn on the computer, boot from the RIS boot disk, press F12 to begin the network service boot, the CIW is downloaded and starts. Once the CIW starts, RIS process is identical to the client computer being booted using a PXE boot ROM. It uses the RBGF utility—the Remote Boot Floppy Generator tool (Rbfg.exe) for Remote Installation.

RGBF creates a Pre-boot Execution Environment (PXE) emulator that works on a supported set of PCI adapters that do not have a PXE ROM embedded on the adapter. This tool is located in the following share on the Remote Installation Service (RIS) server: *Servername*\Reminst\Admin\I386.

To create a RIS boot disk, follow these steps:

1. rom the **Start** menu, choose **Run** and type the **UNC path** of the RBGF utility, for example: \\ server\share\RemoteInstall\Admin\1386\RBFG.EXE

2. Click **OK**.

3. Insert a formatted disk in the floppy drive.

4. Within the **Windows 2000 Remote Boot Disk Generator** page (Figure 4.12) choose the correct floppy drive and select **Create Disk**.

Figure 4.12 Remote Boot Disk

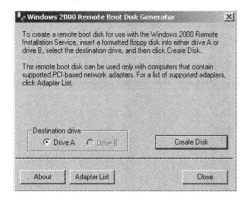

5. Choose **Close** when the disk has finished being created. Remove the disk from the disk drive.

 Note: You can only use the boot disk with computers that have supported PCI-based network adapters. To see the list of adaptors, select Adaptor List in the Windows 2000 Remote Disk Generator page.

Configuring Remote Installation Options

After the installation of RIS, it still needs to be configured to start servicing client computers. The following processes must be completed to configure RIS:

• Authorize RIS servers

• Set RIS server properties

• Set RIS client installation options

• Set RIPrep image permissions

You can specify which RIS servers you want to run on your network, to ensure only those that you authorize can service clients. If an attempt is made to start an unauthorized service, it will be automatically shut down.

Warning: A RIS server must be authorized before it can service client computers.

To authorize RIS servers, follow these steps:

1. From the **Start** menu, choose **Programs**, **Administrative Tools** and select **DHCP**.

2. From the DHCP console tree, choose the **DHCP node** you wish to use.

3. From **Action**, choose **Manage Authorized Services**.

4. Within the **Manage Authorized Services** page, choose **Authorized**.

5. Within the **Authorized DHCP Server** page, type the **Name** or **IP address** of the RIS server you want to authorize, and then click **OK**.

6. Within the **DHCP** message section, choose **Yes**.

7. Within the **Manage Authorized Servers** page, choose the computer, and then click **OK**.

The authorized RIS server is now displayed under the DHCP node (Figure 4.13).

Figure 4.13 RIS Server

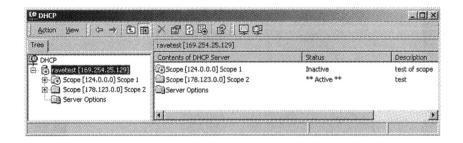

You can control how the RIS server supplies RIS to the clients asking for services by setting the properties on the individual RIS servers. To set RIS server properties, follow these steps:

1. From the **Start** menu, choose **Programs, Administrative Tools** and select **Active Directory Users and Computers**.

2. From the console tree, choose the folder that contains the computer whose configuration you want to confirm or change.

3. From the details pane, right-click the appropriate RIS server, then choose **Properties**.

4. Within the **Properties** page for the server, choose **Remote Install**.

5. Within the **Remote Install** property page (Figure 4.14), set the options as they are described in Table 4.6.

Figure 4.14 Remote Install Property Page

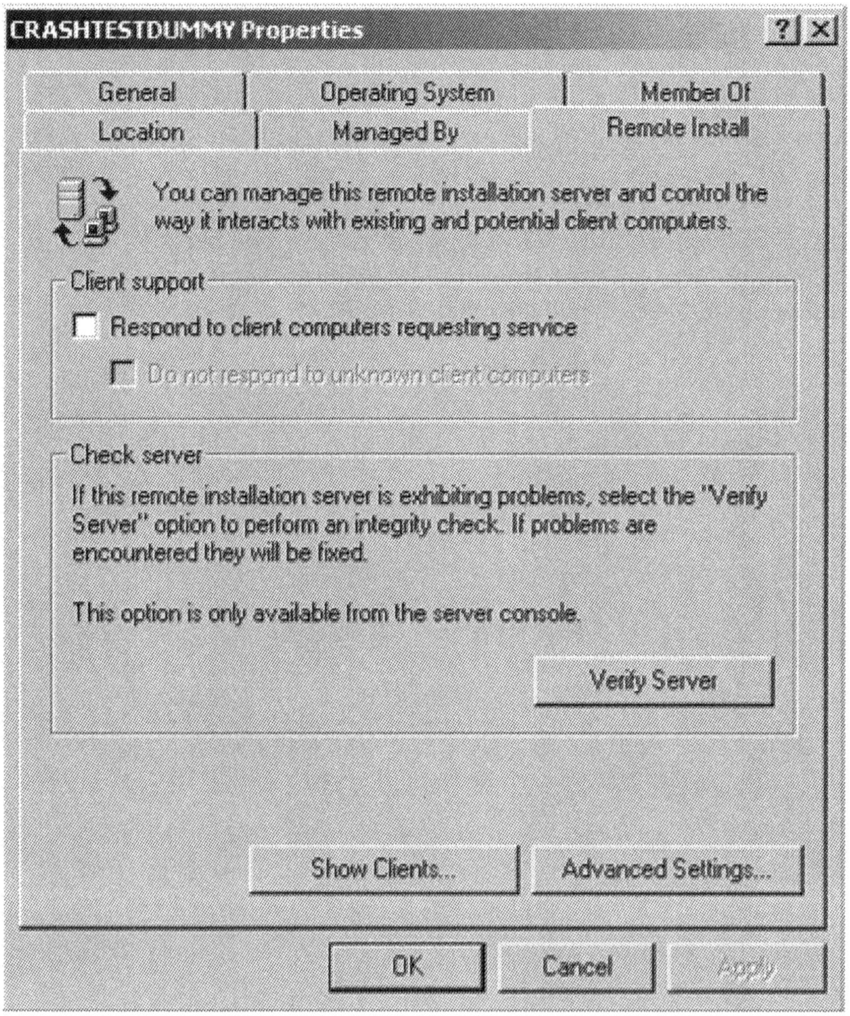

Table 4.6 Options on the Remote Install Property Page

Configuration Option	Description
Respond to Client Computers Requesting Services	The RIS server will respond to all of the clients that request services.
Do Not Respond to Unknown Client Computers	The RIS server will not respond to unknown client computers. This option is offered if the Respond to Client Computers Requesting Service has been enabled.

6. Within the **Remote Install** page, choose **Advanced Settings**.

7. Within the **Remote Installation Services Properties** page for the server, on the **New Clients** property page (Figure 4.15), set the options as described in Table 4.7.

Figure 4.15 New Clients Page

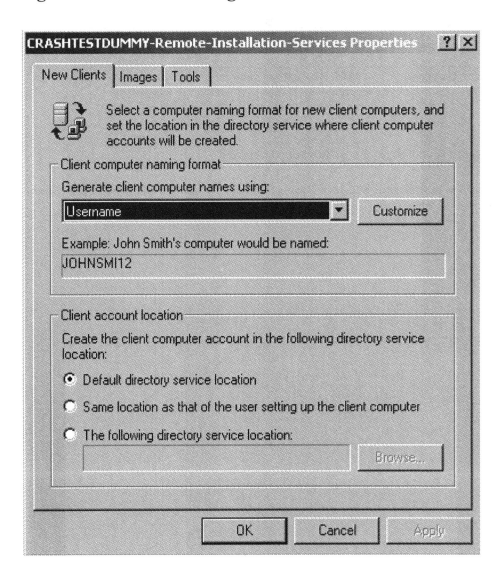

Table 4.7 Options on the New Client Page

Configuration Option	Description
Generate Client Computer Names Using	During the operating system installation, this option will automatically generate the client computer name. It establishes how the name is formatted without end user or administrator involvement.
Customize	Accesses the Computer Account Generation page where you can create a custom naming format for the client computer.
Client Account Location	The directory service location of the client computer account, either: The **Default Directory Service Location** option spells out that the computer account object should be created in the Active Directory location where all computer accounts are created during the domain join operation. The **Same Location As That Of The User Setting Up The Client Computer** option spells out that the computer account object should be created in the same Active Directory container as the user setting up the machine. The **Use The Following Directory Service Location** option lets the administrator set a particular Active Directory container where all the client computer account objects installing from this server are created.

Tip: Most administrators will select the Client Account Location option and stipulate a particular container where all remote installation client computer account objects are to be created.

8. Within the **Remote Installation Services Properties** page for the server, in the **Images** properties page (Figure 4.16) you view the images that have been created and installed in the RIS server. Select **Add** and follow the Wizard directions to install additional RIS images.

Figure 4.16 Images Property Page

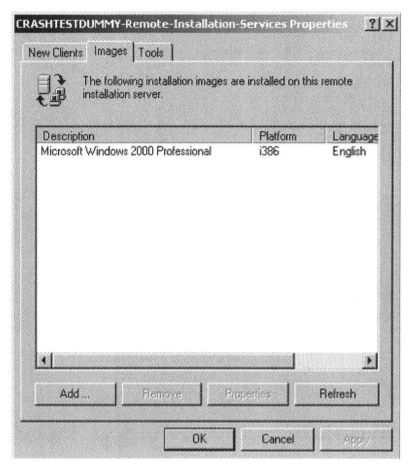

9. Within the **Remote Installation Services Properties** page for the server, in the **Tools** property page as in Figure 4.17, you can view the maintenance and troubleshooting tools that have been installed on the RIS server.

10. Within **Remote Installation and Services Properties,** click **OK**.

Figure 4.17 Tools Property Page

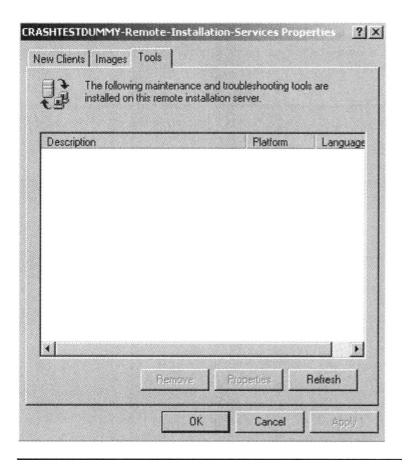

 Note: If you use the Windows 2000 Administration Tools on a system other than the RIS server, the administrator cannot add operating system images or verify the integrity of the RIS server. All other configuration options are available.

Users of a remote boot-enabled client computer can use the Client Installation Wizard (CIW) to select installation options, operating systems, and maintenance and troubleshooting tools. The wizard will ask the user for their user name, password, and domain name. After their credentials have been validated, the wizard displays the installation options available to that user. After the user selects an option, the selected operating system installation image is copied to the client computer's local hard disk. You can predetermine these installation options during the RIS setup process, or by running the RIPrep utility.

 Warning: Since the client computer's hard disk is reformatted during the operating system installation, all locally stored files are removed during installation.

You can manage the options available to different groups of users during the CIW. The following four client installation options are available:

- Automatic setup

- Custom setup

- Restart a previous setup attempt

- Maintenance and troubleshooting

The default is automatic setup. This option allows you to limit the operating system options so when the user logs on, the operating system installation starts right away and does not ask the user for any input during the installations. While restricting installation options, you can still allow users to choose the configured operating system option for installation. The friendly text you entered for the descriptions helps the user select the most appropriate option. This predefinition of configuration options classifies the automatic machine naming format and the location within Active Directory where the client computer accounts will be created.

The Custom Setup option is similar to the Automatic Setup option. It can be used to preinstall a client computer or to predefine the client computer by creating a corresponding computer account in the

Active Directory. With this option, you can override the automatic naming and location. By default, the RIS server will generate a computer name based on the format defined by the Remote OS Installation administrator.

 Note: By default, the automatic computer naming policy creates names based on the person who logs onto the CIW.

The restart a previous setup attempt option is provided in case the installation fails for any reason. The CIW can be customized to ask a series of questions about the specific system being installed. When restarting a failed installation attempt, any questions previously asked will not be asked again. The setup preserves this information, restarts the file copy process, and completes the installation.

The maintenance and troubleshooting makes available access to third-party hardware and software vendor tools. These tools range from virus scans to a range of computer diagnostic tools that check for hardware problems. They are available before starting the installation.

If the option to display the Maintenance and Troubleshooting menu is enabled, the user running the installation can access the individual tool images. These images are controlled in the same way as the operating system installation options.

To set the client installation options, follow these steps:

1. From the **Start menu**, choose **Programs**, **Administrative Tools**, and then select **Active Directory Users and Computers**.

2. From the console tree, right-click the appropriate OU, such as Computers or Domain Controllers, and select **Properties**.

3. From the OU Properties, select the **Group Policy** property page.

4. Select the Group Policy object and then choose **Edit**.

5. From the Tree pane of the Group Policy console, expand **User Configuration**, **Windows Settings**, and then select **Remote Installation Services**.

6. In the Details pane, double-click **Choice Options**.

The Choice options window is displayed (Figure 4.18).

Figure 4.18 Choice Options

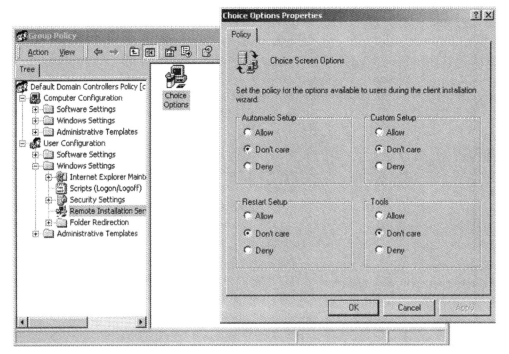

Table 4.8 shows the group policy options.

Table 4.8 Group Policy Options

Option	Description
Allow	This policy option lets the user make use of the options that have this setting.
Don't Care	This option accepts the policy settings of the parent container. For example, if the administrator for the domain has set a group policy specific to RIS, and the administrator has selected this option, the policy set on the domain will apply to all users affected by that policy. This is the default setting.
Deny	This setting denies the users access to the option with this policy setting.

 Warning: The changes that you make to RIS policy do not take effect until the policy is propagated to your computer.

To initiate propagation, choose one of the following:

• Type **secedt/refreshpolicy user_policy** at the command prompt Press Enter and restart the computer

• Wait for automatic policy propagation which occurs at regular intervals and can be configured; by default, propagation takes place every eight hours

Troubleshooting RIS Problems

Troubleshooting RIS problems is covered extensively in Windows 2000 Server and Windows 2000 Advanced Server on-line help as shown in Figure 4.19.

Figure 4.19 Troubleshooting Remote Installation Services

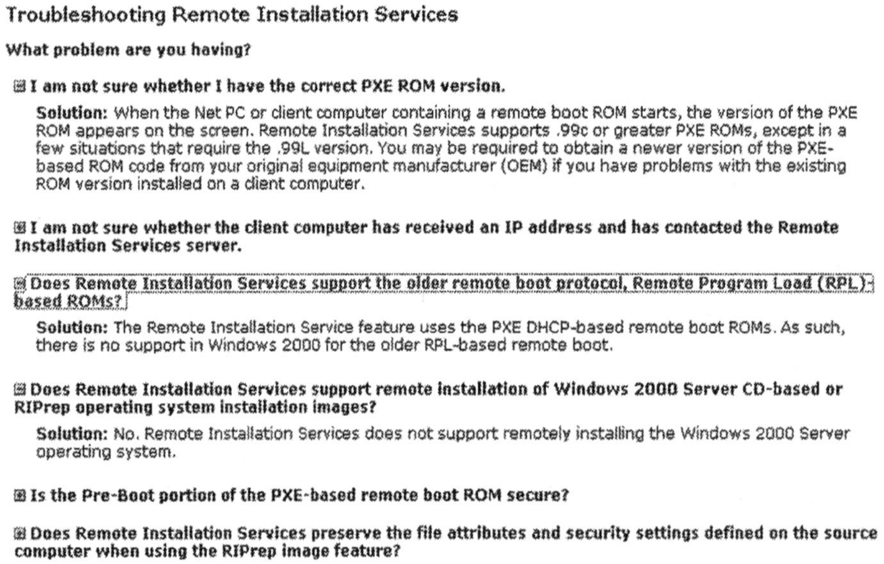

Troubleshooting Remote Installation Services

What problem are you having?

⊞ **I am not sure whether I have the correct PXE ROM version.**

> **Solution:** When the Net PC or client computer containing a remote boot ROM starts, the version of the PXE ROM appears on the screen. Remote Installation Services supports .99c or greater PXE ROMs, except in a few situations that require the .99L version. You may be required to obtain a newer version of the PXE-based ROM code from your original equipment manufacturer (OEM) if you have problems with the existing ROM version installed on a client computer.

⊞ **I am not sure whether the client computer has received an IP address and has contacted the Remote Installation Services server.**

⊞ **Does Remote Installation Services support the older remote boot protocol, Remote Program Load (RPL)-based ROMs?**

> **Solution:** The Remote Installation Service feature uses the PXE DHCP-based remote boot ROMs. As such, there is no support in Windows 2000 for the older RPL-based remote boot.

⊞ **Does Remote Installation Services support remote installation of Windows 2000 Server CD-based or RIPrep operating system installation images?**

> **Solution:** No. Remote Installation Services does not support remotely installing the Windows 2000 Server operating system.

⊞ **Is the Pre-Boot portion of the PXE-based remote boot ROM secure?**

⊞ **Does Remote Installation Services preserve the file attributes and security settings defined on the source computer when using the RIPrep image feature?**

There are also a number of troubleshooter tools available at the Microsoft Web site for Windows 2000. Figure 4.20 shows the RIS Troubleshooter page.

Figure 4.20 RIS Troubleshooter

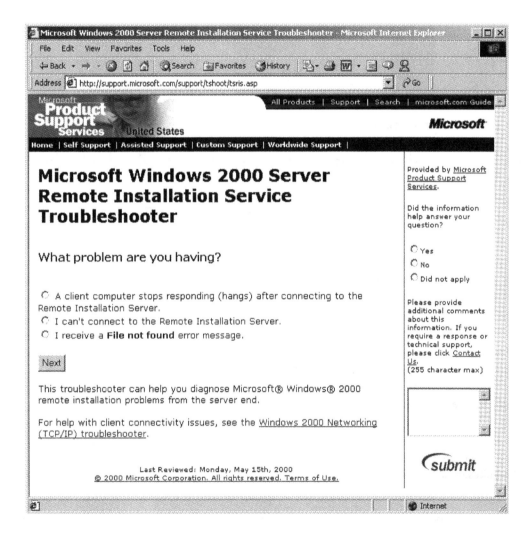

Managing Images for Performing Remote Installations

Managing RIS installation images consists of the following tasks:

- Adding a new client installation image

- Associating unattended setup answer files

To add a new client installation image, follow these steps:

1. From the **Start** menu, choose **Properties**, **Administrative Tools** and then select **Active Directory Users and Computers**.

2. From the console tree, right-click the appropriate RIS server, then choose **Properties**.

3. Choose **Remote Install** and then select **Advanced Settings**.

4. Within the **Remote Installation Services Properties** page, choose the **Images** property page.

5. Choose **Add** to start the Add Wizard.

6. From within the **New Answer File Or Installation Image** page, choose **Add A New Installation Image**, then select **Next** to start the Add Installation Image Wizard.

7. From the **Welcome To The Add Installation Image** page, choose **Next**.

8. From the **Installation Source Files Location** page, type the location of the Windows 2000 Professional installation image, and then choose **Next**.

 Tip: The location of the Windows 2000 Professional Installation image can be found on either a CD-ROM or a network share.

9. From the **Windows Installation Image Folder Name** page, type a name for the Windows installation image, then choose **Next**.

10. From the **Friendly Description And Help Text** page, type a description that is easy to understand and is descriptive for the friendly description and help text for the installation image, then choose **Next**.

11. If a previous set of CIW screens exists, the **Previous Client Installation Screens Found** page is displayed. Choose the CIW screen you would like use for this image, then choose **Next**.

12. From the **Review Settings** page, review the installation summary, then choose **Finish**.

The Remote Installation Wizard completes the addition of the new client installation image. You can also associate an unattended setup answer file to go with the installation image. To do this, follow these steps:

1. From the **Start** menu, choose **Programs, Administrative Tools** and select **Active Directory Users and Computers**.

2. From the console tree, right-click the appropriate RIS server, then select **Properties**.

3. Within the **Properties** page for the server, select the **Remote Install** page, then choose **Advanced Settings**.

4. Within the **Remote Installations Services Properties** page, choose **Images**.

5. Choose **Add** to start the Add Wizard.

6. From the **New Answer File Or Installation Image** page, choose **Associate a New Answer File to An Existing Image**, then select **Next**.

7. From the **Unattended Setup Answer File Source** page, choose the source that has the unattended setup file you wish to copy: Windows Image Sample Files; Another Remote Installation Server; or An Alternate Location.

8. Choose **Next**.

9. From the **Select An Installation Image** page, choose the installation image the answer file will be associated with, then select **Next**.

10. From the **Select A Sample Answer File** page, choose a sample unattended setup file, then select **Next**.

11. From the **Friendly Description And Help Text** page, type a description that is easy to understand and is descriptive, then choose **Next**.

12. From the **Review Settings** page, review the settings summary, then choose **Finish**.

Remote Installation Services (RIS) Security Configuration

Administration of RIS security includes the following:

- Setting permissions for creating pre-staged and user created computer accounts

- Setting permissions for joining computers created in the Computers container and OUs.

For users to create new computer accounts in Active Directory or join them to the domain, they must have the correct rights and permissions. You decide the users who will be performing these functions and set up their rights and privileges.

Authorizing a RIS Server

You set up the RIS authorization using the DHCP server management console. This console is used to authorize both the DHCP and RIS servers to provide services on the network.

When a remote installation server attempts to start on the network, Active Directory is queried and the server computer's name or IP address is compared to the list of authorized remote installation servers. If a match is found, the remote installation server is authorized and started on the network. If a match is not found, the server is not authorized. In this case, Remote Installation Services will not answer.

Granting Computer Account Creation Rights

To set permissions for creating user-created computer accounts, follow these steps:

1. From the **Start** menu, choose **Programs, Administrative Tools** then select **Active Directory Users and Computers**.

2. From the console tree, right-click the appropriate domain and choose **Delegate Control**, to start the Delegation of Control wizard.

3. From the **Welcome** screen, choose **Next**.

4. From the **Users or Groups** page, choose **Add**.

5. Within the **Select Users, Computers or Groups** page, choose the user account or security group containing the users for which you are setting permissions.

6. Choose **Add** and then click **OK**.

7. From **Users or Groups**, choose **Next**.

8. From **Tasks to Delegate**, choose **Delegate the Following Common Tasks**, select **Join A Computer To A Domain** and then choose **Next**.

9. Review the delegation of control summary information that is displayed and choose **Finish**.

Adding Security and Load Balancing for RIS Client Computers

Load balancing is a technique used by Windows Clustering to calculate the performance of a server-based program, such as a Web server and distributes its client requests across multiple servers within the cluster. Each host spells out the load percentage it will handle, or the load can be equally distributed across all the hosts.

If a host fails, Windows Clustering dynamically redistributes the load among the remaining hosts. Network load balancing also supports unattended setup. To do this on a number of computers, you can run the setup unattended by creating an answer file, a customized script that answers the setup questions automatically. Then you run setup from the command line with the RIS options.

You can also predetermine a client computer network account identification to identify and route a client computer during the network service boot request. To define the permissions for creating pre-staged computer accounts, follow these steps:

1. From the **Start** menu, choose **Programs**, **Administrative Tools** and select **Active Directory Users and Computers**.

2. From the **View** menu, enable **Users, Groups And Computers as Containers** and **Advanced Features**.

3. From the console tree, right-click the appropriate client computer account and choose **Properties**.

4. From within **Properties**, choose the **Security** property page and select **Add**.

5. Within **Select User, Computers, Or Groups** page, choose the user or group from the list, select **Add** and then click **OK**.

6. Within the **Properties** page, choose the group that you have added.

7. Within the **Permissions** box, choose **Read, Write, Change Password and Reset Password Permissions** then click **OK**.

Note: If a group is allowed to have these permissions, keep in mind that you must add users to the group.

Vocabulary

Review the following terms in preparation for the certification exam.

Term	Description
BINL	The Boot Information Negotiation Layer service is added during the RIS installation, and supplies management of the RIS environment. BINL is responsible for answering client network requests, querying the Active Directory for the client computer and ensuring the correct policy and configuration settings are put on the client computer during installation. If the client computer has not been set up, BINL creates the client computer account in Active Directory.
CD	CD is an acronym for Compact Disc read-only memory. This form of information storage is characterized by high capacity (roughly 650 megabytes) and the use of laser optics rather than magnetic means for reading data.
CIW	Users of a remote boot-enabled client computer can use the Client Installation Wizard to select installation options, operating systems, and maintenance and troubleshooting tools.
clustering	Grouping computers to work together to provide a service. Using a cluster enhances both the availability of the service and the scalability of the operating system that provides the service. Network Load Balancing provides a software solution for clustering multiple computers.
container	A container is an object containing other linked or embedded objects.
DHCP	The Dynamic Host Configuration Protocol is a networking protocol that provides safe, reliable and simple TCP/IP network configuration. It offers dynamic configuration of IP addresses and ensures that address conflicts do not occur. It also conserves the use of IP addresses through centralized management of address allocation.

Term	Description
Distribution Group	Distribution Groups have only one function, to create e-mail distribution lists. You use distribution groups with e-mail applications, such as Microsoft Exchange. You can add a contact to a distribution group so that the contact receives e-mail sent to the group. As you assign no permissions to distribution groups, they have no function in security.
domain	An administrative and security boundary. Active Directory data is replicated between domain controllers within a domain.
Global Catalog (GC)	Built automatically by the Active Directory replication system, the Global Catalog contains a partial replica of every Windows 2000 domain in the directory. When given one or more attributes of the target object, the GC lets users and applications find objects quickly, without knowing what domain they occupy. The attributes in the global catalog are those used most frequently in search operations, and those required to locate a full replica of the object.
groups	Groups are Active Directory objects that can contain users, contacts, computers and other groups. In Windows 2000. Like user and computer accounts, groups are Windows 2000 security principals; they are directory objects and SIDs are assigned to them at creation.
IP	The Internet Protocol is the routable protocol in the TCP/IP suite that is responsible for the IP addressing, routing, and fragmentation and reassembly of IP packets.
load balancing	Load balancing is a method used by Windows Clustering to gauge the operation of a server-based program, such as a Web server, and spreads out its client requests across multiple servers within the cluster. Each host can spell out the load percentage that it will handle, or the load can be equally distributed across all the hosts. If a host fails, Windows Clustering dynamically redistributes the load among the remaining hosts.

Term	Description
MMC	The Microsoft Management Console is a framework for hosting administrative tools, called consoles. A console may contain tools, folders or other containers, and other administrative tools. The main MMC page provides commands and tools for authoring consoles.
object	An object can be a file, folder, shared folder or printer, described by a named set of attributes. For example, the attributes of a File object include its name, location and size; the attributes of an Active Directory user object could contain the user's first name, last name and e-mail address.
OU	An Organizational Unit is an administrative and security boundary. Active Directory data is replicated between domain controllers within a domain.
PCI	Peripheral Component Interconnect is a personal computer 32-bit local bus designed by Intel, which runs at 33 MHz and supports Plug and Play. It provides a high-speed connection with peripherals and allows the installation of up to ten peripheral devices.
pre-stage	With pre-staging, you can predetermine a client computer network account identification to identify and route a client computer during the network service boot request.
publish	Publishing makes data available for replication.
PXE	Pre-Boot eXecution Environment DHCP-based remote boot ROMS
RBFG.EXE	The Remote Boot Floppy Generator tool (RBFG.EXE) for Remote Installation creates a Pre-boot Execution Environment (PXE) emulator that works on a supported set of PCI adapters that do not have a PXE ROM embedded on the adapter.
RIPrep	Using the Remote Installation Preparation Wizard, an administrator can copy the installation image of an existing Windows 2000 Professional client computer, including any locally installed applications and operating system configuration changes, to an available remote installation server on the network.

Term	Description
RIS	With Remote Installation Services software, an administrator can set up new client computers remotely. The target computer must support remote booting.
ROM	Read-Only Memory is a semiconductor circuit that contains information that cannot be modified.
security group	Security groups have two functions, to manage user and computer access to shared resources and to filter Group Policy settings. You put users, computers and other groups into a security group and then assign permissions to specific resources to the security group. This means you can assign permissions to the group instead of multiple times to each individual user. When you add a user to an existing group, the user automatically gets the rights and permissions assigned to that group.
SID	Security ID is a unique number that identifies user, group and computer accounts. Each account is issued a unique SID when the account is first created. Windows 2000 uses the account's SID rather than the account's user or group name.
SIS	Single Instance Storage is the service that reduces disk space requirements on the volumes used for storing RIS installation images. The SIS service attaches itself to the RIS volume and look for any duplicates. When it finds one, it creates a link to the duplicate, reducing the disk space required.
site	One or more well-connected TCP/IP subnets. A site allows administrators to configure Active Directory access and replication topology quickly and easily to take advantage of the physical network. When users log on, Active Directory clients locate Active Directory servers in the same site as the user.
snap-ins	A type of tool you can add to a console supported by Microsoft Management Console (MMC). A stand-alone snap-in can be added by itself, an extension snap-in can be added to extend the function of another snap-in.
TCP/IP	The Transport Control Protocol/Internet Protocol is a set of protocols that provides communication among diverse networks. Because it accommodates different architectures and operating systems, TCP/IP is the most commonly used Internet protocol.

Term	Description
TFTPD	On the server side, this Trivial File Transfer Protocol Daemon services host's specific file download requests made by the client computer. The TFTPD service is used to download the Client Installation Wizard (CIW) and all of the client pages in the CIW during a single session.
UNC	Universal Naming Convention is the full Windows 2000 name of a resource on a network. It conforms to the \\ servername \ sharename. UNC names of directories or files can also include the directory path under the share name, with the following syntax: \\ servername\ sharename\ directory \ filename.
UPN	The User Principal Name consists of a user account name and a domain name identifying the domain in which the user account is located. This is the standard for logging on to a Windows 2000 domain. The format is: user @ domain.com.

In Brief

If you want to...	Then do this...
Add a new client installation image	1. From the **Start** menu, choose **Programs, Administrative Tools** and select **Active Directory Users and Computers**
	2. From the console tree, right-click the appropriate RIS server, select **Properties**.
	3. From the computer **Properties**, select the **Remote Install** property page and then choose **Advanced Settings**.
	4. In the Remote Installation Services **Properties** page, select the **Images** property page.
	5. Choose **Add** to start the Add Wizard.
	6. On the **New Answer File Or Installation Image** page, select **Add A New Installation Image**, then choose **Next** to start the Add Installation Image Wizard.
	7. Enter the required information on each of the Wizard's pages.
	8. If a previous set of CIW screens exists, the **Previous Client Installation Screens Found** page is displayed. Choose the CIW screen you would like use for this image, then choose **Next**.
	9. On the **Review Settings** page, review the installation summary, then select **Finish**.

If you want to...	Then do this...
Add a new printer	1. From the **Start** menu, **Settings, Printers,** and double-click **Add Printer**. The **Add Printer Wizard** appears. Choose **Next**
	2. Choose **Local Printer,** clear the **Automatically detect and install my Plug and Play printer** checkbox, and select **Next**.
	3. Choose the **Create a new port** option, select **Standard TCP/IP Port,** and choose **Next**.
	4. The **Add Standard TCP/IP Printer Port Wizard** appears. Select **Next**.
	5. On the **Add Port** page, within **Printer Name or IP Address** type the IP address of the printer, the port name in **Port name,** and select **Next**. Choose **Finish**.
	6. On the **Printers** list, choose your printer's manufacturer and model, and select **Next**.
	7. Within **Printer name** type the name of your printer.
	8. On the **Printer Sharing** page, type a name for the printer.
	9. In **Location** and **Comment,** type the appropriate information.
	10. Print a test page and choose **Finish**.
	11. After you create the printer, the printer is automatically published in Active Directory and the **Listed in the Directory** check box is selected.

If you want to...	Then do this...
Add a user to a group	1. From the desktop, right-click **My Computer** and choose **Manage**.
	2. From the console tree of Computer Management, expand **System Tools**, expand **Local Users and Groups**, and then select **Groups**.
	3. From the right pane, right-click the group and choose **Add to Group**.
	4. Choose **Add**, select the user names, choose **Add**, and then click **OK**.
	5. Click **OK** again to save the changes.
Add the RIS component	1. You access the Windows Component Window either: During **Windows 2000 Server Installation** or From the **Start** menu, choose **Settings, Control Panel,** select **Add/Remove Programs**, then **Add/Remove Windows Components**.
	2. In the **Windows Components Wizard** page select the **Remote Installation Services**, choose **Next**.
	3. When prompted, put the Windows 2000 CD in the CD-ROM drive.
	4. Select **Yes** to restart the server before installing RIS.

If you want to...	Then do this...
Authorize RIS servers	1. From the **Start** menu, choose **Programs**, **Administrative Tools** and select **DHCP**. 2. From the DHCP console tree, select the **DHCP node**. 3. On the **Action** menu, select **Manage Authorized Services**. 4. In the **Manage Authorized Services** page, select **Authorize**. 5. In the **Authorize DHCP Server** page, type the **Name** or **IP address** of the RIS server you want to authorize. Then select **OK**. 6. In the **DHCP** message box, select **Yes**. 7. From **Manage Authorized Servers,** select the server, the click **OK**.
Create a nested group	1. From the **Start** menu, choose **Settings**, and then select **Control Panel**. 2. Double-click **Administrative Tools**, and then choose **Computer Management**. 3. Within the **Local Users and Groups** console tree, choose **Groups**. 4. Create a new group by right-clicking the Group you will use as the base, select **New**, and then **Group**. 5. Select the name of the group to which you want to add the new group, choose **Add**, and then select **OK**. 6. Right-click the the new Group, and choose **Properties**. 7. Select the **Members** property page and choose **Add**. 8. Select the name of the group you want to add the new group, choose **Add**, and then select **OK**. 9. Choose **Apply**, and then click **OK**.

If you want to...	Then do this...
Create a RIS boot disk	1. From the **Start** menu, choose **Run** and type the **UNC path** of the RBGF utility, for example: \\ server\share\Remote Install\Admin\1386\RBFG.EXE
	2. Select **OK**.
	3. Put a formatted disk in the floppy drive.
	4. In the **Windows 2000 Remote Boot Disk Generator** page select the correct floppy drive and choose **Create Disk**.
	5. Select **Close** when the disk has finished being created. Remove the disk from the disk drive.
Create an OU	1. Start **Active Directory Users and Computers**.
	2. Select the location where you want to create this OU—either a domain, such as Lightpoint.net or another OU.
	3. On the **Action** menu, select **New** and then choose **Organizational Unit**.
	4. In the **New Object-Organizational Unit** page, Within **Name** type the name of the OU. Click **OK**.

If you want to...	Then do this...
Create user accounts	1. From the **Start** menu, choose **Programs**, **Administrative Tools** and select **Active Directory Users and Computers**
	2. From the console tree, double-click the domain you wish to use.
	3. Right-click the OU where you want to add the user, choose **New**, and then **User**.
	4. Type the User's name information.
	5. In **User logon name**, type the name the user will use to log on with and then select the suffix to be added on to the user logon name (following the @ symbol), and then choose **Next**.
	6. Enter the user's password in both the **Password** and **Confirm password** sections and then choose **Next**.
	7. Choose **Finish** to confirm and accept the new entry.
Define an unattended setup answer file	1. From the **Start** menu, choose **Programs**, **Administrative Tools** and select **Active Directory Users and Computers**
	2. From the console tree, right-click the appropriate RIS server and select **Properties**.
	3. In the **Server Properties** page, select the **Remote Install** page, then choose **Advanced Settings**.
	4. In the **Remote Installations Services Properties** page, select the **Images** page.
	5. Select **Add** to start the Add Wizard.
	6. On the **New Answer File Or Installation Image** page, select **Associate a New Answer File to An Existing Image**, then choose **Next**.
	7. On the **Unattended Setup Answer File Source** page, select the source that has the unattended setup file you wish to copy. Choose **Next**.
	8. On the wizard pages, type the appropriate information.
	9. On the **Review Settings** page, review the settings summary, then select **Finish**.

If you want to...	Then do this...
Define the permissions for creating pre-staged computer accounts	1. From the **Start** menu, choose **Programs**, **Administrative Tools** and select **Active Directory Users and Computers**.
	2. On the **View** menu, enable **Users, Groups And Computers as Containers** and **Advanced Features**.
	3. From the console tree, right-click the appropriate client computer account and select **Properties**.
	4. In the **Properties** page, select the **Security** property page and choose **Add**.
	5. In **Select User, Computers, Or Groups** page, select the user or group from the list, choose **Add** and then **OK**.
	6. In the **Properties** page, select the group that you have added.
	7. In the **Permissions** box, select **Read, Write, Change Password and Reset Password Permissions** then select **OK**.
Install RIS on the server	1. From the **Start menu**, choose **Settings**, and the select **Control Panel**.
	2. Open **Add/Remove Programs**, and then select **Add/Remove Windows Components**.
	3. Select **Remote Installation Services**, and then select **Next**.
	4. Follow through the wizard prompts.
Move a user	1. From the **Start** menu, choose **Programs**, **Administrative Tools** and select **Active Directory Users and Computers**
	2. From the console tree, select **Users** or, select the folder containing the desired user account.
	3. Right-click the user you want to move, and then choose **Move**.
	4. In the **Move** page, choose the folder you want to move the user account into.
	5. Select the appropriate OU, and click **OK**.

If you want to...	Then do this...
Publish the shared folder in the directory	1. In the Active Directory **Users and Computers** snap-in, right-click the selected OU, select **New**, and choose **Shared Folder**. 2. In the **New Object-Shared Folder** page, within **Name** type the name of your shared folder. 3. Within **Network Path**, type the UNC where you want to publish in the directory. 4. Click **OK**.
Set permissions for creating user-created computer accounts:	1. From the **Start** menu, choose **Programs**, **Administrative Tools** and select **Active Directory Users and Computers** 2. From the console tree, right-click the appropriate domain and select **Delegate Control**, to start the Delegation of Control wizard. 3. On the **Welcome** screen, choose **Next**. 4. On the **Users or Groups** page, choose **Add**. 5. In the **Select Users, Computers or Groups** page, select the user account or security group containing the users for whom you will be setting permissions. 6. Choose **Add** and then select **OK**. 7. On the **Users or Groups** page, choose **Next**. 8. On the **Tasks to Delegate** page, select **Delegate the Following Common Tasks**, select **Join A Computer To A Domain** and choose **Next**. 9. Review the delegation of control summary information that is displayed and select **Finish**.

If you want to...	Then do this...
Set the client installation options	1. From the **Start** menu, choose **Programs, Administrative Tools** and select **Active Directory Users and Computers**
	2. From the console tree, right-click the appropriate OU, select **Properties**, then choose the **Group Policy** page.
	3. Choose the **Group Policy** and select **Next**.
	4. From the **Group Policy** console tree, select **User Configuration**, open **Windows Settings** and choose **Remote Installation Services**.
	5. Double-click the **Choice Options** object. The Choice Options page opens. Make the appropriate selections.
Set the OU properties	1. From the **Start** menu, choose **Programs, Administrative Tools** and select **Active Directory Users and Computers**
	2. Expand the domain.
	3. Right-click the correct OU, then select **Properties**.
	4. Select the property page for those you want to include or change for the OU. **Enter** or change the values for each property.
Share a folder	1. In **Windows Explorer**, right-click the folder name that you wish to share and select **Properties**.
	2. Select the **Sharing** page, and then choose **Share this folder**.
	3. Type a name for the shared folder, and then click **OK**.
	4. In Comments, type a description for the share name.
	5. In **Maximum Number Of Users,** type a number.
	6. Everyone has permissions to this shared folder. To limit the access choose **Permissions**. Click **Ok**.

Lesson 4 Activities

Complete the following activities to prepare for the certification exam.

1. Describe the two-step process that you need to do to create a shared folder object.

2. Explain what RIS is and the types of remote booting that RIS supports.

3. List the components of a user account.

4. When you share folders, you should use centralized data folders. Explain why.

5. Explain why you would use security groups rather than distribution groups.

6. Describe what publishing a resource means.

7. Explain how to publish a printer.

8. Describe how OUs have a place in defining your Active Directory structure.

9. Explain the purpose of OU properties.

10. Describe the RIS boot disk.

Answers to Lesson 4 Activities

1. Creating a shared folder object in Active Directory does not automatically share the folder. You first share the folder, and then publish it in Active Directory.

2. Remote Installation Services (RIS) are software services that let administrators set up client computers without having to visit each client. The remote client must support remote booting. There are two types of remote boot enabled computers: those with Pre-Boot eXecution Environment (PXE) DHCP based remote ROMs and those with network cards supported by the RIS boot disk.

3. A User Account is a record of all the information that identifies a user to Windows 2000 and includes the following components:

    • Username

    • Password required to log on

    • Groups which the user account is a member of group

    • Rights and permissions the user has for accessing the computer, the network, and its resources

4. Centralized data folders can be backed up easily.

5. You use security groups to assign permissions. You cannot use a distribution list to assign security. You use distribution groups when the only function of the group is not security related (e.g. e-mail distribution list).

6. Publishing information about shared resources such as printers and file folders makes it uncomplicated for users to find them on the network. Information about Windows NT 4.0 printers and shared folders can be published in the directory using Active Directory Users and Computers.

7. You can publish a printer using the Sharing page of the printer Properties page. By default, Listed in the directory is enabled. The directory is the Active Directory data store. This means that Windows 2000 Server publishes the shared printer by default. The print subsystem automatically propagates any changes made to the printer attributes (location, description, loaded paper, and so forth) to the directory.

8. You should make OUs that represent your organization's business or operative structure. Each domain can put into operation it own OU hierarchy. If there are several domains, you can create OU structures inside each domain that are independent from each of the other domains.

9.   It is important that you supply comprehensive property definitions for each OU that you create. For example, when you search, you can use an OU's description.

10.   If the computer you wish to set up does not have a PXE-based remote boot ROM, Windows 2000 provides a tool to create a remote boot disk. The RIS remote boot disk can work with a number of PCI network cards. Using the RIS boot disk removes the need to upgrade existing computers with new network cards that contain a PXE remote boot ROM to use the remote operating system installation feature. The RIS boot disk simulates the PXE remote boot and supports a number of network cards.

Lesson 4 Quiz

These questions test your knowledge of features, vocabulary, procedures and syntax.

1.   Why should you use groups?
      A.   Groups simplify administration by granting rights and assigning permissions to the
            group instead of individually to each member.
      B.   You create groups according to the access the group members require for
            resources.
      C.   Groups can be used to create distribution lists.
      D.   Use groups so that members can access resources in any domain.

2.   What is the purpose of adding a group to another group?
      A.   Nesting creates consolidated groups.
      B.   You can model your organization's management hierarchy.
      C.   They perform transfers.
      D.   Reduces the number of times you have to assign permissions.

3.   What is DHCP?
      A.   It is a remote boot-enabled client service to select installation options, operating
            systems and troubleshooting tools.
      B.   It offers dynamic configuration of IP addresses and ensures that address conflicts do
            not occur.
      C.   It also conserves the use of IP addresses through centralized management of address
            allocation.
      D.   A networking protocol that provides safe, reliable and simple TCP/IP network
            configuration.

4.   What is RIS?
      A.   Lets administrators set up new client computers remotely
      B.   Imaging option that allows the administrator to clone a standard desktop image
      C.   A new form of remote boot technology
      D.   A tool for creating a remote boot disk

5.   You have deleted a user account. Can you recreate it?
      A.   A new user account with the same name as a deleted user account does not
            automatically take on the permissions and memberships of the deleted account.
      B.   To duplicate a deleted user account, all permissions and memberships must be
            manually recreated.
      C.   You do not need to duplicate a deleted user account. No permissions and
            memberships need to be manually recreated.
      D.   A new user account with the same name as a deleted user account automatically
            takes on the permissions and memberships of the deleted account.

6. A user account is a record of all the information that identifies a user to Windows 2000. What must it include?
    A.   Password required to log on
    B.   User name
    C.   Groups in which the user account has membership
    D.   Rights and permissions the user has for using the computer and network and accessing their resources

7. What are the Group Policy Options?
    A.   Allow
    B.   Deny
    C.   Valid
    D.   Don't Care

8. What are the default accounts created?
    A.   Domain User Accounts
    B.   Local User Accounts
    C.   Administrator and Power User
    D.   Administrator and Guest

9. You have created a shared folder. Can others access it?
    A.   No, you will still need to publish it.
    B.   No. You will need to assign permissions to it.
    C.   Yes. As soon as you have created it, it is shared.
    D.   Yes. A shared folder is created in a special way and everyone has access to it.

10. Installing RIS is a two-step process. What are the steps?
    A.   Add the RIS component.
    B.   Authorize RIS servers.
    C.   Install RIS.
    D.   Set RIS client installation options.

Answers to Lesson 4 Quiz

1. Answers A, B and C are correct. Windows 2000 has two kinds of groups: distribution groups, which are used by applications for non-security related functions and security groups to assign permissions to gain access to resources.

   Answer D is partly correct. If you create a Universal Group, members can come from any domain and members can access resources in any domain.

2. Answers A and D are correct. You create nested groups to creates consolidated groups and reduce the number of times you have to assign permissions.

   Answer B is incorrect. The domain models your organization's hierarchy.

   Answer C is incorrect. Name servers perform transfers.

3. Answers B, C and D are correct. The Dynamic Host Configuration Protocol is a networking protocol that provides safe, reliable and simple TCP/IP network configuration. It offers dynamic configuration of IP addresses and ensures that address conflicts do not occur. It also conserves the use of IP addresses through centralized management of address allocation.

   Answer A is incorrect. The definition described is for CIW.

4. Answer A is correct. The Remote Installation Service (RIS) is software services that allow administrators to set up new client services remotely. The target must support remote booting.

   Answer B is incorrect. A Remote Installation Preparation (RIPrep) imaging option allows the cloning of a desktop image.

   Answer C is incorrect. PXE is a new form of remote boot technology.

   Answer D is incorrect. A RIS boot disk is a Windows 2000 tool provided to create the remote boot disk.

5. Answers A and B are correct. A new user account with the same name as a deleted user account does not automatically take on the permissions and memberships of the deleted account. To duplicate a deleted user account, all permissions and memberships must be manually recreated.

6.   Answers A, B, C and D are correct. A User Account is a record of all the information that identifies a user to Windows 2000--User name, password required to log on, groups the user account has membership, rights and permissions the user has for using the computer and network and accessing their resources. Additional information can be entered in Properties.

7.   Answers A, B and D are correct. The three Group Policy options are: Allow, Don't Care and Deny.

      Answer C is incorrect. Valid is not an option.

8.   Answer A is correct. With a domain user account the user can log onto the domain to gain access to network resources.

      Answer B is correct. A local user account allows a user to log onto specific computer to use the resources of that computer.

      Answer D is correct. Administrator and Guests are part of the built-in user accounts.

      Answer C is incorrect. Power Users are a group not a user account.

9.   Answer A is correct. Creating a shared folder object in Active Directory does not automatically share the folder. You must first share the folder, and then publish it in Active Directory.

      Answer B is partly correct. You provide the following information when you share a folder: share name, comments on its content, the number of users who have access to the folder and permissions.

      Answers C and D are incorrect. Creating the shared folder is only the first step.

10.   Answers A and C are correct. You first add the RIS component and then install RIS.

      Answers B and D are incorrect. They are the configuration steps you perform after installing RIS.

Administrative Control of Active Directory Objects

In a Windows 2000 network, you organize the component objects into Organizational Units (OUs) within a domain. You link domains together to form trees, and join the trees together to create a forest.

The administration of objects includes locating objects, assigning permissions to objects, moving objects within and between domains, delegating administrative control to OUs, and creating Global Catalog (GC) servers. This is done using a number of system and command-line tools. This lesson will cover, in depth, the processes and tools.

After completing this lesson, you should have a better understanding of the following topics:

• Active Directory Administrative Control

• Global Catalog Servers

• Manual and Scripted Account Creation and Management

Active Directory Administrative Control

In networks running Windows 2000, you can be specific in delegating administrative authority to both individual OUs and individual domains. You can delegate administrative control to any level of a domain tree by creating OUs within domains and delegating administrative control for specific OUs to particular users or groups. In doing so, you can reduce the number of administrators in an organization, which otherwise would require far-reaching administrative authority.

Since a domain is a security boundary, administrative permissions for a domain are limited, by default, to the domain. For example, an administrator with permissions to set security policies in one domain is not automatically granted authority to set security policies in any other domain in the directory.

By delegating administrative responsibilities, you can eliminate the need for multiple administrative accounts that have broad authority. You will still use the predefined Domain Admins group for administration of the entire domain, but you can limit the accounts that are members of the Domain Admins group to highly trusted administrative users.

Delegating Administrative Control of Active Directory Objects

Windows 2000 comes with the Delegation of Control Wizard to help administrators assign the management of certain kinds of objects to individuals or groups within the organization.

This delegation of administration of specific resources to an individual or group does away with a number of administrators needing to have authority over an entire domain or site. By choosing the appropriate user or groups and giving them the correct permissions, they, in turn, will be able to delegate administration of a subset of their accounts and resources. You can configure the scope of delegated administrative responsibility in many ways. Although you generally grant permissions at the Organizational Unit level by applying inheritance, you can also delegate administration for an entire domain within a forest.

Table 5.1 contains only the most common OU-level administrative tasks. However, you do have the ability to delegate administration down to the per-user per-property level. For example, a user object has more than 300 individual properties. Each property is secured by an access mask, which defines who can read or write to it. In other words, you could potentially define more than 600 possible permissions for each user object.

Table 5.1 Options for Delegating Administrative Tasks

Alternative	Description
Delegate complete administrative control over an OU and its contents to a user	This assigns a user the capability to change properties on the OU itself and to create, delete, or modify any objects in the OU
Delegate administrative control over objects of a specific type in an OU to a user	This allows a user to manage only certain objects in a specific OU, such as group, printer, or file share objects
Delegate the ability to create and delete objects in a particular OU to a user	This assigns a user the ability to create and delete every object in a specific OU, including users, groups, and printers
Delegate the ability to create and delete objects of a specific type in an OU to a user	This allows a user to create and delete certain objects in a specific OU, such as user or printer objects
Delegate administrative control over specific properties of objects in an OU to a user	This assigns a user the ability to manage specific properties of objects in an OU, such as the password property of user objects

The Delegation of Control Wizard does not deny permissions, remove previously delegated control, delegate control over individual objects, or apply special permissions. Its greatest strength is to apply permissions to multiple users and groups at the same time. There are three ways to define the delegation of administration responsibilities:

- Delegate permissions to change properties on a particular container

- Delegate permissions to create and delete objects of a specific type, such as users, groups, or printers, under an Organizational Unit

- Delegate permissions to update specific properties on objects of a specific type under an Organizational Unit

Table 5.2 describes the Delegation of Control Wizard options.

Table 5.2 Delegation of Control Wizard Options

Option	Description
Users or Groups	Select the users, accounts, or groups to which you want to delegate control
Tasks to Delegate	Choose the common tasks from the pre-defined list or create custom tasks
Active Directory Object Type Only available when custom tasks are selected	Choose the scope of the tasks you want to delegate: • This Folder, Existing Objects in This Folder • Only the Following Objects In This Folder
Permissions Only available when custom tasks are selected	Select one of the following permissions: • General, the most commonly assigned permissions available for the object • Property Specific, permissions you assign to the attributes of the object • Creation/Deletion of Specific Child Objects, the permission to create and delete child objects

To use the Delegation of Control Wizard, follow these steps:

1. From the **Start** menu, choose **Programs**, **Administrative Tools**, and then select **Active Directory Users and Computers**.

2. In the left pane of **Active Directory Users and Computers**, right-click the object to which you want to delegate administration, and then choose **Delegate control**. The Delegation of Control Wizard appears (Figure 5.1).

Figure 5.1 Delegation of Control Wizard

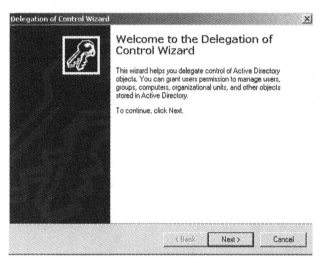

3. From **Delegation of Control**, choose **Next.**

4. From **Users or Groups,** specify the groups or users to whom you are granting control of this OU (Figure 5.2).

Figure 5.2 Users or Groups

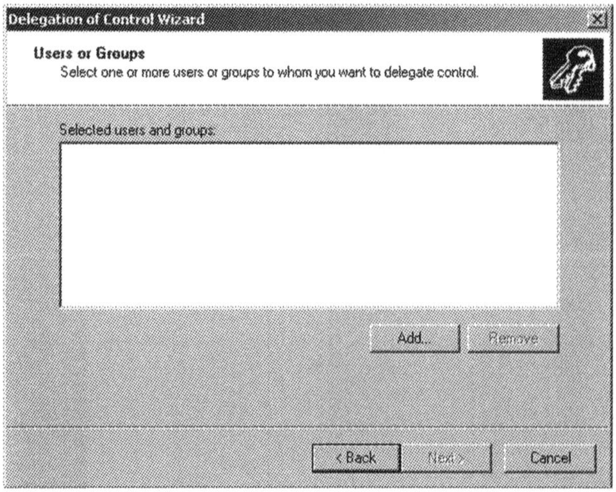

5. Choose **Add**, and a list of Users and Groups appears (Figure 5.3).

Figure 5.3 Select Users

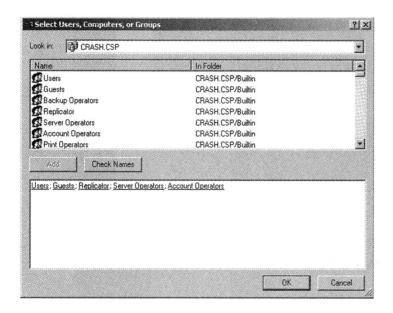

6. From **Users, Groups and Computers**, choose the users and groups to whom you want to delegate control of the specifc tasks, click **OK**, and select **Next**.

7. From **Tasks to Delegate** (Figure 5.4), choose the appropriate tasks and then **Next**.

Figure 5.4 Tasks to Delegate

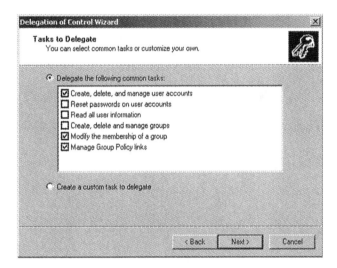

8. Choose **Finish**.

Decentralizing Windows 2000 Network Administration

Before implementing Active Directory, you must have examined your organization's business structure and operations to plan the needed domain structure, domain namespace, OU structure, and site structure. Assessing your network resources helps you identify the method of network administration that is most suitable for your organization. In decentralized network administration, a number of administrative teams or administrators provide network services.

Global Catalog Servers

To make it easy to search the Active Directory, all objects and their frequently used attributes are stored as a partial replica in a directory in each Windows 2000 domain. This directory is the Global Catalog (GC). The GC is built automatically during Active Directory replication. A user finds objects by using the Lightweight Directory Access Protocol (LDAP) to query a GC server. The GC server works like an index. Just as you would use an index to locate information about a topic such as the solar system in an encyclopedia, you can use the GC to find the location of an object such as a color printer in Active Directory. Since the GC server indexes the entire forest, you can find objects throughout your forest, no matter where they physically exist (Figure 5.5).

Figure 5.5 Global Catalog Attributes

During the logon process, GC servers also provide group information to domain controllers. A network user would not be able to log on if a GC server is not available. However, once logged on, a user with the appropriate permissions can access resources anywhere inside a Windows 2000 forest.

 Note: You have to publish network resources, such as shared folders and printers, before a user can access them.

Active Directory automatically builds the GC. For each object in a tree or forest, there is a subset of object properties that is useful to the global community for location of objects. These are values such as the Logon Name property for a user or the Members property in a universal group.

Each property of every object in the Windows 2000 Schema has a variable attribute that is used to indicate if an attribute should be contained in the GC. If you request the value of an object that is not in the GC, the object's Distinguished Name (DN) is retuned. The DN assigns you enough information to find a domain controller containing the partition holding that particular object and its values. The information returned by the GC is called a referral. Referrals are valid only for the domain partitions in a single tree; other trees are not searched. As a result, you need to closely examine object search and retrieval requirements when building a forest.

Tip: The larger a GC gets, the longer each search will take and the more bandwidth will be consumed because these extra attributes will be replicated each time they change.

The GC performs two key Active Directory roles:

• It facilitates network logon by supplying universal group information to a domain controller when a logon procedure is started

• It facilitates querying or the finding of directory information no matter which domain in the forest contains the data

Figure 5.6 describes how the GC is the central repository for information.

Figure 5.6 Global Catalog is the Central Repository for Information

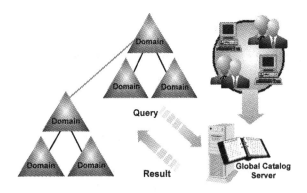

Creating Global Catalog Servers

To configure a Windows 2000 domain controller as a Global Catalog server, perform the following steps:

1. From the **Start menu**, choose **Programs**, **Administrative Tools**, and then select **Active Directory Sites and Services**.

2. From the Tree pane, expand **Sites**, expand the site that owns the server, expand **Servers**, and then expand the server.

3. Right-click **NTDS Settings** and choose **Properties** (Figure 5.7).

Figure 5.7 NTDS Settings General Property Page

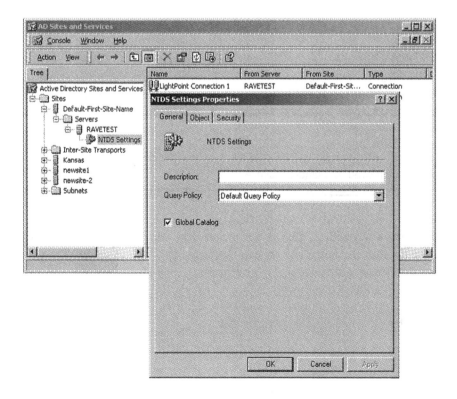

4. Select **Global Catalog**, choose **Apply**, and then click **OK**.

Moving Server Objects Between Sites

A forest site topology is very flexible and easily changed after you set up your network. As your physical network evolves, you will need to evaluate and tune your site topology. Before you effect any changes to your site topology, you need to anticipate the impact of the change on availability, replication latency and replication bandwidth, and how that might affect end-users. Since site topology is stored in the Configuration container, changes will replicate to every domain controller in the forest.

Frequent changes to the site topology will cause a large amount of replication traffic, so changes should be rolled up into fewer, larger changes instead of many, smaller changes. Depending on your replication topology and schedule, site topology changes can take a long time to reach every domain controller in the forest.

If you have not organized your Windows 2000 network into sites, information exchange among domain controllers and clients can be disorganized. Sites improve the efficiency of network usage.

Site membership is determined in a different way for domain controllers and clients. A client decides what site it is in when it is turned on, and the site location will often be dynamically updated. A domain controller's site location is determined by the site to which its Server object belongs.

 Note: A domain controller's site location will be consistent unless the domain controller's server object is intentionally moved to a different site.

If a domain controller or client has an address that is not included in any site, then the client or domain controller is contained within the initial site created (Default-First-Site). All activity is then handled as though the client or domain controller activity is a member of Default-First-Site, in spite of the actual Internet Protocol (IP) address or subnet location. All sites will always have an associated domain controller, since the nearest domain controller will associate itself with a site that has no domain controller—unless you have deleted the Default-First-Site.

If you have configured sites and subnets, then new servers are automatically added to the site that owns the subnet. To manually move a server to a different site, follow these steps:

1. From the **Start** menu, choose **Programs**, **Administrative Tools**, and then **Active Directory Sites and Services Manager**.

2. Expand the **Sites** container, the site that currently contains the desired server, and the **Servers** container.

3. Right-click the server name, and then choose **Move** (Figure 5.8).

Figure 5.8 Move a Site

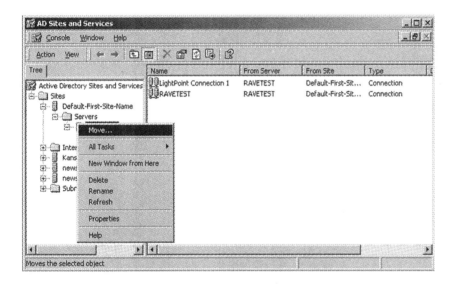

4. A list of all sites is displayed. Select the new target site and click **OK**.

Locating Objects in Active Directory

Rather than browsing a list of objects, it is often more efficient to find objects that meet a certain criteria. To find objects follow these steps:

1. From the **Start** menu, select **Programs**, **Administrative Tools**, and then select **Active Directory Users and Computers**.

2. Choose a domain or container in the console tree.

3. From the menu bar, select **Action**, and then choose **Find**. Alternately, right-click the container and then choose **Find.** Find creates an LDAP query that will be executed against the selected domain or container. Table 5.3 describes the options available.

4. If available, type in further information to refine your search in the appropriate places on the Advanced or Users, Contacts, and Groups property pages.

5. Choose **Find Now**.

6. A list of the objects that match the selected criteria displays, as illustrated in Figure 5.9.

Figure 5.9 Find Users Contacts and Groups

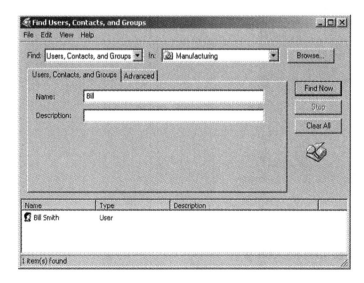

Table 5.3 Options in Find

Search Criteria	Description
Find	A list of the object types that you can search for: • Users, contacts, and groups • Computers • Printers • Shared folders • OUs • Custom search
In	A list of the locations that you can search. This could be the entire Active Directory, a specific domain, or an OU.
Browse	Selecting Browse lets you select the path of your search.
Advanced	On this property page, you can define the search criteria to locate the object you need. This property page has a number of choices: • Users, contacts, and groups • Computers • Printers • Shared folders • OUs If you select Custom Search, you must type in the search criteria manually or use the common attributes on the Custom Search property page.
Field list	A context-sensitive list of the methods available to refine the search further on the object type you select. Located on the Advanced property page
Condition list	A context-sensitive list of methods available to further refine your search for an attribute. Located on the Advanced property page
Value list	In this area, you can enter the value for the condition of the attribute you are using to search the Directory. You can search for an object by using an attribute of the object, but only if you enter a value for that attribute. Located on the Advanced property page

Search Criteria	Description
Search Criteria	On the Advanced property page, Search Criteria displays your selections. To define a search criterion, use the Field list, Condition list, and Value list, and select Add. To remove a criterion, select the criterion and then choose Remove.
Find Now	Select Find Now after you have defined your criteria to begin a search.
Stop	Select Stop to halt the search. Items that match the criteria up until the search is stopped will display.
Clear All	Select Clear All to clear the specified Search Criteria.
Results	A display at the bottom of the window showing the results of your search after you have selected Find Now.

Filtering a List of Objects

Being able to filter the list of returned objects from the directory can help you manage the directory more efficiently. With the filtering option, you can restrict the types of objects returned. For example, you can choose to view only users and groups. You can also design a more complex filter.

You can also restrict the number of objects displayed, if an Organizational Unit has more than a specified number of objects. You use the filter to configure this option.

For example, to create a filter that retrieves only users, you would follow these steps:

1. From the **Start menu,** choose **Programs, Administrative Tools,** and then select **Active Directory Users and Computers.**

2. From the menu bar, select **View,** and then choose **Filter Options.**

Figure 5.10 Filter Options

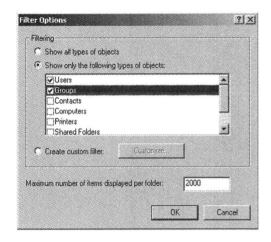

3. From **Filter Options** (Figure 5.10), choose **Show only the following types of objects**, and then select **Users**.

4. Click **OK** to save the filter changes.

After you have defined your filter, whenever you view a container, it will retrieve only the objects you have selected. In Figure 5.10, the user and group objects are selected. If you also enable the description bar, there will be a visual indication that a filter has been applied, as shown in Figure 5.11.

Figure 5.11 Filter Activated Indicator

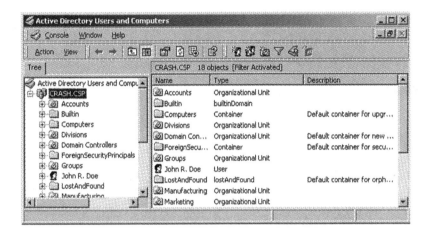

Manual and Scripted Account Creation and Management

In large networks, companies can have thousands of computers supported by hundreds of servers in an organization that spans many sites. Windows 2000 Active Directory will add to this complexity. Managing complex setups can take a lot of time, and setting up management can be unwieldy.

Windows 2000 provides the administrator with a number of tools. However, to manage some tasks, there are no tools on a large number of objects and computers. No administrator would manually create thousands of users using the Active Directory Users and Computers tool. However, you can manage large numbers of objects and computers using scripts. You can write scripts to manipulate any object and its properties.

Table 5.4 describes and briefly explains the common scripting tools you can use.

Tip: More information about scripting can be found on the Microsoft Developer Network (MSDN) library documentation.

Table 5.4 Scripting Overview

Name	Description
VB Script	The Visual Basic Scripting language is based on the Visual Basic programming language, but it is much simpler and is similar to JavaScript.
HTML	The Hypertext Markup Language is used to create Web pages with hyperlinks and markup for text formatting.
JScript	JavaScript is a cross-platform programming language from Sun Microsystems that can be used to create animations and interactive features.
ActiveX Data Objects (ADO)	ADO is a general technology that lets developers write scripts and applications to access and manipulate data held in a database server. ADO is used with Active Directory Service Interface (ADSI).
Remote Data Service (RDS)	RDS uses a technique where data is retrieved in a client from a server, updated and manipulated in the client, and returned to the server in a single round trip. You will often see ADO/RDS together as they are two components of Microsoft Data Access Components (MDAC).

Table 5.5 describes the underlying technology used in scripting.

You can also interface these scripts to Web pages and perform administration through a browser interface.

Table 5.5 Technology Overview

Name	Description
ActiveX	ActiveX allows software components to work together in a network, regardless of the language in which they are created. Microsoft currently provides the following three hosts that run scripts to manipulate Active X objects: Internet Information Server (IIS) webserver; Internet Explorer browser; and Windows Scripting Host (WSH)
Active Server Pages (ASPs)	When VB Scripts are inside an HTML page, they are called ASPs. They are dynamic, meaning the Web page displayed differs depending on the results of a script incorporated as part of that Web page.
Active Directory Service Interface (ADSI)	ADSI provides a simple, powerful, object-oriented interface to Active Directory. With ADSI, programmers and administrators can create programs utilizing directory services by using high-end tools, such as Visual Basic, Java, C or Visual C++. ActiveX scripting languages such as VB Script, Jscript or PerlScript can be used as well. With ADSI, you can build (or buy) programs that give you a single point of access to multiple directories in your network environment. ADSI supports Lightweight Directory Access Protocol (LDAP).
Windows Scripting Host (WSH)	WSH comes with Windows 2000 and Windows 98, and it can be installed on Windows 95 and Microsoft Windows NT machines as well.

Windows Scripting Host (WSH) is an important tool for the following reasons:

• No new software needs to be purchased to use scripting

• It supports scripts without the need for Web pages, meaning anyone can quickly write a script in the scripting language and execute it on Windows 98, Microsoft Windows NT 4.0 or Windows 2000

• Any text editor can be used

• Scripts can be executed from the command line, directing output to the command line

You can run command-line scripts because WHS has two interpreters, one called WSCRIPT.EXE that deciphers the scripts in the 32-bit Windows environment and the other called CSSCRIPT.EXE that deciphers the scripts in the command line environment of the command prompt window. By default, if you launch a script called MYSCRIPT.VBS with a double-click, Windows 2000 would pass the script to WSCRIPT.EXE as though you had typed **WSCRIPT.EXE MYSCRIPT.VBS** at the command line.

WSH comes with a series of procedures defined to run the following script interactions with the host computer:

- Running programs

- Reading and writing to the registry

- Creating and deleting files

- Manipulating the contents of files

- Reading and writing environment variables

- Mapping and removing drives

- Adding, removing, and setting default printers

When configuring user environments, accessing these scripts is useful since you can write logon scripts using VB Script or Jscript if you wish.

 Note: WSH comes with Windows 2000 and Windows 98. It can be downloaded from the Microsoft Web site and installed on Windows 95 and Microsoft Windows NT workstations.

Active Directory Command-Line Tools

There are a number of command-line tools to configure, manage and troubleshoot Active Directory. These tools are known as the Support Tools and are available on the Windows 2000 Server compact disc in the \SUPPORT\ folder. The two following tools can be used to automate the creation of computer accounts:

- NETDOM (a Windows 2000 Resource Kit tool also available in X86\Support\Tools\Support.cab on the operating system CD-ROM)

- Scripting the computer account using ADSI and WSH

To create a computer account using NETDOM, follow these steps:

1. From the **Start** menu, choose Programs, Accessories, and then select Command Prompt.

2. From the command prompt, type the following:

NETDOM ADD computer_name /DOMAIN:domain_name /USERD:user /PASSWORDD:password

Where **computer_name** is the name of the account to add, **domain_name** is the name of the domain in which the computer account will be added, **user** is the username of an account with domain administrative rights, and **password** is the password for that user account.

 Note: You should only use the Windows 2000 version of NETDOM, which is included with the Windows 2000 Resource Kit. Previous versions are not compatible with some Windows 2000 features.

You can use NETDOM from the command line or call it from a batch file. The example above will create only the computer account and display how credentials of an authorized user who has permissions to create computer accounts in the domain can be specified.

To create a computer account running scripting using ADSI and Windows Script Host, an administrator can create a Visual Basic Script (VB Script). For more information about Visual Basic Scripting, visit the following Microsoft Web site:

http://msdn.microsoft.com/scripting

Controlling Access to Active Directory Objects

Every Active Directory object has a security descriptor that identifies who has permission to gain access and what type of access is allowed. However, before anyone can access the object, the administrator or the owner of the object assigns the permissions. Windows 2000 stores a list of user access permissions, called Access Control Lists (ACL), for every Active Directory object.

You can use permissions to assign administrative privileges to a specific user or group for an OU or single object, without assigning administrative permissions for controlling other Active Directory objects.

The type of object also determines which permissions you can select; they vary for different objects. For example, you can assign the Reset Password permission to a user object but not a printer object.

A user can be a member of multiple groups. Each of these groups can have different levels of access to objects. When you assign a permission to a user for an object, and they are a member of a group that has a different level of permissions, that user will have a combination of the user and group permissions.

For example, if you assign Read permissions for an object to Joe, and he is a member of a group that has Write permissions to that object, then Joe's permissions would be Read and Write to that object.

When defining permissions, you can allow or deny them. Deny always takes priority over any permissions that you have allowed for any user or group. If you deny access to an object, the user will not be able to access it, even if they belong to a group that has permissions for that object.

You can also set standard and special permissions on an object. Standard permissions are those most often given to objects. Special permissions give you a finer degree of control. Table 5.6 describes the standard permissions and the type of access.

Table 5.6 Standard Object Permissions

Object Permission	Allows the user to...
Full Control	Change permissions, take full ownership, perform all the other tasks specified in the other permissions
Read	View objects, object attributes, object owner, and Active Directory permissions
Write	Change object attributes
Create All Child Objects	Add any type of child objects to an OU
Delete All Child Objects	Remove any type of object from an OU

Managing Active Directory Performance

Monitoring performance is integral to maintaining and administering your Active Directory. You use Active Directory performance data for the following tasks:

- Understand Active Directory performance and its impact on your system resources

- Track changes and trends to plan for future upgrades

- Test changes and tune results by monitoring the results

- Detect problems and determine which components or processes will need to be optimized

The Active Directory has powerful administration tools. Objects can be hierarchically ordered so that they model large organizations, and the Windows 2000 Graphical User Interface (GUI) provides a drag-and-drop control console, giving an object-view of administration. For example, to do pruning and grafting, the administrator would grab the top of the merge-from tree, and then drag it to the target domain. The administrator is asked to confirm the action. The administrator must have rights in the merge-from tree to merge it with another tree and in the merge-to domain to bring new trees into it.

Anything that can be done through a graphical interface can also be done programmatically or from a script. To allow an administrator to write command- line procedures, the Active Directory provides full support for automation and scripting. This makes it possible to add, change, move, copy, and perform other administrative functions by scripted manipulation, using Active Directory and a scripting language, such as Visual Basic or Java.

Monitor, Maintain, and Troubleshoot Domain Controller Performance

One reason to use multiple Windows 2000 domains is to support decentralized administration. Your organization's offices may not accept a domain design that assigns them limited administrative control. Instead, they may want complete and total control over their local resources.

Under Windows 2000, domain controllers hold the Active Directory and perform the authentication and security services within domains, trees, and forests. In Microsoft Windows NT 4.0 and earlier versions there are two types of domain controllers—Primary Domain Controllers (PDCs) and Backup Domain Controllers (BDCs). A domain only had a single PDC and usually one or more BDCs. When changes were made, such as a new user being added to the domain or a password change for an existing user, all changes had to take place on the PDC. Updates were then replicated out to all the BDCs.

Under Windows 2000, there is no real concept of a PDC or BDC—all domain controllers are the same. Under Windows 2000, every domain controller can accept any changes to Active Directory and send those changes out to the other domain controllers to accept. Updates are passed around using multimaster replication, until all domain controllers are brought up to date.

Any Windows 2000 Server can become a domain controller without having to reinstall the operating system. Under Microsoft Windows NT 4.0 and earlier, a complete Operating System (OS) reinstall was required to turn a regular server into a PDC or BDC. Similarly, a Windows 2000 domain controller can be downgraded to a regular server without a reinstall.

Windows 2000 provides the following tools for monitoring resource usage on your computer:

• System Monitor

• Performance Logs and Alerts

Monitoring system performance is an important part of maintaining and administering Windows 2000. You use performance data to accomplish the following tasks:

• Understand your network's workload and the corresponding impact on your system's resources

• Test configuration changes or other tuning efforts by monitoring the results

- Diagnose problems and target components or processes for optimization

- Observe changes and trends in workloads and resource usage so that you can plan for future upgrades

The System Monitor and Performance Logs and Alerts give you comprehensive data about the resources used by specific components of the operating system and by server programs that have been designed to collect the following performance data:

- Graphs provide a display for performance-monitoring data

- Logs provide recording capabilities for the data

- Alerts send notification to users through the Messenger service when a counter value is reached, exceeded, or falls below a defined limit

Task Manager is another tool that gives you performance information about systems running Windows 2000. Task Manager presents a snapshot of programs and processes that are running on your computer, plus a summary of its processor and memory usage.

Monitor, Maintain, and Troubleshoot Active Directory Components

Windows 2000 comes with the Event Viewer console and the Performance console to monitor Active Directory. The Event Viewer console is a tool to monitor events, such as a service starting or application and system errors. The Performance Monitor console lets you monitor conditions within local and remote computers on your network and to summarize performance at selected intervals. The Performance Monitor contains two snap-ins—System Monitor and Performance Logs and Alerts. With System Monitor, you can measure Active Directory performance on any computer in the network. With the Performance Logs and Alerts snap-in, you can create counter logs, trace logs, and system alerts.

Tip: If you experience problems with Active Directory, it is recommended that you investigate potential causes of the problems first within the directory service event logs.

The event logs that monitor Active Directory are described in Table 5.7.

Table 5.7 Active Directory Event Logs

Log	Description
Application	Contains errors, warnings, or information that applications generate. The application developer presets which events are recorded.
Directory Service	Contains errors, warnings, and information that Active Directory generates (Figure 5.12).
File Replication Service	Holds the warnings, errors, and information that are generated by the File Replication Service.
System	Windows 2000 predefines what events to record. The System log contains errors, warnings, and information that Windows 2000 generates.

Figure 5.12 Directory Service Log

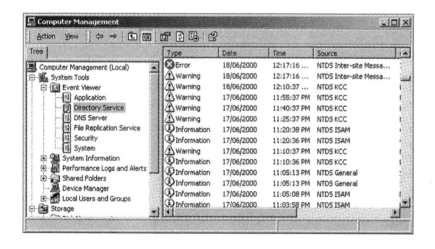

The Performance console lets you monitor conditions in any computer in the network and summarize performance at selected intervals. The Performance console uses various counters for monitoring resource usage. It logs results into a file for viewing and diagnosing performance problems. The Performance console can be used to collect baseline performance data and then to send alerts to the Event log about exceptions to the baseline.

The System Monitor is a snap-in to the Performance console. With the System Monitor, you can measure Active Directory performance on any computer on the network. With it, you can accomplish the following tasks:

- Collect and view real-time performance data on a local computer or several remote computers

- View data collected either currently or previously recorded in a counter log

- Present data in a printable graph, histogram, or report view

- Create HTML pages from performance views

- Create reusable monitoring configurations that can be installed on other computers using the Microsoft Management Console (MMC)

The Performance Logs and Alerts snap-in allows you to create counter logs, trace logs, and system alerts automatically from local or remote computers.

Counter Logs—Similar to the system monitor, counter logs support the definition of performance objects, performance counters, and system sample intervals for monitoring data about hardware resources and system services.

Trace Logs—Trace logs record data collected by the operating system provider or non-system providers when certain activities, such as a disk error or page fault, occur. When these events take place, the provider sends the data to the Performance Logs and Alerts services.

Vocabulary

Review the following terms in preparation for the certification exam.

Term	Description
ACL	An Access Control List details which users can access a network resource.
ActiveX	ActiveX is a set of technologies that allow the software components to work together in a network, regardless of the language in which they are created.
ADO	ActiveX Data Objects is a general technology that lets developers write scripts and applications to access and manipulate data held in a database server. ADO is used with ADSI.
ADSI	The Active Directory Services Interface is the programming interface that applications use to access the Active Directory.
API	The Application Programming Interface is the interface that applications use to send requests to the operating system.
ASP	Active Server Pages are VB Scripts, which are inside an HTML page. They are dynamic, meaning that the Web page displayed differs, depending on the results of a script incorporated as part of that Web page.
attribute	A parameter describing an object.
BDC	Backup Domain Controller is a computer in Microsoft Windows NT 4.0 or earlier versions which has a copy of the domain's directory database.
container	An Active Directory object that holds other objects and containers. Sites, domains, and OUs are all containers.
DN	The Distinguished Name naming convention uses particular abbreviations to define the path for an Active Directory object. For example a distinguished name is: domain controller=com/domain controller=Corp/CN=Users1

Term	Description
domain	In Active Directory, a boundary for security and administrative purposes.
domain controller	A domain controller is a server that authenticates users to the domain.
forest	A Forest is a number of domain trees joined in transitive trust relationships.
GC	The Global Catalog is a specialized domain controller that contains a partial copy of every domain database in the Active Directory. It has two key roles: logon and querying. The Global Catalog must be available for every directory logon by a client. Otherwise, the user will be limited to logging on to the local computer. Global Catalogs also streamline domain-wide searches, eliminating the need to search each domain individually.
GUI	Graphical User Interface is the computer environment that uses graphical image interface.
HTML	The HyperText Markup Language is used to create Web pages with hyperlinks and markup for text formatting.
IIS	The Internet Information Server is a software service that supports Web site creation, configuration, and management, along with other Internet functions.
JScript	Java Script is a cross-platform programming language from Sun Microsystems that can be used to create animations and interactive features.
LDAP	The Lightweight Directory Access Protocol is an Internet standard that makes it possible for Web browsers to find and access information in a directory service database.
MDAC	Microsoft Data Access Components are technologies that allow Universal Data Access. You can use these data-driver client/server applications through the Web or a LAN to easily integrate information from a variety of sources, both relational (SQL) and nonrelational.
MMC	The Microsoft Management Console provides a common structure in which administrative tools (snap-ins) can run.

Term	Description
MSDN	The Microsoft Developer Network is a resource for developers when they want to find timely, comprehensive development resources for creating applications. It includes software subscription programs, technical Web sites, conferences, membership programs, communities, and more.
object	The term object can refer to a user, a group, a printer, or any other real component and its accompanying attributes. Active Directory is a database containing all the objects in your Windows 2000 environment.
OS	Operating System of Windows 2000 is a master control program written for a computer so it can manage the computer's internal functions. It allows a user to control the computer' operations.
OU	An Organizational Unit is a logical container within a domain. You use an OU to organize objects for easier administration and access.
PDC	A Primary Domain Controller authenticates domain logons and maintains the directory database for a domain in a Microsoft Windows NT 4.0 server or earlier.
RDS	Remote Data Service uses a technique where data is retrieved in a client from a server, updated and manipulated in the client, and returned to the server in a single round trip. You will often see ADO/RDS together since they are two components of Microsoft Data Access Components (MDAC).
Schema	Definition of all objects or object classes and their attributes stored in the Active Directory.
tree	A hierarchical group of domains, in a contiguous namespace.
VB Script	The Visual Basic Scripting language is based on the Visual Basic programming language, but it is similar to JScript and much simpler.
WSH	Windows Scripting Host is language independent so that you can write scripts in languages such as VB Script and JScript. Using WSH, you can automate specific actions.

In Brief

If you want to...	Then do this...
Configure a Windows 2000 domain controller as a Global Catalog server	1. From the **Start menu**, choose **Programs, Administrative Tools**, and then select **Active Directory Sites and Services**.
	2. From the console tree, expand **Sites**, expand the site that contains the server, expand **Servers**, and then expand the server.
	3. Right-click **NDTS Settings** and choose **Properties**.
	4. Select **Global Catalog** and then choose **OK**.
Delegate control of objects using the Delegation of Control Wizard	1. From the **Start** menu, choose **Programs, Administrative Tools**, and **Active Directory Users and Computers**.
	2. In the left pane of **Active Directory Users and Computers**, right-click the object to which you want to delegate administration, and select **Delegate control**.
	3. From **Delegation of Control**, select **Next**, and from **Users or Groups**, specify the groups or users to whom you are granting control of this OU.
	4. Select **Add**.
	5. From **Users, Groups and Computers**, select the users and groups to whom you want to delegate control of the specifc tasks, click **OK**, and then select **Next**.
	6. From **Tasks to Delegate**, select the appropriate tasks, and select **Next**.
	7. Your selections display for review; if the information is correct, select **Finish**

If you want to...	Then do this...
Manually move a server to a different site	1. From the **Start menu**, choose **Programs, Administrative Tools,** and then select **Active Directory Sites and Services.**
	2. From the console tree, expand **Sites,** expand the site that contains the server, expand **Servers,** and then select the server.
	3. Right-click the server and choose **Move.**
	4. Select the new target site and choose **OK.**
Find objects in the Active Directory:	1. From the **Start** menu, choose **Programs, Administrative Tools,** and **Active Directory Users and Computers.**
	2. Select a domain or container in the console tree.
	3. Either select **Find** on the toolbar, or right-click and select **Find** from the context menu.
	4. If available, type in further information to refine your search in the appropriate places on the Advanced or Users, Contacts, and Groups property pages.
	5. Select **Find Now.**
	A list of the objects that match the selected criteria will display
Filter a search in Find window	1. From the menu bar of Active Directory Users and Computers, choose **View,** and then select **Filter Options.**
	2. Select **Show only the following types of objects,** select the filter criteria you want, and then choose OK.

Lesson 5 Activities

Complete the following activities to prepare for the certification exam.

1.   Describe how the Global Catalog helps users find Active Directory objects.

2.   You want the Accounting Human Resources Manager to create, modify, and delete users for the accounting department. Detail what you need to do to accomplish this.

3.   Explain the difference between a counter log and a trace log.

4.   Describe how the logical structure elements are organized and what relationships they form in Active Directory.

5.   You want to find all users in the Accounting OU who have a surname of "Smith". Describe the steps you would perform.

6.   Explain the differences between site membership for domain controllers and clients.

7.   Monitoring the performance of the Active Directory is important. Describe the information that performance data gives you.

8.   Explain what the Delegation of Control Wizard does.

9.   Describe the four event logs for monitoring Active Directory performance.

10.   List the standard object permissions.

Answers to Lesson 5 Activities

1. The Global Catalog contains a partial replica of the entire directory, storing information about every object in the domain, tree, or forest. Since there is information about every object, a user can find the object, no matter where it actually resides in the domain, tree, or forest.

2. First, put all the user accounts for the staff in the Accounting department in an OU. Then delegate the control of the OU to the Accounting Human Resources Manager.

3. Counter logs collect performance counter data for a specified interval. Trace logs record data collected by the operating system provider or non-system providers when certain activities, such as a disk error or page fault, occur.

4. Elements are organized into OUs within a domain. Domains link together to form trees, and trees join to create a forest.

5. To find all users who have a surname of "Smith" and are in the Accounting Organizational Unit, you would follow these steps:

    1. From the **Start** menu, choose **Programs**, **Administrative Tools**, and **Active Directory Users and Computers**.

    2. Select the Accounting Organizational Unit.

    3. Either select **Find** on the toolbar, or, within the context menu, right-click and select **Find**.

    4. In the **Name** box, type Smith.

    5. Select **Find Now**.

    6. A list of those users that match the search will appear in the bottom portion of the window.

6. Site membership is determined in a different way for domain controllers than for clients. A client decides what site it is in when it is turned on, and the site location will often be dynamically updated. A domain controller's site location is determined by which site its Server object belongs to in the directory.

7.   Monitoring performance is integral to maintaining and administering your Active Directory. You use Active Directory performance data to accomplish the following tasks:

   • Understand Active Directory performance and its impact on your system resources

   • Track changes and trends to plan for future upgrades

   • Test changes and tune results by monitoring the results

   • Detect problems and determine which components or processes will need to be optimized

8.   Using the Delegation of Control Wizard, you can delegate control of very specific objects. This delegation of administration of specific resources to an individual or group does away with a number of administrators needing to have authority over an entire domain or site. By choosing the appropriate user or groups and giving them the correct permissions, they, in turn, will be able to delegate administration of a subset of their accounts and resources. You can configure the scope of delegated administrative responsibility in many ways. Although you generally grant permissions at the Organizational Unit level by applying inheritance, you can also delegate administration for an entire domain within a forest.

9.   The following four event logs for monitoring Active Directory performance exist:

   Application logs—The Application log contains errors, warnings, or information that applications generate. The application developer presets which events are recorded.

   Directory Service logs—The Directory Service log contains errors, warnings, and information that Active Directory generates.

   File Replication Service logs—The File Replication Service log holds the warnings, errors and information that are generated by the File Replication Service.

   System logs—In the System log, Windows 2000 predefines what events to record. The System log contains errors, warnings, and information that Windows 2000 generates.

10.   The following standard object permissions exist: Full Control, Read, Write, Create All Child Objects, and Delete All Child Objects.

Lesson 5 Quiz

These questions test your knowledge of features, vocabulary, procedures and syntax.

1. At what level does the Delegation of Control Wizard allow you to set administrative control?
    A. Container
    B. Domain
    C. OU
    D. Forest

2. Who can create child OUs within an existing OU?
    A. Members of the Admins groups
    B. Any user in the OU
    C. The OU manager
    D. Users who have been assigned the Read, List Contents, and Create Child (OU) permissions on the parent OU

3. Which of the following are options for the delegation of control?
    A. Delegate complete administrative control over an OU and its contents to a user
    B. Delegate administrative control over objects of a specific type in an OU to a user
    C. Delegate the ability to create and delete objects in a particular OU to a user
    D. Delegate administrative control over specific properties of objects in an OU to a user

4. What is the Global Catalog?
    A. It contains definitions of all object categories and their attributes that are stored in the Active Directory.
    B. It is a searchable index that lets users search for network objects without knowing their domain locations.
    C. It is a group of IP subnets connected by a high-speed link.
    D. It is the entire path leading to a network object.

5. What object types can you select for a search?
    A. Users, Contacts, and Groups
    B. Computers, Printers, Shared Folders
    C. Trees, Forests
    D. OUs, Custom Searches

6.   What are the key roles a Global Catalog server performs?
    A.   It hosts tools, including snap-ins, which you can use to administer both local and remote computers.
    B.   It facilitates network logon by supplying universal group information to a domain controller when a logon procedure is started.
    C.   It facilitates querying or the finding of directory information no matter which domain in the forest contains the data.
    D.   With it, administrators can monitor access to specific objects in Active Directory.

7.   Why is Windows Scripting Host (WSH) important to Windows 2000?
    A.   You can automate specific actions.
    B.   WSH is language-independent so you can write scripts in languages such as VB Script and JScript
    C.   You can execute scripts from the command line.
    D.   You can use any text editor.

8.   What are some of the tools you can use to manage Active Directory Performance?
    A.   MMCs, Task Manager, Performance and System Logs
    B.   Scripts
    C.   The Global Catalog, the Schema Master, the Infrastructure Master
    D.   The Administrators group.

9.   What can you do with the System Log snap-in?
    A.   Create HTML pages from performance views
    B.   Used to load configure and run the operating system.
    C.   Store messages generated by an application, service, or operating system.
    D.   Records events in the system, security, and applications.

10.   How do you control access to Active Directory objects?
    A.   ADSI
    B.   API
    C.   ACLs
    D.   ASP

Answers to Lesson 5 Quiz

1.   Answers A and C are correct. Using the Wizard, you can set control at the container or OU level.

      Answer B is incorrect. A domain is a boundary encompassing objects for security and administrative purposes.

      Answer D is incorrect. A forest is a grouping of domain trees joined together by transitive trust relationships.

2.   Answers A and D are correct. Members of the Admins group and any users who have been assigned the Read, List Contents, and Create Child (OU) permissions on the parent OU can create child OUs within existing OUs.

      Answer B is incorrect. Any user in the OU can create child OUs only if they have the correct permissions assigned.

      Answer C is incorrect. OU Manager is not a real position.

3.   Answers A, B, C, and D are correct. All four of the following options are options for the delegation of control:
      • Delegate complete administrative control over an OU and its contents to a user
      • Delegate administrative control over objects of a specific type in an OU to a user
      • Delegate the ability to create and delete objects in a particular OU to a user
      • Delegate administrative control over specific properties of objects in an OU to a user

4.   Answer B is correct. The Global Catalog is a searchable index that lets users search for network objects without knowing their domain locations.

      Answer A is incorrect. It is the definition of the Schema.

      Answer C is incorrect. It is the definition of a Site.

      Answer D is incorrect. It is the definition of a Fully Qualified Domain name (FQDN).

5.   Answers A, B, and D are correct. The object types you can select for a search include Users, Contacts, Groups, Computers, Printers, Shared Folders, OUs, and Custom Searching.

      Answer C is incorrect. A Tree is a set of Domains and a Forest is made up of interrelated Trees.

6.   Answers B and C are correct. A GC facilitates network logon by supplying universal group information to a domain controller when a logon procedure is started, and it facilitates querying or the finding of directory information no matter which domain in the forest contains the data.

      Answer A is incorrect. A Microsoft Management Console (MMC) hosts tools, including snap-ins, which you can use to administer both local and remote computers.

      Answer D is incorrect. Using auditing, administrators can monitor access to specific objects in Active Directory.

7.   Answers A, B, C, and D are correct. WSH is important to Windows 2000 because you can automate specific actions, it is language-independent so that you can write scripts in languages such as VB Script and JScript, you can execute scripts from the command line, and you can use any text editor. In addition, WSH comes with Windows 2000 and Windows 98 and can be used and installed on Windows 95 and Microsoft Windows NT computers.

8.   Answer A is correct. Microsoft Management Consoles, the Task Manager and Performance and System Logs are all tools for management of Windows 2000.

      Answer B is correct. By using scripts, you can automate large-scale management.

      Answer C is incorrect. The Global Catalog is an index of all the objects in the database, the Schema Master is one of the forest-wide operations master roles, the Infrastructure Master is responsible for updating the Group-to-user references.

      Answer D is incorrect. Administrators do the administration, but are not an Active Directory tool.

9. Answer A is correct. With the System Log Snap-in you can create HTML pages from performance views. You can also collect and view real-time performance data on a local computer or several remote computers, view data collected either currently or previously recorded in a counter log, present data in a printable graph, histogram, or report view, and create reusable monitoring configurations that can be installed on other computers using the MMC.

    Answer B is incorrect. Systems files are used to load, configure, and run the operating system.

    Answer C is incorrect. It is a definition of a log file and is not specific to system logs.

    Answer D is incorrect. It is a definition of an Event log service.

10. Answer C is correct. Every Active Directory object has a security descriptor that identifies who has permission to gain access and what type of access is allowed. However, before anyone can access the object, the administrator or the owner of the object assigns the permissions. Windows 2000 stores a list of user access permissions, called Access Control Lists (ACL), for every Active Directory Object.

    Answer A is incorrect. The Active Directory Services Interface is the programming interface that applications use to access the Active Directory.

    Answer B is incorrect. The Application Programming Interface is the one applications use to send requests to the operating system.

    Answer D is incorrect. When VB Scripts are inside an HTML page, they are called Active Server Pages. They are dynamic, meaning the Web page displayed differs, depending on the results of a script incorporated as part of that Web page.

Group Policy Implementation

By using Group Policy, you can define your users' environments once, and then rely on the operating system to ensure that all users receive the same environment. You, as the administrator, manage and maintain Group Policy, a Microsoft Management Console (MMC) administrative tool, to set policies on groups of users and computers. Instead of managing user accounts and access privileges individually, by using Group Policy you can administer users and computers in volume. Each group policy is known as a Group Policy Object (GPO), and it is stored in the Active Directory. By giving administrators the ability to add to and control the users' desktops, Group Policy allows an organization to reduce the Total Cost of Ownership (TCO).

Group Policy is inherited from the site, to the domain, and finally to the Organizational Unit (OU) level. The order and level in which you apply GPOs, through linking them to their targets, determines the Group Policy settings a user or computer actually receives.

After completing this lesson, you should have a better understanding of the following topics:

- Implementation of Group Policy

- Group Policy User Environments

- Group Policy Filtering

- Group Policy Modification

- Administrative Templates

- GPO Security Group Assignment

266

- Software Deployment and Management

- Group Policy Security

- Audit Policy Implementation

Implementation of Group Policy

In Windows 2000, you use Group Policies to define user and computer configurations for groups of users and computers. You create a specific desktop configuration for a particular group of users and computers by using the Group Policy MMC snap-in. The Group Policy settings that you create are contained in a GPO, which is associated with these Active Directory objects: sites, domains or OUs. By default, Group Policy affects all the relevant users and computers in the specified site, domain or OU, but does not affect any other objects in that site, domain or OU.

Using Group Policy provides the following advantages:

- Capitalizes on the Windows 2000 Active Directory services

- Allows for centralized or decentralized management of policy options

- Offers flexibility and scalability

- Handles a wide range of implementation scenarios that can be applied to both small businesses and large corporations

- Provides an integrated tool for managing policy

- Allows administrators to delegate control of GPOs

- Provides reliability and security

After you define Group Policy for groups of users and computers, you can rely on the system to enforce those policy settings.

You manage policy settings using the Group Policy snap-in. The Group Policy

snap-in extends other administrative tools, such as the Active Directory Users and Computers snap-in and the Active Directory Site and Services Manager snap-in. All policy settings created by the Group Policy snap-in are stored in a GPO.

A Group Policy snap-in is shown in Figure 6.1.

Figure 6.1 Group Policy Snap-In

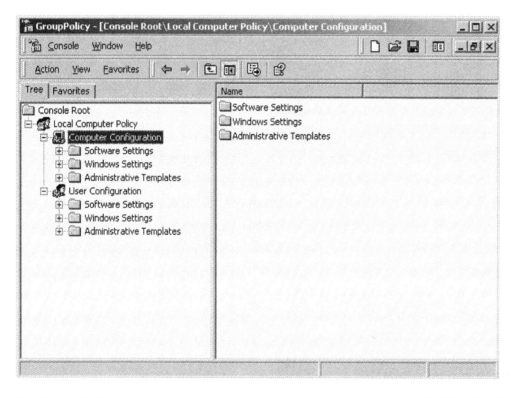

The Group Policy snap-in includes several snap-in extensions giving you added functionality. Table 6.1 contains a brief description of the snap-in extensions.

Table 6.1 Group Policy Snap-in Extensions

Extension	Description
Administrative Templates	This extension manages registry-based settings that govern the behavior and appearance of the desktop, including applications. It also manages disk quotas.
Security Settings	This extension defines security configuration options for local computer, domain and network security settings.
Software Installation	This extension is used to centrally manage application installation, updates and removal.
Scripts	This extension gives access to the scripts available, including scripts for computer startup and shutdown, and user logon and logoff. These scripts are compatible with the Windows Scripting Host (WSH).
Folder Redirection	This extension helps administrators redirect users' special folders to the network.

The registry-based policy settings are stored in the REGISTRY.POL files. The Group Policy snap-in creates two REGISTRY.POL files and stores them in a GPO. One file contains user settings and the other file contains computer settings.

 Note: Using Group Policy, you can define the state of users' work environments once and rely on the system to enforce the policies you define.

Implementing Group Policy

By default, when you select Group Policy for a container there will be no GPO and you will be given the option of either adding an existing GPO to the container or creating a new one. To create a new GPO, select New and type a name for the GPO. Once created, by choosing Edit you can modify the specified policy.

GPOs are stored in a Windows 2000 domain, and their effects are enabled on sites, domains or OUs to which they are linked. Following are definitions of the linkages:

- A GPO linked to a site, using Active Directory Sites and Services, will apply to all the domains at the site

- A GPO applied to a domain, applies directly to all users and computers in the domain and, by inheritance, to all users and computers in OUs farther down the Active Directory tree

- A GPO applied to an OU, applies directly to all users and computers in the OU and, by inheritance, to all users and computers in OUs farther down the Active Directory tree

Creating a Group Policy Object (GPO)

A GPO is a collection of policy settings you give a unique name, such as a Globally Unique Identifier (GUID). A GPO can represent policy settings in up to three locations: the registry, the file system and the Active Directory. The structure of a GPO is described in Figure 6.2.

Figure 6.2 Group Policy Object

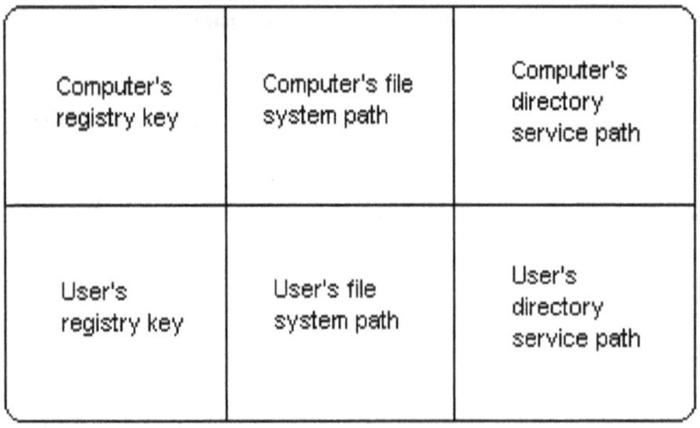

Computer's registry key	Computer's file system path	Computer's directory service path
User's registry key	User's file system path	User's directory service path

Group Policy Object (GPO)

A GPO can be linked to one or more Active Directory containers, such as a site, domain or OU. Multiple containers can be linked to the same GPO, and a single container can have more than one linked GPO, as shown in Figure 6.3.

Figure 6.3 Group Policy and the Active Directory

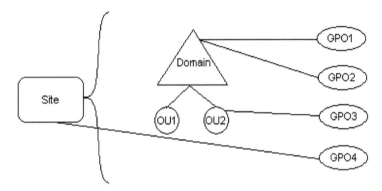

Group Policy and the Active Directory

The administrator can further define the users and computers affected by a GPO by using member-ship in security groups. Starting with Windows 2000, the administrator can add both users and com-puters to security groups. Then the administrator specifies which security groups are affected by the GPO by using the Access Control List (ACL) editor. In addition, every computer receives a local GPO that contains registry-based policy settings and security-specific policy settings, by default. This is par-ticularly useful for computers that are not members of a domain.

To create a group policy for a site, domain or OU, follow these steps:

1. From the **Start menu**, choose **Programs**, **Administrative Tools**, and then select **Active Directory Users and Computers**.

2. From the console tree, right-click the desired container, and then select **Properties**.

3. Choose the **Group Policy** property page, and then select **New**.

Figure 6.4 Group Policy Property Page

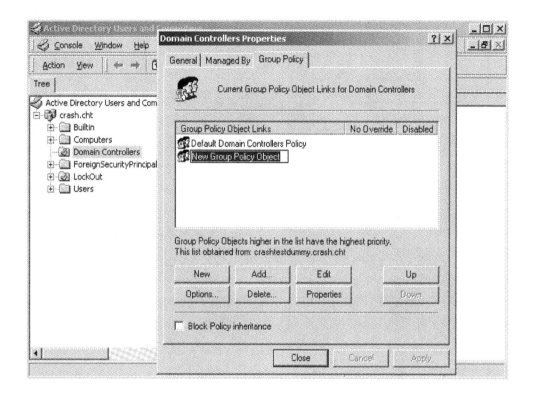

Type a name for the new Group Policy object, and then press **ENTER** (Figure 6.4).

 Warning: Group policies can have a negative effect on your network. If they are configured improperly, you can prevent users from logging on to the network. Plan group policies carefully and test them extensively before implementing them.

After you have created the GPO, you add the Group Policy snap-in to an MMC, and create a stand-alone GPO console. After you have saved the console, you will be able to open it, whenever it is required, from the Administrative Tools menu.

To open Group Policy as a stand-alone MMC snap-in, follow these steps:

1. From the **Start** menu, choose **Run**.

2. Type **MMC**, and then press **ENTER**.

3. From the menu bar of the empty MMC console, choose **Console**, and then select **Add/Remove Snap-in**.

4. From the **Standalone** property page, choose **Add**.

5. From **Add Standalone Snap-in**, choose **Group Policy**, and then select **Add**.

6. From **Select Group Policy Object**, choose **Local Computer** to edit the local Group Policy object, or select **Browse** to find a different computer on the network.

7. Select **Finish**, choose **Close**, and then select **OK**.

8. From the Menu bar, choose **Console**, and then select **Save As**.

9. Type a name for the console (such as Group Policy Snap-in), and then choose **Save**. The console you have created now appears in the Administrative Tools menu (Figure 6.5).

Figure 6.5 Group Policy Snap-In

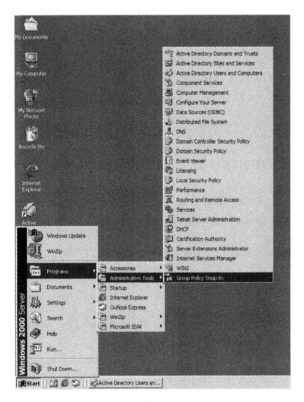

Linking an Existing GPO

Each GPO is created as a standalone object in the Active Directory. This object can then be linked—one or more times—to sites, domains and OUs. GPOs for domains and OUs are kept in the domain relating to their application but GPOs for sites are stored in the root domain of the forest. By linking GPOs to specific sites, domains or OUs, you maximize and extend the power of Active Directory. GPOs are actually applied to a site, domain or OU by using a link. A non-local GPO that is not linked to a site, domain or OU has no effect on any user or computer.

A GPO is a policy unit and can be applied to a site, domain or OU. Often a user or computer will have multiple GPOs applicable to them. In the event of a clash of a setting, the order of precedence is Site, Domain, then OU (SDOU). Any setting defined at a site level can be overwritten by a domain setting, and anything defined on a domain can be overwritten by an OU setting. There is a fourth type of policy, the Local computer policy. This has the lowest priority, so any Local computer policies will be overwritten by any of the other policies giving us an order of Local computer, Site, Domain then OU (LSDOU).

Following are the three major points about GPOs and how they are used in Active Directory:

• GPOs only apply to sites, domains and OUs

• A single GPO can be linked to multiple locations in the tree

• By default, GPOs affect all of the users and computers in a container

To link a GPO to a site, domain or OU, follow these steps:

1. From the **Start** menu, choose **Programs** and **Administrative Tools**, and then select **Active Directory Users and Computers** to link a GPO to a domain or OU; or choose **Active Directory Sites and Services** to link a GPO to a site.

2. From the console tree, right-click the desired site, domain or OU you want to link to the GPO; Choose **Properties** and then select the **Group Policy** page.

3. If the GPO already appears in the **Group Policy Object Links** list, choose **Cancel**; if the GPO does not appear in the **Group Policy Object Links** list, choose **Add**.

4. From **Add A Group Policy Object Link**, (Figure 6.6) choose **All**, choose the desired GPO and then select **OK**.

Figure 6.6 Group Policy Link Management

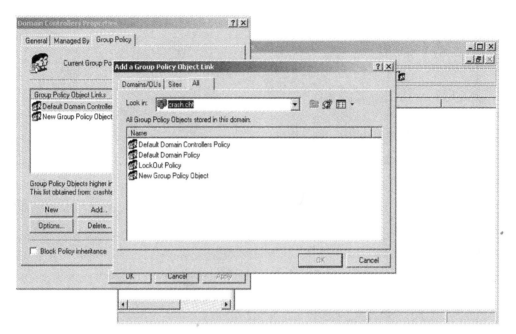

Group Policy User Environments

Group Policy settings affect both user and computer accounts. They can be used to configure security options, manage applications, manage desktop appearance, assign scripts, and redirect folders from local computers to network locations. All of these settings affect how users interact with their environments.

Following are some examples of how Group policy can be used to manage user environments:

• For an entire domain, the minimum password length and the maximum length of time that a password will remain valid can be defined

• Applications can be automatically installed on every computer in a particular domain or on all computers assigned to a particular group in a particular site

- Unique logon and logoff scripts can be assigned to the user accounts in each OU

- If members of a particular group often use different computers, administrators can install the necessary applications on each of those computers

- So users can have access to their own files anywhere in the network, any user's My Documents folder can be redirected to a network location

This type of configuration control means that any user can log on to any machine in the network and their desktop will remain the same, whether they are in Hong Kong, London or New York.

Managing User Environments with Group Policy

Group policies are collections of user and computer configuration settings to specify the behavior of users' desktops. You then link the policies to computers, sites, domains and OUs. Using group policies, you determine the programs available to users.

To define a particular desktop configuration for a group of users, you create GPOs. GPOs are collections of group policy settings. There are two types of group policy settings—user configuration and computer configuration settings.

User Configuration Settings (Figure 6.7) sets group policies applied to users. It does not matter which computer the user logs onto—the settings are applied when the user logs on.

Figure 6.7 User Configuration

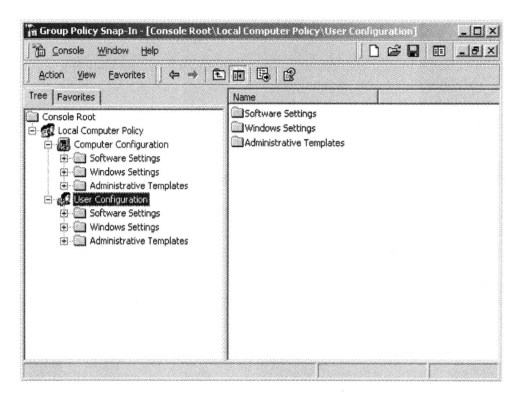

Computer configuration settings (Figure 6.8) are applied to computers, no matter who logs onto them. Computer configuration settings are applied when the operating system starts.

Figure 6.8 Computer Configuration

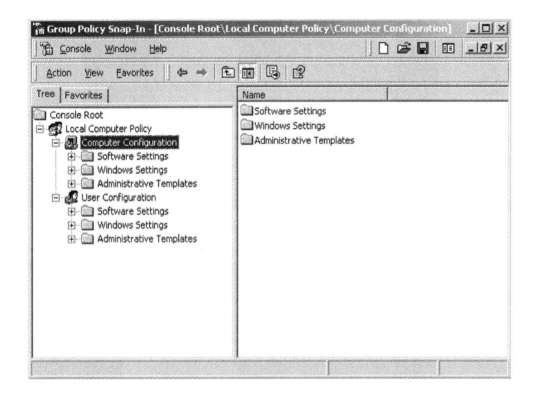

Delegating Administrative Control of Group Policy

In Windows 2000 one of the administrative tasks that can be delegated is Group Policy. To delegate control of Group Policy, you first create and save Group Policy Microsoft Management Consoles.

Next, you need to determine which users and groups have access permissions to the Group Policy object and the site, domain and organizational unit.

To set read and write permissions for Group Policy, follow these steps:

1. From the **Start** menu, choose **Programs**, **Administrative Tools**, and then select **Active Directory Users and Computers**.

2. From the console tree, right-click the container that is associated with the Group Policy object on which you wish to delegate control, and then choose **Properties**.

3. Choose the **Group Policy** property page, select the **Group Policy** object, and then select **Properties**.

4. From **Group Policy Object Properties**, select the **Security** property page.

5. Use this page to allow and deny permissions to the GPO to individual users or groups of users. When finished, choose **OK** in each open window to save the changes.

You use the **Security** property page to set permissions on a selected GPO. These permissions allow or deny access to the Group Policy object by specified groups.

 Note: The security ACL for a GPO is found in the Properties of that GPO.

Members of the Domain Administrators group can use the ACL editor to determine which administrator groups can modify policies in Group Policy objects. To do this, the network administrator can define specific groups of administrators and give them Read/Write access to selected Group Policy objects. In this way, the network administrator can delegate control of the Group Policy object policies.

 Warning: A user or administrator who does not have Write access (but does have Read access) to a Group Policy object cannot use the Group Policy snap-in to see the settings that it contains. Every MMC extension to Group Policy expects it has Write access to the GPO storage locations. As a result, Group Policy does not open a GPO when the current user does not have Write access to it.

Modifying Group Policy Inheritance

GPOs can have unintended effects. This generally occurs when the settings that you configure through a GPO pass down to child domains and OUs—the child domains and OUs inherit these settings. You can link multiple GPOs to a single container and you can link a single GPO to more that one container.

If multiple GPOs affect a computer or a user, group policies apply in the following order:

- Site

- Domain

- OU

When you configure a domain GPO and a child OU GPO, if the settings are compatible, both sets of configurations apply. However, if the settings conflict, the configuration of the OU GPO applies. The OU settings override the domain settings because inherited settings from the domain come into play.

In certain circumstances you may want to alter the inheritance of GPOs. For example, if you want a GPO to apply to all the containers in one branch of a tree—except one—you can block the inheritance to that one container. Or if you do not want the GPO settings of an OU to override the settings from the domain GPO, you can configure the GPO so the OU settings will not override those of the domain.

By setting No Override on a specific GPO link, the GPOs linked at a lower level of Active Directory—closer to the receiving user or computer—cannot override that policy. By doing this, GPOs linked at the same level, but not as No Override, will not be able to override the GPO settings. If you have several links set to No Override, at the same level in Active Directory, you need to prioritize them. Links higher in the list have priority on all configured (that is, Enabled or Disabled) settings.

If you have linked a specific GPO to a domain, and set the GPO link to No Override, then the configured Group Policy settings that the GPO contains apply to all OUs under that domain. GPOs linked to OUs cannot override that domain-linked GPO.

You can also block the inheritance of Group Policy from above in Active Directory. Selecting Block Policy inheritance on the Group Policy page of the Properties of the domain or OU does this. This option does not exist for a site. Following are some important facts about No Override and Block Policy:

- No Override is set on a link, not on a site, domain, OU or GPO

- Block Policy Inheritance is set on a domain or OU, and therefore applies to all GPOs linked at that level or higher in Active Directory, which can be overridden

- No Override takes precedence over Block Policy Inheritance if the two are in conflict

To block the policy inheritance from a parent domain, follow these steps:

1. From the **Start** menu, choose **Programs**, **Administrative Tools** and then select **Active Directory Users and Computers**.

2. From **Active Directory Users and Computers**, right-click the desired container and then choose **Properties**.

3. Choose **Group Policy**, and then enable **Block Policy Inheritance**, as in Figure 6.9.

4. Click **OK**.

Figure 6.9 Group Policy Permissions Block Inheritance

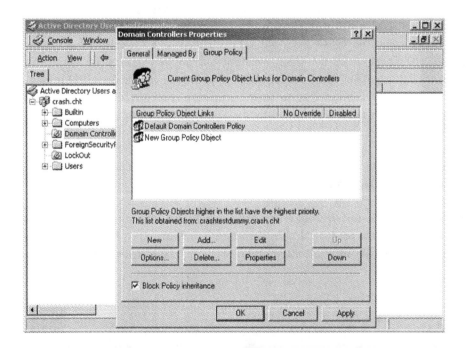

To specify no override policies by a child domain's GPO, follow these steps:

1. From the **Start** menu, choose **Programs**, **Administrative Tools** and then select **Active Directory Users and Computers**.

2. From **Active Directory Users and Computers**, right-click the desired container and then choose **Properties**.

3. Choose **Group Policy** and then select **Options**.

4. Choose **No Override: prevents other Group Policy objects from overriding policy set in this one** (Figure 6.10).

5. Click **OK**.

Figure 6.10 Group Policy Permissions Options Window

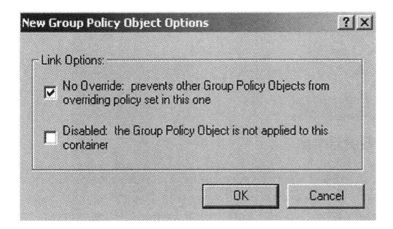

Group Policy Filtering

The effects of Group Policy can be filtered on users and computers by using membership in security groups and setting Discretionary Access Control List (DACL) permissions. By doing this you can ensure faster processing of GPOs. Also, you can limit who in your organization can create Active Directory links to GPOs and who has access to create and modify GPOs, by using security groups, as shown in Figure 6.11.

Figure 6.11 Inclusive and Exclusive Filtering

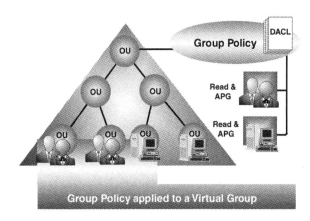

Filtering Group Policy Settings

A GPO can be used to filter objects based on security group membership, which allows administrators to manage users and computers in either a centralized or a de-centralized manner. To do this, administrators can use filtering based on security groups to define the scope of Group Policy management, so that Group Policy can be applied centrally at the domain level, or in a decentralized manner at the OU level, and can then be filtered again by security groups. Administrators can use security groups in Group Policy in the following ways:

Filter the scope of a GPO—This defines which groups of users and computers a GPO affects.

Delegate control of a GPO—Managing the group policy links and managing who can create and edit GPOs are the two aspects of managing and delegating Group Policy.

You can further refine which groups of users and computers a particular GPO influences by using Windows 2000 security groups. To do this, you use the Security tab on the Properties page of the GPO.

 Note: Having full control of a GPO does not enable you to link it to a site, domain or OU. However, you can grant that ability using the Delegation of Control Wizard.

By default, Group Policy affects all computers and users in a selected Active Directory container. However, you can filter the effects of Group Policy based on users' or computers' membership in a Windows 2000 Security Group. Figure 6.12 illustrates a Group Policy and Active Directory scenario.

Figure 6.12 Group Policy and Active Directory

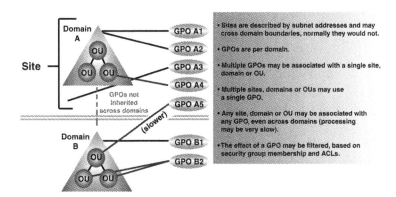

Computer Configuration and User Configuration are two parent nodes that are at the root of the Group Policy snap-in namespace. These are the parent folders that configure specific desktop environments and enforce policy settings on groups of computers and users on the network.

Group Policy Modification

To modify a group policy, you would perform any of the following tasks:

- Removing a GPO link

- Deleting a GPO

- Editing a GPO setting

Modifying Group Policy

Removing a GPO simply unlinks the GPO from the selected site, domain or OU. Deleting a GPO removes it from the Active Directory and any sites, domain or OUs to which it was linked will no longer be affected by it. Editing a GPO merely changes its settings.

To remove a GPO link, follow these steps:

1. From the **Start** menu, choose **Programs, Administrative Tools** and then select **Active Directory Users and Computers**.

2. From the console, right-click the site, domain or OU from which the GPO should be unlinked.

3. Choose **Properties**, and then select **Group Policy**.

4. From **Group Policy**, choose the GPO that you wish to unlink, and then select **Delete**.

5. From **Delete**, choose **Remove The Link From The List**, and then click **OK**.

Note: The GPO remains in the Active Directory but is no longer linked.

If you delete a GPO, it is removed from the Active Directory and no longer affects any of the sites, domains or OUs to which it was previously linked. Rather than deleting a GPO, removing the link will keep the GPO intact but remove its effect from the sites, domains or OUs to which it was linked.

To delete a GPO, follow these steps:

1. From the **Start** menu, choose **Programs**, **Administrative Tools** and then select **Active Directory Users and Computers**.

2. From the console, right-click the site, domain or OU from which the GPO should be deleted.

3. Choose **Properties**, and then select **Group Policy**.

4. From **Group Policy**, choose the GPO that you wish to delete, and then select **Delete**.

5. From **Delete**, choose **Remove The Link And Delete The Group Policy Object Permanently**, and then click **OK.**

 Warning: The Deleted GPO is removed permanently from Active Directory.

To edit a GPO or its settings, follow these steps:

1. From the **Start** menu, choose **Programs**, **Administrative Tools**, and then select the **Group Policy Snap-in** for the GPO (Figure 6.13).

Figure 6.13 Group Policy Snap-in

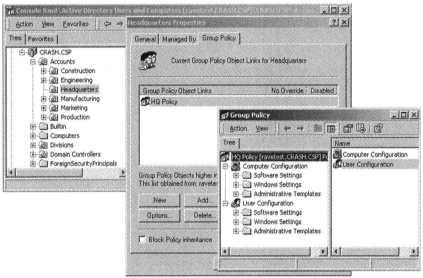

2. From the console tree, expand the item that represents the particular policy you want to set.

3. From **Details**, right-click the policy you want to set and then choose **Properties**.

4. In Figure 6.14, the **Hide Screen Saver** page policy was chosen from **Details**.

Figure 6.14 Hide Screen Saver Page Properties

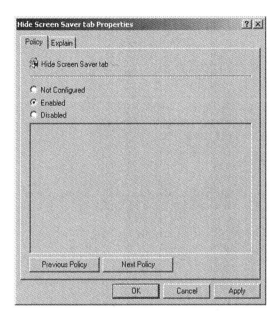

5. Choose **Enabled** to apply the policy to users or computers that are subject to the GPO, and then select **OK**.

Administrative Templates

In previous versions of Windows, Administrative Templates were ANSI-encoded text files. They created a namespace within System Policy Editor for convenient editing of the registry. In Windows 2000, for both user and computer configurations, five Administrative templates, as described in Table 6.2, contain all registry-based group policy settings.

Table 6.2 Windows 2000 Default Administrative Templates

Administrative Template	Description
SYSTEM.ADM	This template is installed for Windows 2000 clients in Group Policy.
INETRES.ADM	This template has Internet Explorer policies for Windows 2000 clients and is installed in Group Policy.
WINNT.ADM	This template has user interface options specific to Windows NT 4.0. You use this particular template with the System Policy Editor (POLEDIT.EXE).
WINDOWS.ADM	This template has user interface options specific to Windows 95 and 98. You use this particular template with the System Policy Editor (POLEDIT.EXE).
COMMON.ADM	This template has user interface options specific to Windows NT 4.0, 95 and 98. You use this particular template with the System Policy Editor (POLEDIT.EXE).

SYSTEM.ADM and INETRES.ADM use the four reserved Group Policy registry areas. Although the last three .ADM files can be loaded into Group Policy, you should limit their use to the administration of earlier versions of Windows through System Policy Editor.

Administrative Templates provided a friendlier user interface than the Registry Editor (Regedit.exe). They also added a degree of safety by exposing only the registry keys explicitly mentioned in the .ADM file.

To add administrative templates (.ADM files), follow these steps:

1. From the Group Policy console double-click **Active Directory Users and Computers**, choose the domain or OU for which you want to set policy, choose **Properties**, and then select **Group Policy.**

2. From **Properties**, choose the GPO you want to edit from the **Group Policy objects links** list, and then select **Edit** to open the Group Policy snap-in.

3. From **Group Policy**, select the plus sign (+) next to either **User Configuration** or **Computer Configuration**.

4. The .ADM file defines which of these locations the policy is displayed from, so it does not matter which node you choose.

5. Right-click **Administrative Templates**, and then choose **Add/Remove Templates**.

6. A list of the currently active template files for this Active Directory container will display, as in Figure 6.15.

Figure 6.15 Computer Administrative Templates

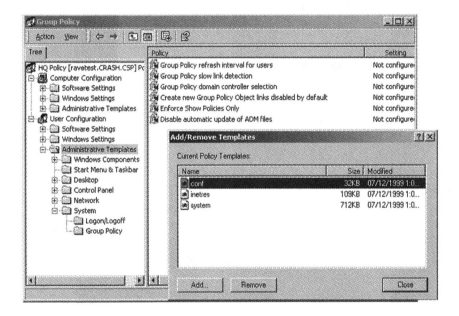

7. Choose **Add**, and a list of the available .ADM files in the %systemroot%\inf directory of the computer where Group Policy is being run is displayed.

8. You can also choose an .ADM file from another location; once chosen, the .ADM file is copied into the GPO.

Controlling User Environments with Administrative Templates

Group Policy requires a source to generate the user interface settings that an administrator can set. For this purpose, Group Policy can use either a snap-in extension to Group Policy or an .ADM file. The .ADM file specifies the registry settings that can be modified through the Group Policy interface. It is made up of a hierarchy of categories and subcategories defining how the options are displayed through the Group Policy user interface. It also indicates the registry locations where changes should be made if a particular selection is made, and specifies any options or restrictions that are associated with the selection.

You can extend the Group Policy functionality by creating either an MMC extension snap-in to Group Policy or by using custom .ADM files.

Assigning Script Policies to Users and Computers

Script policies are a component of Group Policy. With script policies, you can develop, define and run scripts based on key system events. For example, you can create startup and shutdown scripts, and assign these scripts to one or more users or computer objects.

You perform Group Policy configuration for a site using the Active Directory Sites and Services MMC snap-in. You perform Group Policy configuration for a domain or OU using the Active Directory Users and Computers MMC snap-in. In the \%systemroot%\sysvol\sysvol *domain.com*\policies*GUID* folder, the \machine\scripts\startup, \machine\scripts\shutdown, \user\scripts\logon, and \user\scripts\logoff folders store the scripts that you configure as part of Group Policy. Windows 2000 Group Policy includes the following four new script types:

- Logon and logoff for user objects

- Startup and shutdown for computer objects

Logon and logoff scripts are part of the Group Policy user configuration. Group Policy logon and logoff scripts give you a way to define and apply common scripts to multiple users.

Startup and shutdown scripts are part of the Group Policy computer configuration. You run startup and shutdown scripts on each computer to which you apply the script policy—either directly or through Group Policy inheritance.

Note: The Group Policy logon script is not related to the logon script defined as part of a user's profile.

Group Policy logon scripts will affect multiple user objects in the site, domain or OU to which you apply Group Policy. Any user from the configured container who logs on will trigger Group Policy logon scripts.

The computer runs startup scripts when it starts and shutdown scripts when it shuts down. Startup scripts run after the computer initializes network connections, and shutdown scripts run before the computer deletes network connections. You can access network-based resources from the startup and shutdown scripts.

Logon scripts run when a configured user logs on to the computer, and logoff scripts run when the user logs off. Logon scripts will always run after startup scripts, and logoff scripts always run before shutdown scripts. Also, you can have multiple scripts for each script type. Windows 2000 will execute the scripts in the order they appear in the Script Properties window.

Scripts can be written in any language Windows 2000 supports. For example, you can continue to use batch files or write Windows Scripting Host (WSH) scripts in VBScript or JScript. You can also use the new Extensible Markup Language (XML)-based Windows Script (.ws) file type.

To modify the Default Domain Policy definition by installing scripts such as STARTUP.WS saved in C:\, follow these steps:

1. From the **Start** menu, choose **Programs**, **Administrative Tools** and then select **Active Directory Users and Computers**.

2. Right-click your domain name, choose **Properties** and then select **Group Policy**.

3. Choose **Default Domain Policy** and then select **Edit**. The Group Policy Editor (GPE) will appear with Default Domain Policy loaded.

4. From **Default Domain Policy**, choose the plus sign (**+**) to expand **Computer Configuration** and the plus sign (**+**) to expand **Windows Settings**.

5. Choose **Scripts (Startup/Shutdown)**, as in Figure 6.16.

Figure 6.16 Windows Settings Scripts (Startup/Shutdown)

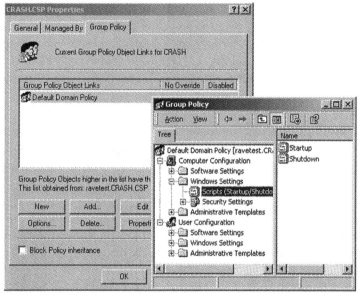

6. Double-click **Startup**.

7. From the Startup **Properties**, choose **Show Files**.

8. Using **My Computer**, copy the script that you want to apply to the Default Domain Policy startup script folder (STARTUP.WS).

9. **Close** the startup script folder.

10. From Startup **Properties**, choose **Add**.

11. From **Add a Script**, choose **Browse**, and you will see the name of your selected script (STARTUP.WS).

12. Choose the script that you want to add, and then select **Open**.

13. From **Add a Script**, click **OK** and you will see your new script (STARTUP.WS) in the list of scripts (Figure 6.17 shows the scripts Startup.ws and Dell610.vbs).

Figure 6.17 Startup Properties

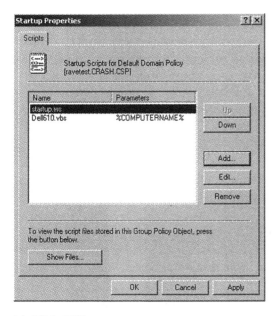

14. Click **OK**.

15. Close the Group Policy Editor.

16. From **Domain Properties**, choose **OK**, and then close the **MMC** and **My Computer**.

When you restart the computer, the results of the script policy change will be applied.

Warning: You need to take precautions when you implement script policies as a script may not complete and will cause systems to hang.

GPO Security Group Assignment

Security groups are the most effective way to manage permissions. You can assign permissions to individuals, but usually it is easier to grant permissions to a group and then add or remove users as members of the group. By using security groups, you can assign the same security permissions to large numbers of users at the same time, ensuring consistent security permissions for all members of a group. By using security groups to assign permissions, the access control on resources remains consistent and easy to control and audit. Those users who need access are added or removed from the appropriate security groups.

When you create a new user, you can add the user to an existing security group to completely define the user's permissions and access limits. Changing a permission for the group affects all users in the group. Windows 2000 comes with several predefined security groups.

Domain local groups—These security groups are used to give access rights to resources, such as printers, that are located on any computer in the domain where common access permissions are required. Members of the domain local groups can come from inside and outside the domain.

Global groups—These security groups are used for joining users sharing a common access profile based on their job function. Usually an organization will use global groups for all groups where it is expected that membership could change often. Only members whose user accounts are in the same domain as the global group can belong to global groups. They can be nested, allowing for overlapping access needs or scaling for very large group structures.

Universal groups—These security groups are used in multi-domain organizations where access to similar groups of accounts defined in multiple domains needs to be granted. You use global groups as members of universal groups to reduce overall replication traffic from changes to universal group membership. Users can be added and removed from the corresponding global group within their account domains, and only a small number of global groups are the direct members of the universal group. Universal groups are easily granted access by making them a member of a domain local group used to grant access permissions to resources.

Universal groups are used only in multiple domain trees or forests that have a global catalog. A Windows 2000 domain must be in native mode to use universal groups. A domain model that has only a single domain does not need or support universal groups.

Computer local groups—These are security groups specific to a computer and are not recognized elsewhere in the domain.

You use security groups in Group Policy for two purposes:

* To filter the scope of a GPO

* To delegate control of Group Policy

 Note: Group Policy does not affect security groups.

Associating Security Groups to GPOs

It is not possible to apply a group policy to a security group. However, you can filter a group policy by changing the permissions on the Group Policy so that only certain groups have Read and Apply privileges.

To associate a security group to a GPO, follow these steps:

1. From the **Start menu**, choose **Programs**, **Administrative Tools**, and then select **Active Directory Users and Computers**.

2. From the console tree, right-click the container that is associated with the Group Policy object to which you wish to assign a security group, and then choose **Properties**.

3. Choose the **Group Policy** property page, select the **Group Policy** object, and then select **Properties**.

4. From **Group Policy Object Properties**, select the **Security** property page.

5. Use this page to allow and deny permissions to the GPO to the appropriate security group. When finished, select **OK** in each open window to save changes.

You can filter the scope of a GPO by creating security groups and assigning Read permissions to the selected groups. This way, you can prevent a policy from applying to a specific group by denying that group Read permissions.

To filter the scope of a GPO, follow these steps:

1. From the **Start menu**, choose **Programs, Administrative Tools**, and then select **Active Directory Users and Computers**.

2. From the console tree, right-click the container that is associated with the Group Policy object to which you wish to assign a security group, and then choose **Properties**.

3. Choose the **Group Policy** property page, select the **Group Policy** object, and then select **Properties**.

 Note: you need to change the list of security groups you wish to filter the GPO through, you can add or remove groups using Add and Remove

4. Set Permissions as shown in Table 6.3 and click **Ok**.

5. From **Group Policy Object Properties**, select the **Security** property page.

Figure 6.18 GPO Properties

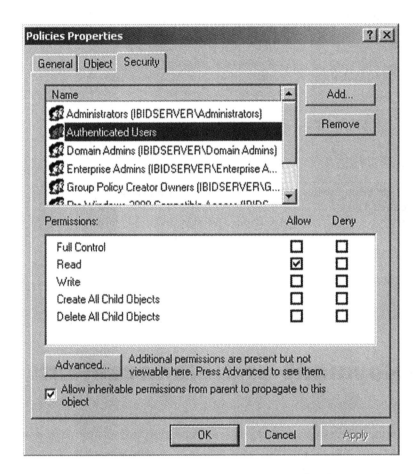

6. Use this page to allow and deny permissions to the GPO to the appropriate security group. When finished, select **OK** in each open window to save changes.

Now only the selected users will run the GPO.

Table 6.3 Permissions for GPO Scopes

GPO Scope	Set these Properties	Result
Members of this group should have this GPO applied to them	Set Apply Group Policy to Allow Set Read to Allow	This GPO applies to members of this security group unless they are members of at least one other security group with AGP set to Deny or Read set to Deny or both
Members of this security group are exempt from this GPO	Set Apply Group Policy to Deny Set Read to Deny	This GPO never applies to members of this security group, regardless of the permissions these members have in other security groups
Membership in this security group is irrelevant to whether the GPO should be applied	Set Apply Group Policy to neither Allow or Deny Set Read to neither Allow or Deny	This GPO applies to members of this security GPO only if they have both Apply Group Policy and Read set to Allow as members of at least one other security group. They must also not have Apply Group Policy or Read set to Deny as members of any other group.

Software Deployment and Management

You can use the Software Installation snap-in to centrally manage software distribution in your organization. With this tool, you can assign and publish software for groups of users, and you can assign software for groups of computers. You assign applications to groups of users so all the users who require them have them on their desktops, without you having to install the application on each desktop.

When users log on to Windows 2000, the application shortcut appears on the Start menu, and the registry is updated with information about the application, including the location of the application package and the location of the source files for the installation. The application is installed the first time users activate the application. Users can remove assigned applications using Add/Remove Programs in Control Panel, but only for the duration of a logon session. The next time they start their computer, the application icon reappears.

You can also publish applications to groups of users, making the application available for users to install if they choose to do so. When you publish an application, no shortcuts to the application appear on users' desktops, and no local registry entries are made. That is, the application has no presence on the user's desktop. Information needed to publish applications is stored in the GPO.

To install a published application, users can use the Add/Remove Programs in Control Panel, which includes a list of all published applications that are available for them to use. Users can open a document file associated with a published application (for example, a .doc file to install Microsoft Word).

Deploying and Managing Software with Group Policy

Software installation works in conjunction with Group Policy and Active Directory. It is one of the three Software Installation and Maintenance tools provided with Windows 2000 Server (Table 6.4).

Table 6.4 Software Installation and Maintenance Tools

Component	Role
The Software Installation extension of the Group Policy snap-in	Used by administrators to manage software.
Windows Installer	Installs software packaged in Windows Installer files.
Add/Remove Programs in Control Panel	Used by users to manage software on their own computers.

Configuring Deployment Options

When choosing software deployment options (Figure 6.19), you can choose one of the following options:

- Assign to users

- Assign to computers

- Publish to users

- Application assignment scripts

Figure 6.19 Software Deployment MMC

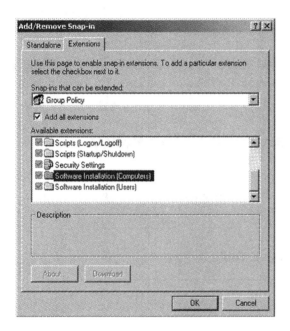

 Note: The first time the user selects the application from the Start menu, it sets up automatically and then opens.

An Application Assignment Script (.AAS file) is created and stored in the particular domain's GPO for every published or assigned application GPO. These script files contain the advertisement information about the application configuration.

To create the Software Installation Snap-in, follow these steps:

1. From the **Start** menu, choose **Programs**, **Administrative Tools** and then select **Active Directory Users and Computers**.

2. Open **Group Policy**.

3. To assign software to computers, double-click **Computer Configuration**.

4. To assign or publish software to users, double-click **User Configuration.**

5. Double-click **Software Settings.**

6. From the console tree, choose **Software Installation**.

To reconfigure the software installation defaults, follow these steps:

1. Open the Software Installation snap-in you created in the previous steps.

2. Right-click **Software Installation**, and then choose **Properties**.

3. Choose the **General** page and then select the settings as defined in Table 6.5.

Table 6.5 Software Installation Properties

Option	Description
Default Package Location	Specifies the software distribution point.
New Packages	Packages can either be published or assigned by default. You can choose to make decisions about each package by selecting Display the Deploy Dialog Box. You can define further by choosing Advanced Assign or Publish.
Installation User Interface Options	Depending on how apparent you want the installation to be to the users, choose Basic or Maximum.
Uninstall the Applications when this GPO no longer applies to the Users or Computers	You can select this option if you want software to be removed at logon (for users) or startup (for computers) if the user or computer moves to a site, domain or OU to which the software is not applicable.

Troubleshooting Software Deployment Problems

A number of common problems with software deployment can occur. A few of these are covered in Table 6.6. For current information on troubleshooting, visit the Microsoft Personal Support Site http://www.microsoft.com/support/default.asp on the Internet.

Table 6.6 Software Deployment Troubleshooting

Problem	Cause	Solution
Published applications do not appear in Add/Remove Programs in Control Panel.	Following are several causes: Group Policy was not applied, Active Directory cannot be accessed, User does not have any published applications in the GPOs that apply to them, or the Client is running Terminal Server.	You investigate each possibility. Software Installation is not available for Terminal Server clients.
The published application does not install.	The administrator did not set autoinstall.	Set autoinstall.
The user receives an error message such as "The feature you are trying to install cannot be found in the source directory."	This could be caused by network or permissions problems.	Ensure the network is working correctly.
A user receives an error message such as "Another installation is already in progress".	An un-installation could be taking place in the background and the interface is being presented to the user, or the user has accidentally started two installations.	The user should try again later.

Group Policy Security

With the right combination of security settings, you can audit and control membership to administrative groups, limit access to computer registries, limit remote and local access to computers, and more. If you use them correctly, group policies are a powerful tool for streamlining administration.

You can filter Group Policy by using membership in Security Groups and setting DACL permissions. This process makes fast processing of GPOs possible and allows Group Policy to be applied to Security Groups. By using ACLs and Security Groups, you can modify the scope of GPOs. For example, when you use Security Groups to filter Group Policy, you can adjust the use of the policy for specific users within an OU.

Managing Security with Group Policy

Make certain you plan group policies thoroughly. Besides creating an unintended effect on your network, group polices can add significant overhead to the Domain Controllers and the network. Because Windows 2000 stores the event logs in the Active Directory, they are replicated to the Domain Controllers. When a strict audit policy is implemented, frequent Active Directory changes occur. This results in frequent replication and a great increase in overhead. Security logging is turned off by default. You can use Group Policy to enable security logging.

To turn on security logging, follow these steps:

1. From the **Start** menu, choose **Run**, type **mmc /a**, and then choose **OK**.

2. On the **Console** menu, choose **Add/Remove Snap-in** and then select **Add**.

3. From **Snap-in**, choose **Group Policy** and then select **Add**.

4. From **Select Group Policy Object**, choose **Local Computer**, **Finish**, **Close**, and then select **OK**.

5. From the console tree, expand **Local Computer Policy**, expand **Computer Configuration**, expand **Windows Settings**, expand **Security**, expand **Local Policies**, and then select **Audit Policy**.

6. From the details pane, choose the attribute or event you want to audit.

7. From the menu bar, choose **Action**, and then select **Security**.

8. From **Local Security Policy Setting**, choose the options you want and then click **OK**.

An administrator can also set auditing policies in the registry that cause the system to halt when the security log is full. Table 6.7 describes the Group Policies and their security settings.

Table 6.7 GPO Security Settings

Policies	Settings
Account Policies	Configure password, account lockout and Kerberos policy.
Event Log	Configure application, system and security logs.
File System	Control security on folders.
IP Security Policies	Control IP security settings throughout the network.
Local Policies	Configure audit policies, user rights assignments and security options.
Public Key Policies	Configure trusted certificate authorities.
Registry	Configure security on the registry.
Restricted Groups	Control group memberships for key groups, such as Administrator and Schema Administrator.
System Services	Control security settings for system service.

Managing Network Configurations with Group Policy

TCO is the cumulative cost involved in administering computer networks. One of the highest component costs in TCO is lost productivity at the desktop. Lost productivity can be credited to user errors, such as modifying system configuration files that make their computer unworkable.

In Windows 2000, administrators can manage desktops centrally. One of the ways to address TCO is to use Group Policy to create managed desktop environments customized to the users' jobs and level of experience with computers. You can use the Group Policy MMC snap-in and its extensions defining

Group Policy options to manage desktop configurations for specific groups of users and computers. With the Group Policy snap-in you can specify policy settings for the following:

Registry-based policies—These policies include Group Policy and applications. To manage these settings, use Administrative Templates in the Group Policy snap-in.

Security options—These options include those for local computers, domains and network security settings.

Software installation and maintenance options—These options are used to centrally manage application installation, updates and removal.

Scripts options—These options include scripts for user logon and logoff and computer startup and shutdown.

Folder redirection options—These options allow an administrator to redirect users' special folders to the network.

Tip: By using Group Policy, you can define the state of users' work environments once and the system will enforce the policies you define.

Administering a Security Configuration

The term security configuration is interchangeable with security settings. Security settings include Security Policies (account and local policies), access control (services, files, registry), event log, group membership (restricted groups), Internet Protocol security, Security policies and Public Key policies.

To configure and analyze security locally, administrators use the Security Configuration and Analysis snap-in.

To configure security centrally in Active Directory, administrators use the Group Policy snap-in.

Applying Security Policies with Group Policy

The security behavior of the network system is defined by the security policy settings. Through the use of GPOs, you can apply explicit security profiles to various classes of computers from a central location. For example, Windows 2000 comes with a default Group Policy object called Default Domain Controllers Policy that governs the security behavior of domain controllers.

You can import a security profile into a GPO and apply it to groups of users or computers. You can also import the template into a personal database and use it to examine and configure the security policy of a local computer. Security templates provide standard security settings to use as a model for your security policies. They help you troubleshoot computers whose security policies do not comply with your current policy or are unknown. Security templates are inactive until imported into a Group Policy object or the Security Configuration and Analysis snap-in to MMC.

To import a security template into a Group Policy object, follow these steps:

1. From the **Start** menu, choose **Programs, Administrative Tools** and then select **Active Directory Users and Computers**.

2. From the console tree, right-click the desired container, and then choose **Properties**.

3. Choose the **Group Policy** property page.

4. Select the GPO and choose **Edit**.

5. From the Group Policy console, expand **Computer Configuration**, expand **Windows Settings**, right-click **Security Settings**, and then choose **Import Policy**.

6. Select a template, and then click **OK**.

Analysis and Security Templates

The status of the operating system and applications on a computer is dynamic. Through regular analysis you can track and ensure an adequate level of security on each computer as part of your risk management program. Analysis can be done on highly specific information about all system aspects related to security. With this information, you can tune the security levels and detect any security flaws that may occur in the system over time.

Security Configuration and Analysis gives you the ability to compare the security settings of a computer to a standard template, view the results, and resolve any discrepancies revealed by the analysis. You can also import a security template into a Group Policy object and apply that security profile to many computers at once. Windows 2000 contains several predefined security templates appropriate to different levels of security and to different types of clients and servers on the network.

To start Security Templates, follow these steps:

1. Decide if you wish to add Security Templates to an existing console or create a new console.

2. From the **Start** menu, choose **Run**, type **MMC** and then select **OK**.

3. To add Security Templates to an existing console, open the console: from the **Console** menu, choose **Add/Remove Snap-in** and then select **Add**.

4. Choose **Security Templates**, **Add**, **Close**, and then select **OK**.

5. From the **Console** menu, choose **Save**.

Enter the name to assign to this console and then choose **Save**.

 Note: The console will appear in My Documents and will be accessible either on the desktop or from the Start menu.

To define a security template, follow these steps:

1. From the **Security Templates** snap-in, double-click **Security Templates**.

2. Right-click the template path folder where you want to store the new template and then choose **New Template**.

3. Type the name and description for your new security template; the new template is then displayed in the console tree.

4. Double-click the new security template to display the security policies.

5. Double-click the security policy, such as **Account Policies,** you wish to customize, and then choose the security area, such as **Password Policy**.

6. Double-click the security attribute you wish to configure.

7. Enable **Define this policy setting in the template**.

Modifying Security Configurations

A security template is a profile of security settings appropriate to a specific level of security on a Windows 2000 network. A number of predefined templates are installed with Windows 2000. You can change the templates and then import them into a GPO.

To customize a predefined security template, follow these steps:

1. From the **Security Templates** snap-in, double-click **Security Templates**.

2. Double-click the default path folder where the templates are stored (*Systemroot*\Security\ Templates), and right-click the template you wish to modify.

3. Choose **Save As** and type a file name for the new security template.

4. Double-click your new template to display the security policies, and double-click the security policy you wish to modify.

5. Choose the security area to customize and then double-click the security attribute to modify.

6. Enable **Define this policy setting in the template** to edit the template.

To import a security template to a Group Policy object, follow these steps:

1. From a console where you manage Group Policy settings, choose the GPO to which you want to import the security template.

2. From the console tree, right-click **Security Settings**.

3. Choose **Import Policy**.

4. Choose the security template you want to import.

 Note: Security settings are applied when the computer starts or as the Group Policy settings dictate.

Audit Policy Implementation

Before you implement auditing, you must choose an auditing policy. An auditing policy defines the categories of security-related events that you wish to audit. When you first install Windows 2000, all of the auditing categories are turned off. By turning on auditing event categories, you can implement an auditing policy to suit the security needs of your organization. You can turn the auditing categories on and off with Computer Management. The most common types of events to audit are:

• Access to objects, such as files and folders

• Management of user and group accounts

• Users' log ons and log offs of the system

If you choose to audit access to objects as part of your audit policy, you must turn on either the audit directory service access category, for auditing objects on a domain controller, or the audit object access category, for auditing objects on a member server. Once you have turned on the correct object access category, you can use each object's properties to choose to audit successes or failures for the permissions you give to each group or user.

Implementing an Audit Policy

An audit records specific user actions that have been predefined. You can audit both successful and failed attempts at actions. For example, changing a file or a policy can create an audit entry. This shows the action performed, the user account, and the date and time of the action. Actions are not audited by default. You can specify what types of actions are audited. When you enable auditing, you:

- Establish a local audit policy on the computer where the actions occur

- Choose the actions to audit

There are different auditing tools, depending on whether you want to audit Active Directory objects or local objects.

- For Active Directory objects, use Active Directory Users and Computers

- For files and folders, registry keys, and network printers, use the Security tab from the object's properties; this allows you to specify which types of access to those objects you would like to audit

Following are the event categories that you can choose to audit:

- Audit account logon events

- Audit account management

- Audit directory service access

- Audit logon events

- Audit object access

- Audit policy change

- Audit privilege use

- Audit process tracking

- Audit system events

Monitoring and Analyzing Security Events

After you have enabled auditing in Group Policy, you can track security events. You can specify that an audit entry is to be written to the security event log when certain actions are performed or files are accessed. Before Windows 2000 will audit access to files and folders, you must use the Group Policy snap-in to enable the Audit Object Access setting in the Audit Policy. If you do not define this setting, you will receive an error message when you set up auditing for files and folders, and no files or folders will be audited. Once you have auditing enabled in Group Policy, you can view the security log in Event Viewer for successful or failed attempts to access the audited files and folders.

Vocabulary

Review the following terms in preparation for the certification exam.

Term	Description
ACE	Access Control Entry or permission entry is the allocation of permissions to a user or group and can be inherited by a specific object type. Each ACE contains a security identifier (SID), which identifies the principle (user or group) to whom the ACE applies, and what type of access the ACE grants or denies.
ACL	An Access Control List details which users can access a network resource.
ActiveX	ActiveX is a set of technologies that allow the software components to work together in a network, regardless of the language in which they are created.
administrative templates (.adm files)	The .ADM file specifies the registry settings that can be modified through the Group Policy snap-in user interface.
attribute	An attribute is a parameter describing an object.
authentication	In network access, authentication is the process by which the system validates the user's logon information.
container	A container is an object that can contain other objects. For example, a domain is a container that can contain users, computers and other objects. Unlike other objects, a container is a logical not a physical construct.
DACL	The Discretionary Access Control List contains the access control permissions for an object and its attributes, and the SIDs, which determine who can use the object.
domain	In Active Directory, a domain is a boundary for security and administrative purposes. Active Directory data is replicated between domain controllers within a domain.
GPE	The Group Policy Editor is run from the command line. It is a user interface to modify policy for objects.

Term	Description
GPO	Group Policy Objects are a collection of Group Policy settings and the documents created by the Group Policy snap-in. They are stored at the domain level, and they affect users and computers contained in sites, domains and OUs. Each Windows 2000 computer has one group of settings stored locally, called the local Group Policy object.
Group Policy	A Group Policy is a tool defining and controlling how programs, network resources, and the operating system operate for users and computers in an organization. Group Policy is applied to users or computers on the basis of their membership in sites, domains or OUs.
groups	Groups are Active Directory objects that can contain users, contacts, computers and other groups. Like user and computer accounts, groups are Windows 2000 security principals; they are directory objects and SIDs are assigned to them at creation.
GUID	The Globally Unique Identifier distinguishes the type of object or attribute, and is part of the ACE.
Jscript	Java script is a cross-platform programming language from Sun Microsystems that can be used to create animations and interactive features.
MMC	The Microsoft Management Console is a framework for hosting administrative consoles. A console is defined by the items on its console tree. It has windows that provide views of the tree as well as the administrative properties, services and events that are acted on by items in the console tree.
object	Objects can be a file, folder, shared folder or printer, described by a named set of attributes. For example, the attributes of a file object include its name, location and size; the attributes of an Active Directory User object could contain the user's first name, last name and e-mail address.
OU	An Organizational Unit is a logical container within a domain. You use an OU to organize objects for easier administration and access.
permission	A permission is a rule associated with an object to regulate which users can gain access to the object and in what manner.

Term	Description
SACL	The System Access Control List contains a list of events that can be audited for an object. An administrator can audit all attempts to create a user object in a given organizational unit (OU) by creating an auditing entry for the OU. If the audit directory service access policy is enabled on a domain controller, then access to the audited objects appear in the security log of the domain controller.
security groups	The two functions of security groups are to manage user and computer access to shared resources and to filter Group Policy settings. You put users, computers and other groups into a security group and then assign permissions to the specific resources to the security group. This means you can assign permissions to the group instead of multiple times to each individual user. When you add a user to an existing group, the user automatically gets the rights and permissions assigned to that group.
site	A site is one or more well-connected TCP/IP subnets. A site allows administrators to configure Active Directory access and replication topology quickly and easily to take advantage of the physical network. When users log on, Active Directory clients locate Active Directory servers in the same site as the user.
snap-in	A snap-in is a type of tool you can add to a console supported by Microsoft Management Console (MMC). A stand-alone snap-in can be added by itself, while an extension snap-in can be added to extend the function of another snap-in.
snap-in extension	An extension to a snap-in can only be added to extend the function of another snap-in.
TCO	The Total Cost of Ownership includes the total amount of money and time associated with purchasing, configuring and maintaining hardware and software. This includes updates, maintenance, administration and technical support.
VBScript	The Visual Basic Scripting language is based on the Visual Basic programming language, but is much simpler. It is similar to JScript.
WSH	Using Windows Scripting Host, you can automate specific actions. WSH is language independent so you can write scripts in languages such as VBScript and JScript.

In Brief

If you want to...	Then do this...
Add administrative templates	1. From **Active Directory Users and Computers**, right-click the domain or OU on which you want to set policy, and then select **Properties**.
	2. Select the **Group Policy** property page, select the **GPO**, and then choose **Edit**.
	3. From the **Group Policy** console, expand either **User Configuration** or **Computer Configuration**, right-click **Administrative Templates**, and then choose **Add/Remove Templates**.
	4. Choose **Add** and select the template you wish to add.
Associate a security group to a GPO	1. From **Active Directory Users and Computers**, right-click the domain or OU on which you want to modify the **GPO**, and then choose **Properties**.
	2. Choose the **Group Policy** property page, select the **GPO**, and then choose **Properties**.
	3. Choose the **Security** property page, and then assign the appropriate permissions to the user or group.
Block the policy inheritance from a parent domain	1. Start **Active Directory Users and Computers**.
	2. In **Active Directory Users and Computers**, right-click the desired container and select **Properties**.
	3. Choose **Group Policy**, and enable **Block Policy Inheritance**.
	4. Select **OK**, then **Close**.
Create a group policy for a site, domain or OU	1. Start **Active Directory Users and Computers**.
	2. From the console tree, right-click the desired container, and select **Properties**.
	3. Choose the **Group Policy** page and select **New**.
	4. Within **Group Policy Name** type the name for the new group policy.
	5. Select **OK,** then **Close**.

If you want to...	Then do this...
Create the Software Installation Snap-in	1. From Active Directory Users and Computers, right-click the domain or OU on which you want to set policy, and then select **Properties**. 2. Select the Group Policy property page, select the GPO, and then choose **Edit**. To assign software to computers, double-click **Computer Configuration**. 3. To assign or publish software to users, double-click **User Configuration.** 4. Double-Click **Software Settings.** 5. Right-click **Software Installation**, choose **New**, and then select **Package**.
Customize a predefined security template	1. From the **Security Templates** snap-in, double-click **Security Templates**. 2. Double-click the default path folder for where the templates are stored (*System root*\Security\Templates), and right-click the template you wish to modify. 3. Choose **Save As** and type a file name for the new security template. 4. Double-click your new template to display the security policies, and double-click the security policy you wish to modify. 5. Choose the security area to customize and double-click the security attribute to modify. 6. Enable **Define this policy setting in the template** to edit the template.

If you want to...	Then do this...
Define a security template	1. From the Security Templates snap-in, double-click Security Templates. 2. Right-click the template path folder where you want to store the new template and click **New Template**. 3. Type the name and description for your new security template; the new template is then displayed from the console tree. 4. Double-click the new security template to display the security policies. 5. Double-click the security policy, such as **Account Policies**, that you wish to customize, and then select the security area, such as **Password Policy**. 6. Double-click the security attribute you wish to configure. 7. Enable **Define this policy setting in the template**.
Delete a GPO	1. Start **Active Directory Users and Computers**. 2. From the console, right-click the site, domain or OU from which the GPO should be deleted. 3. Choose **Properties**, and then select **Group Policy**. 4. From **Group Policy**, choose the GPO that you wish to delete, and then select **Delete**. 5. From **Delete**, choose **Remove The Link And Delete The Group Policy Object Permanently**, and then click **OK**.

If you want to...	Then do this...
Edit a GPO or its settings	1. Start the **Group Policy Snap-in** for the GPO. 2. From the console tree, expand the item that represents the particular policy you want to set. 3. From **Details**, right-click the policy you want to set and then choose **Properties**. 4. Choose the appropriate Policies. 5. Choose **Enabled** to apply the policy to users or computers that are subject to the GPO, and then select **OK**.
Filter the scope of a GPO	1. Start Active Directory Users and Computers. 2. From the console tree, right-click the root of Group Policy, choose **Properties** and then select **Security**. 3. Choose the security group through which you want to filter this GPO. 4. Set the **Permissions** and then choose **OK**. 5. Choose **OK** and then click **Close**.
Import a security template into a Group Policy object	1. Start **Active Directory Users and Computers**. 2. From the console tree, right-click the desired container, and then choose **Properties**. 3. Choose the **Group Policy** property page, select the **GPO**, and then choose **Edit**. 4. From the **Group Policy** console, expand **Computer Configuration**, expand **Windows Settings**, right-click **Security Settings**, and then choose **Import Policy**.

If you want to...	Then do this...
Link a GPO to a site, domain or OU	1. Start **Active Directory Users and Computers** to link a GPO to a domian or OU; or choose **Active Directory Sites and Services** to link a GPO to a site.
	2. From the console tree, right-click the desired site, domain or OU to which you want to link the GPO, choose **Properties** and then select the **Group Policy** page.
	3. If the GPO already appears in the **Group Policy Object Links** list, choose **Cancel**; if the GPO does not appear in the **Group Policy Object Links** list, choose **Add.**
	4. From **Add A Group Policy Object Link**, choose **All**, choose the desired GPO and then select **OK.**
	5. From the **Properties** for the site, domain or OU, choose **OK.**
Modify the Default Domain Policy definition by installing scripts	1. From **Active Directory Users and Computers**, right-click the domain and choose **Properties**
	2. Select the **Group Policy** property page.
	3. Select **Default Domain Policy**, and then choose **Edit.**
	4. From the **Group Policy** console, expand **Computer Configuration**, expand **Windows Settings**, and then select **Scripts (Startup/Shutdown).**
	5. Double-click **Startup**.
	6. Choose **Add** to add a new startup script.

If you want to...	Then do this...
Open Group Policy as a stand-alone MMC snap-in	1. From the **Start menu**, choose **Run**, type **MMC**, and then choose **OK**.
	2. From the menu bar of the empty MMC console, choose **Console**, and then select **Add/Remove Console**.
	3. Choose **Add**, select **Group Policy**, and then choose **Add**.
	4. Select **Finish** to modify the Group Policy for the local computer, or select **Browse** to select a different computer.
	5. Choose Close, and then choose OK.
Remove a GPO link	1. Start Active Directory Users and Computers.
	2. From the console, right-click the site, domain or OU from which the GPO should be unlinked.
	3. Choose **Properties**, and then select **Group Policy**.
	4. From **Group Policy**, choose the GPO that you wish to unlink, and then select **Delete**.
	5. From **Delete**, choose **Remove The Link From The List**, and then click **OK**.
Set read and write permissions for Group Policy	1. From **Active Directory Users and Computers**, right-click the container or OU on which you wish to set permissions, and then choose **Properties**.
	2. Select the **Group Policy** property page, select the GPO, and then choose **Properties**.
	3. Select the **Security** property page, and then set permissions to the appropriate users and groups.
	4. Click **OK** to save the changes.

If you want to...	Then do this...
Specify no override policies by a child domain's GPO	1. Start Active Directory Users and Computers.
	2. From within **Active Directory Users and Computers**, right-click the desired container and then choose **Properties**.
	3. Choose **Group Policy** and then select **Options.**
	4. Choose **No Override.**
	5. Click **OK**, and then select **Close.**
Start Security Templates	1. From the **Start menu**, choose **Run**, type **MMC**, and then click **OK**.
	2. From the menu bar, choose Console, and then select Add/Remove Console.
	3. Choose **Add**, select **Security Templates**, and then choose **Add**.
	4. Choose **Close**, and then click **OK**.
Turn on security logging	1. From the **Start** menu, choose **Run**, type **mmc /a**, and then choose **OK**.
	2. From the **Console** menu, choose **Add/Remove Snap-in** and then select **Add**.
	3. From **Snap-in**, choose **Group Policy** and then select **Add**.
	4. From **Select Group Policy Object**, choose **Local Computer, Finish, Close**, and then select **OK**.
	5. From **Local Computer Policy**, choose **Audit Policy**.
	6. From the details pane, choose the attribute or event you want to audit.
	7. From the menu bar, choose **Action**, and then select **Security**.
	8. From **Local Security Policy Setting**, choose the options you want and then click **OK**.

Lesson 6 Activities

Complete the following activities to prepare for the certification exam.

1.   Explain why you should use groups.

2.   A user cannot gain access to a resource. Name two things that you should check.

3.   Explain what a GPO is.

4.   There are two types of group policy settings. Describe what they are and how they are used.

5.   Explain how user permissions are different from user rights.

6.   Define a security template and how it is used.

7.   Explain linking as it relates to GPOs.

8.   List the Group Policy console extensions.

9.   There are four new group policy script types. Explain what they are and what they do.

10.   Explain the use of security groups in Group Policy.

Answers to Lesson 6 Activities

1.   Groups simplify administration. You can grant rights and assign permissions once to a group instead of multiple times to each user.

2.   Any of the following could be checked to determine why a user would have problems with access to a resource:

    1. Check the permissions assigned to the user's account and the groups to which the user is a member.

    2. Check if any of the above accounts have been denied permissions for the file or folder.

    3. Check if the file or folder has been copied or moved. If it has, the permissions will have changed (only if moved to a different partition - at least in NT 4.0).

3.   A GPO is a Group Policy Object. GPOs are a collection of Group Policy settings and the documents created by the Group Policy snap-in. They are stored at the domain level, and they affect users and computers contained in sites, domains, and OUs. Each Windows 2000 computer has one group of settings stored locally, called the local Group Policy object.

4.   The two types of group policy settings are user configuration settings and computer configuration settings. User configuration settings are used to set group policies and are applied when a user logs onto the network, no matter which computer they log onto. Computer configuration settings are used to apply group policies to a computer, regardless of who logs onto it. They are applied when the computer is booted up.

5.   User permissions are different from user rights, as permissions are attached to objects and rights apply to user accounts.

6.   A security template is a physical representation of a security configuration. It is a file containing a group of security settings. This simplifies and streamlines administration by locating the settings in one place.

7.   Each GPO is created as a standalone object in the Active Directory. This object can then be linked—one or more times—to sites, domains and OUs. GPOs for domains and OUs are kept in the domain relating to their application, but GPOs for sites are stored in the root domain of the forest. By linking GPOs to specific sites, domains, or OUs, you maximize and extend the power of Active Directory. GPOs are actually applied to a site, domain, or OU by using a link. A non-local GPO that is not linked to a site, domain, or OU has no effect on any user or computer.

8.   The Group Policy snap-in includes the following snap-in extensions: Administrative Templates, Security Settings, Software Installation, Scripts and Folder Redirection

9.   Group Policy includes the following four new script types:
     • Logon and logoff for user objects
     • Startup and shutdown for computer objects

     Logon and logoff scripts are part of the Group Policy user configuration. Group Policy logon and logoff scripts give you a way to define and apply common scripts to multiple users.

     Startup and shutdown scripts are part of the Group Policy computer configuration. You run startup and shutdown scripts on each computer to which you apply the script policy—either directly or through Group Policy inheritance.

10. Security groups in Group Policy are used to:
     Filter the scope of a GPO—This defines which groups of users and computers a GPO affects.
     Delegate control of a GPO—The two aspects to managing and delegating Group Policy are managing the group policy links and managing who can create and edit GPOs.

Lesson 6 Quiz

These questions test your knowledge of features, vocabulary, procedures, and syntax.

1. In what order is Group Policy implemented in Active Directory?
   A. Site, Domain and OU
   B. OU, Site, and Domain
   C. Zone, Site and OU
   D. Root, tree and forest

2. How can using GPOs reduce the total cost of ownership?
   A. Managed desktop environments tailored to users' job responsibilities and level of experience with computers.
   B. Administrators can manage desktops centrally.
   C. Centrally manage application installation, updates, and removal.
   D. Define the state of users' work environment once and rely on the system to enforce the policies you define (lack of parallel structure in responses).

3. Which of the following is the correct answer to this definition: Includes all computer-related policies that specify operating system behavior, desktop behavior, application settings, security settings, assigned applications options, and computer startup and shutdown scripts?
   A. User Configuration
   B. Computer configuration
   C. Scripts
   D. Administrative Templates

4. Which of the following are Security Groups?
   A. Domain local groups
   B. Global groups
   C. Universal groups
   D. Computer local groups

5. What are the common events you would audit?
   A. When users log on and log off the system
   B. Management of user and group accounts
   C. Software installation
   D. Access to objects and folders

6. How can security groups be used to filter group policy?
   A. By setting the appropriate permissions
   B. Permissions are passed down from parent to child
   C. Security Settings determine the user's desktop environment.
   D. Security groups are stored on each computer, whether or not they are part of a network.

7.   If you apply policies to an OU that contains only groups and no users, are the policies applied to the members of the group?
    A.   Yes. Any members of the groups are affected by the GPOs.
    B.   Yes. But only those users who become part of the groups.
    C.   No. There are no users.
    D.   No. GPOs are applied only to the users and computers that are members of the OU.

8.   How can you apply a GPO to a Security Group?
    A.   Use the Group Policy Snap-in
    B.   Use the Active Directory Users and Computers MMC snap-in
    C.   From the Users and Computers console window, right click on the Security Group to which you want to add the Group Policy Object.
    D.   It is not possible

9.   What is stored in the GPO?
    A.   A searchable index that enables users to search for network objects.
    B.   A set of user and computer configuration settings.
    C.   An object that holds other objects.
    D.   The definitions of all object classes and their attributes.

10.   What is the difference between assigning and publishing software?
    A.   Assign a software application when you want everyone to have the application on their computers. An application can be published to both computers and users.
    B.   There is no difference between assigning and publishing.
    C.   When you assign an application to a computer, it will install itself when there are no competing processes. Computers can not install published software.
    D.   Publish a software application when you want the application available to people managed by a GPO, and they can choose to install the application. Assigning means that the software will be installed automatically.

Answers to Lesson 6 Quiz

1. Answer A is correct. Site, Domain and OU is the correct order.

   Answer B is incorrect. The local GPO is processed first and the GPOs linked to the OU of which the GPO is a member are processed last, overwriting the previous GPOs.

   Answer C is incorrect. Zones have no part in the processing of GPOs.

   Answer D is incorrect. Root, tree and forest are the domain hierarchy.

2. Answers A, B, C and D are correct. The total cost of ownership encompasses the costs involved in administering distributed networks. Anything that reduces administrator maintenance and workload decreases the TCO.

3. Answer B is correct. A Computer configuration is what was defined.

   Answer A is incorrect. User configurations are the policies that relate to a user.

   Answer C is incorrect. You can use scripts to automate computer startup and shutdown, and user logon and logoff.

   Answer D is incorrect. Administrative templates include registry-based policy settings, which you use to mandate registry settings that govern the behavior and appearance of the desktop, including the operating system components and applications.

4. Answers A, B, C and D are correct. Domain local groups give access rights to resources located on any computer in the domain where common access permissions are required. Global groups are used to join users sharing a common access profile based on their job function. Usually, membership changes often. Universal groups are used in multi-domain organizations where access to similar groups of accounts defined in multiple domains needs to be granted. Computer local groups are security groups specific to a computer and are not recognized elsewhere in the domain.

5. Answers A, B and D are correct. The most common types of events to audit are access to objects, such as files and folders, management of user and group accounts, and when users log on and log off the system.

   Answer C is incorrect. Software installation is usually tightly controlled in network environments.

6.   Answer A is correct. By setting the appropriate permissions for security groups, you can filter group policy to influence only those users and computers that you have specified.

Answer B is incorrect. In general, Group Policy is passed from parent to child but does not filter.

Answer C is incorrect. Group Policy settings are contained in a GPO and determine the user's desktop environment.

Answer D is incorrect. One local GPO is stored on each computer, whether or not it is part of the network.

7.   Answer D is correct. GPOs are applied only to the users and computers that are members of the organizational unit. A different mechanism is used to filter the effect of GPOs, based on membership in security groups.

Answer A and B are incorrect. Users must be part of the OU to be affected by the GPO.

Answer C is incorrect. Only groups were mentioned in the question as being in the OU. The groups could have users outside of the OU.

8.   Answer D is correct. It is not possible to apply a group policy to a security group. However, you can filter a group policy by changing the permissions on the Group Policy so that only certain users/groups have read and apply privileges.

Answer A is incorrect. The Group Policy snap-in does not exist. You can create custom GPO consoles.

Answers B and C are incorrect. They are incorrect and incomplete procedures.

9.   Answer B is correct. A Group Policy Object is a set of user configuration settings that you store as an object in the Active Directory.

Answer A is incorrect. A global catalog is a searchable index that enables users to search for network objects without knowing their domain locations.

Answer C is incorrect. A container is an object that holds other objects.

Answer D is incorrect. A schema contains the definitions of all object classes and their attributes that are stored in the Active Directory.

10.   Answers A, C and D are correct. When assigning a software application to a computer or a user the software will install automatically. With publishing, the user chooses to install the application onto the computer.

Answer B is incorrect. There is a difference between assigning and publishing an application as described in Answers A, C and D.

Lesson 7

Active Directory Replication

Replication is the periodic exchange of information between the domain controllers within a domain. This ensures that all domain controllers have the same data. Your job as an administrator is to plan and control replication traffic. Too much traffic can bog down a network. This results in slow response and application timeouts. Aside from controlling replication traffic, sites can group computers for efficient and fast authentication. Replication occurs in two different forms, inter-site (between sites) and intra-site (within sites). A Windows 2000 service called the Knowledge Consistency Checker (KCC) will automatically generate replication links between intra-site domain controllers. The KCC will also create links inter-site, but you need to specify the sites that are to be linked. Every aspect of the KCC and the links that it creates is configurable.

Windows 2000 replication is very economical. Only the changed properties are replicated, instead of entire objects. Replication can also take place over Transmission Control Protocol/Internet Protocol (TCP/IP) transports. TCP/IP is a set of protocols that provides communication among diverse networks. Because it accommodates different architectures and operating systems, TCP/IP is the most commonly used Internet protocol. This enables you to find a replication protocol suitable to a particular site's requirements. Active Directory uses multi-master replication, which means any domain controller can respond to service requests.

After completing this lesson, you should have a better understanding of the following topics:

- Active Directory Replication Within a Site

- Active Directory Replication Between Sites

Active Directory Replication within a Site

The KCC is a built-in process that creates and maintains replication connections between domain controllers. It uses site topology information to guide the creation of these connections. Intra-site replication is tuned to minimize replication latency, and inter-site replication is tuned to minimize bandwidth usage.

Directory updates between domain controllers in the same site is known as intra-site replication (see Figure 7.1). Information exchanged between domain controllers within a site occurs more often and more efficiently than between domain controllers in different sites. These frequent updates keep information in a site and between the domain controllers new. Updates to domain controllers outside a site happen less frequently, but those controllers are less likely to need as frequent updates.

Figure 7.1 Intra-Site Replication

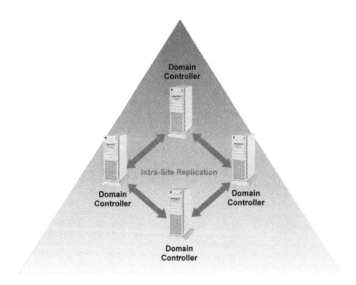

These frequent intra-site updates are why sites play such an important role in network traffic flow. Sites let you physically group together computers that need to share information. By introducing a change notification mechanism, intra-site replication prevents unnecessary network traffic. This replaces the usual polling of replication partners for updates.

Managing Active Directory Replication within a Site

Domain Controllers within sites have links created between them by the KCC. These links use the domain controller's Globally Unique Identifier (GUID) as the unique identifier. A bi-directional ring topology is used intra-site, using Remote Procedure Call (RPC) over TCP/IP without compression. This is because domain controllers within a site are presumed to be on a fast network, according to the definition of a site.

The KCC runs every 15 minutes, adjusting the topology as needed. As new domain controllers are created, they are automatically placed in the ring (Figure 7.2). You can view these links using the Active Directory Sites and Services MMC snap-in.

Figure 7.2 Rings of Replication

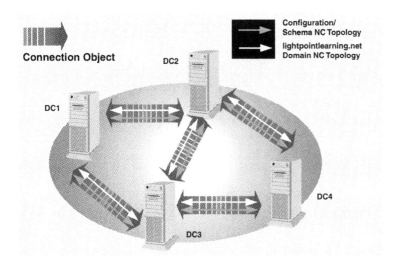

To start Active Directory Sites and Services to view links, follow these steps:

1. From the **Start** menu, choose **Programs, Administrative Tools** and then select **Active Directory Sites and Services**.

2. Expand the **Site**, expand the **Servers** container, expand the **Server**, and the created connection objects are displayed from **NTDS Settings**, as in Figure 7.3.

Figure 7.3 Connection Objects

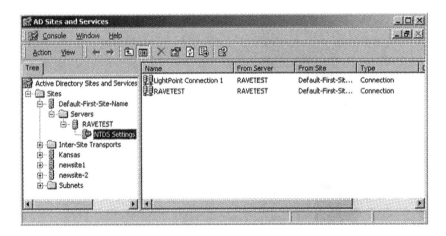

The rings are ordered by the domain controller's GUID to ensure convergence on a single topology as the KCC runs on all domain controllers. There is an exception to the ring rule. There can never be more than three hops between any two domain controllers within the ring and so, if there are 7 or more domain controllers, extra links are added to protect the three-hop rule. Notice in Figure 7.4, two extra non-ring links have been added to enable no more than 3 hops to any domain controller.

Figure 7.4 Three-Hop Rule

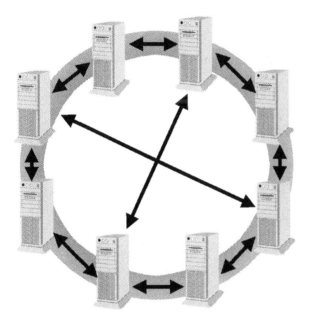

These rings are for the same domains in a single site. If you had multiple domains in a site, there would be rings for each domain within the site.

Tip: Use the Active Directory Replication Monitor to view the site rings or to check connection objects and incoming replication.

Intra-Site Replication

Any manual configuration of intra-site replication should not be needed and is not recommended. The only task you may ever find yourself performing is to add extra connection objects to reduce the hop count between domain controllers.

The KCC, which manages the connection objects for inter and intra-site replication, by default, runs every 15 minutes. This can be changed as follows:

1. From the **Start** menu, choose **Run** and type **REGEDIT.EXE** to start the registry editor.

2. Move to HKEY_LOCAL_MACHINE\SYSTEM\CurrentControlSet\Services\NTDS\Parameters

3. From the **Edit** menu, choose **New - DWORD value**.

4. Type the **Repl topology update period (secs)** and then choose **Enter**.

5. Double click the new value, set it to the number of seconds you wish the KCC to wait before executing again, and then click **OK**.

6. Close the registry editor, and restart your computer.

There are a number of registry settings under HKEY_LOCAL_MACHINE\SYSTEM\CurrentControlSet\Services\NTDS\Parameters that can be used to modify some elements of the Active Directory replication. When a change is made to the Active Directory, a timer is started tracking how long the domain controller will wait before notifying its first replication partner. By default this is 5 minutes and can be modified by changing the Replicator notify pause after modify (secs) value. Once it notifies the first replication partner, there is a default 30 second wait to notify each of its other replication partners. This stops simultaneous replies by the replication partners. You can modify this value by changing the Replicator notify pause between DSAs Definition (secs) value (Figure 7.5).

Figure 7.5 Registry Editor

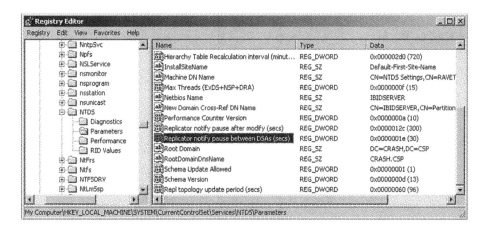

Following are other available values:

- Replication thread priority high, set to 1 to have replication run at high priority. If not set or set to 0, it runs at low priority.

- Replication thread priority log, set to 1 to have replication run at low priority. If set to 1, it is ignored.

 Note: Using the replication topology generator, which is part of the KCC, is strongly recommended: it simplifies a complex task, has a flexible architecture that reacts to failures and to changes you make later in the network topology, and helps compute the lowest-cost topology.

The KCC then figures out the best connection between each domain controller. If replication within a site fails or has a single point of failure, the KCC automatically establishes new connection objects to resume Active Directory replication. You use Active Directory Sites and Services to modify replication topology when adding or removing connection objects and establishing connections that are beyond the KCC.

Tip: In addition to creating and modifying connection objects, you can use Active Directory Sites and Services to force replication and run KCC manually.

When you modify the connection objects, the following rules apply:

• The KCC will never delete a connection object that has been manually created

• If you create a connection that is identical to one the KCC would create, it will not delete the connection that you created

• If the replication within a site fails, the KCC will step in and establish any necessary connections to resume Active Directory replication

Active Directory Replication between Sites

Inter-site replication or replication between domain controllers in different sites, works differently than intra-site replication, as shown in Figure 7.6. In the figure, the inter-site links are arrows between the sites and the intra-site links are the arrows inside the sites, between the controllers.

Figure 7.6 Inter-Site Replication

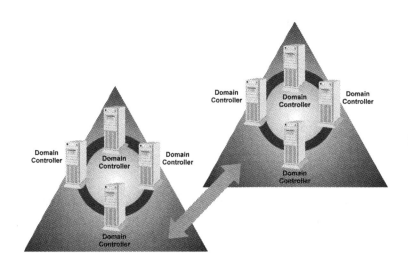

Active Directory does not create the links between sites automatically. You create the site links based on the actual network links in your network environment. After your site links are in place, you assign a cost to each site link. This cost helps the KCC determine which site link to make a primary route between sites, to which you have assigned a cost of 1, and which site link to make a secondary route, to which you have assigned a higher cost, such as 100. The KCC also determines the usage schedule for the site links—the window when replication is allowed over the link.

The value of replication is improved by a replication topology that reflects the structure of an existing network. The Active Directory's replication topology generator runs as part of the KCC. You enter information on the cost of sending data from one location to another and which domain controllers are running in the same location into the KCC. Using this, an inter-site replication topology is built that spans a tree, based on low-cost routing decisions between remote locations and a more strongly connected intra-site topology.

You can also disable the KCC topology generator and manually create the connection objects required for replication. During this process, the Active Directory logging mechanism identifies domain controllers that appear to be isolated from the enterprise-wide replication.

Unlike intra-site replication, inter-site replication does not use a notification process. Inter-site replication can be scheduled by the administrator on a per site link basis. Since there is no notice between replication partners, a domain controller does not know which naming context was updated on the source replication partner. The domain controller has to check all existing naming contexts on the source machine.

While intra-site replication supports only replication based on Remote Procedure Calls (RPCs), Windows 2000 offers the following two methods for inter-site replication:

- Synchronous (scheduled) using RPC over TCP/IP

- Asynchronous using Simple Mail Transfer Protocol (SMTP)

SMTP transport has limits. It can be used to replicate configuration and Global Catalog information. It cannot be used for replication between domain controllers that belong to the same domain and need to replicate the full domain-naming context.

Managing Active Directory Replication Between Sites

When you need to connect two sites, you manually create a site link using the Sites and Services Manager and specify a transport to use. When you do this, inter-site link connection objects are automatically created by the KCC in Active Directory.

To ensure replication between sites, you must customize how Active Directory replicates information using site links to represent network connections. Active Directory uses the network connection information to generate connection objects that provide efficient replication and fault tolerance.

You provide the information about the replication protocol used, the cost of a site link, the times when the link is available for use and how often the link should be used. Active Directory uses the information you enter to determine which site link will be used to replicate information. Customizing replication schedules so replication occurs during specific times, such as when network traffic is light, makes replication more efficient (Figure 7.7).

Figure 7.7 Site Links

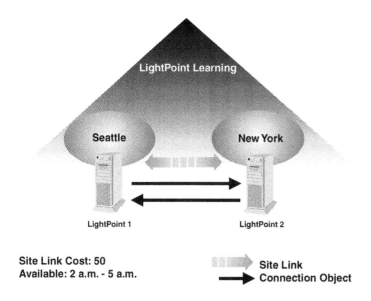

Site Link Cost: 50
Available: 2 a.m. - 5 a.m.

Site Link
Connection Object

Inter-Site Replication

To configure inter-site replication, you must complete the following actions:

- Create site links

- Configure site link attributes

- Configure site link bridges

To create a site link, follow these steps:

1. From the **Start** menu, choose **Programs**, **Administrative Tools** and then select **Active Directory Sites and Services**.

2. Expand **Sites**, expand **Inter-Site Transports**, right-click the protocol you want the site link to use, and then choose **New Site Link**.

3. From within **Name**, type the name to be given to the link.

4. Choose two or more sites to connect, and then select **Add**.

5. Configure the site link cost, frequency and availability.

As part of inter-site replication, you need to configure the site link cost, frequency and availability. All of these are defined through the Properties window for the site link you are configuring.

First, you need to assign a value for the cost of each available connection. Active Directory always chooses the connection on a per-cost basis, so cheaper connections are used when they are available. The default is 100. The lower the cost the lower the value, with a corresponding higher priority.

To configure a site link cost, follow these steps:

1. From the **Start** menu, choose **Programs, Administrative Tools** and then select **Active Directory Sites and Services**.

2. Open **Inter-Site Transports** and either the **IP** or **SMTP**.

3. Right-click the site for which you want to configure the site link cost, and then choose **Properties**.

4. From the **Properties** for the site link, as shown in Figure 7.8, from within **Cost**, type in a value.

Figure 7.8 Cost Properties for a Site Link

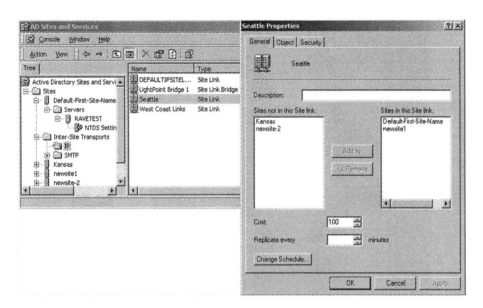

You then need to configure the replication frequency for site links by providing a value telling Active Directory how many minutes it should wait before any replication is to occur. The replication interval must be at least 15 minutes and no more that 10,080 minutes (1 week).

To configure replication frequency, follow these steps:

1. From the **Start** menu, choose **Programs**, **Administrative Tools** and then select **Active Directory Sites and Services**.

2. Open **Inter-Site Transports** and either the **IP** or **SMTP**.

3. Right-click the site for which you want to configure the site link cost, and then choose **Properties**.

4. From the **Properties** for the site link, as shown in Figure 7.9, from within **Replicate Every**, type in the number of minutes.

Figure 7.9 Site Link Properties Replication

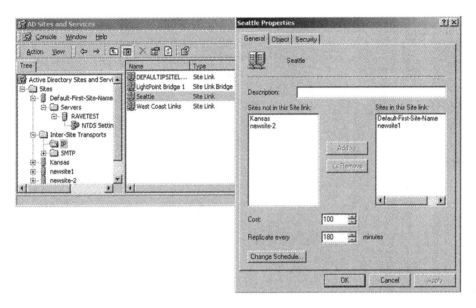

You then configure replication availability to define when the site link is available for replication. Because SMTP is asynchronous, it ignores schedules. You do not need to configure SMTP site links unless:

- The site links use scheduled connections

- The SMTP queue is not on a schedule

- Information is being directly exchanged from one server to another

To configure site link replication availability, follow these steps:

1. From the **Start** menu, choose **Programs**, **Administrative Tools** and then select **Active Directory Sites and Services**.

2. Open **Inter-Site Transports** and either the **IP** or **SMTP**.

3. Right-click the site for which you want to configure the site link cost, and then choose **Properties**.

4. From the **Properties** for the site link, choose **Change Schedule**.

5. From **Schedule For**, shown in Figure 7.10, choose the block of time the connection is available to replicate information, and then select **OK**.

Figure 7.10 Schedule for a Site Link

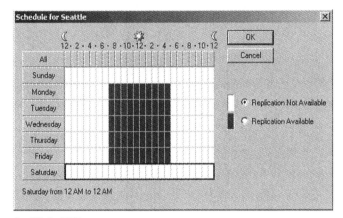

6. Click **OK**.

Site links are transitive. For example, if you have a Site A that is linked to Site B and there is another link between Site B and Site C, the link between Site A and Site C is a transitive link. Figure 7.11 shows this relationship.

Figure 7.11 Transitive Site Links

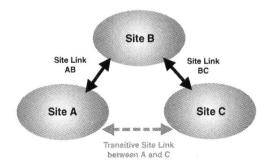

To enable transitive site links, follow these steps:

1. Form the **Start menu**, choose **Programs**, **Administrative Tools**, and then select **Active Directory Sites and Services**.

2. Expand **Sites**, expand **Inter-Site Transports**, right-click either **IP** or **SMTP**, and then choose **Properties**.

3. From the **General** property page, enable **Bridge All Site Links**.

4. Click **OK**.

When two or more sites are linked for replication and use the same transport, they are bridged, in terms of cost. In other words, all site links for a specific transport belong to the same site link bridge. For the transport in a fully routed IP network, you do not need to configure any site link bridges. If your IP network is not fully routed, you can turn off the transitive site link feature and you will need to configure all your site link bridges. In Figure 7.12, you see the site link bridge that enables the connections between the Vancouver and New York sites.

Figure 7.12 Site Link Bridge

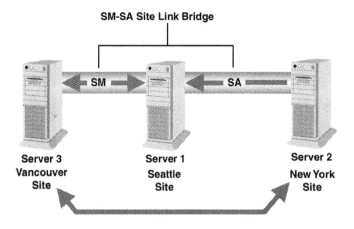

To create a site link bridge, follow these steps:

1. From the **Start** menu, choose **Programs**, **Administrative Tools** and then select **Active Directory Sites and Services**.

2. Open **Inter-Site Transports** and either **IP** or **SMTP**.

3. Right-click either **IP** or **SMTP** and select **New Site Link Bridge**.

4. From **New Object-Site Link**, shown in Figure 7.13 from within **Name**, type a name for the site link bridge.

Figure 7.13 New Object Site Link

5. Choose two or more sites to connect and then select **Add**.

6. Click **OK.**

Table 7.1 shows the differences between intra-site and inter-site replication.

Table 7.1 Intra-Site vs. Inter-Site Replication

Intra-Site replication	Inter-Site replication
Replication traffic is not compressed to save processor time.	Replication traffic is compressed to save bandwidth.
Replication partners notify each other when changes need to be replicated, to reduce replication latency.	Replication partners do not notify each other when changes need to be replicated, to save bandwidth.
Replication partners poll each other for changes on a periodic basis.	Replication partners poll each other for changes on a specified polling interval, during scheduled periods only.
Replication uses the Remote Procedure Call (RPC) transport.	Replication uses the TCP/IP or SMTP transport.
Replication connections can be created between any two domain controllers located in the same site. The KCC creates connections with multiple domain controllers to reduce replication latency.	Replication connections are only created between bridgehead servers. One domain controller from each domain in a site is designated by the KCC as a bridgehead server. The bridgehead server handles all inter-site replication for that domain. The KCC creates connections between bridgehead servers using the lowest cost route, according to the site link cost. The KCC will only create connections over a higher cost route if all of the domain controllers in lower cost routes are unreachable.

Vocabulary

Review the following terms in preparation for the certification exam.

Term	Description
certificate	A certificate is a file used for authentication that secures the exchange of data on non-secured networks, such as the Internet. A certificate securely binds a public encryption key to the entity that holds the corresponding private encryption key. Certificates are digitally signed by the issuing certification authority and can be managed for a user, a computer or a service.
encryption	Encryption is the process of disguising a message or data in such a way as to hide its substance.
GUID	The Globally Unique Identifier that distinguishes the type of object or attribute. Part of the Access Control Entry (ACE).
inter-site	Term used for replication that occurs between sites.
intra-site	Term used for replication that occurs between controllers in the same site.
IP	Internet Protocol is a routable protocol in the TCP/IP protocol suite responsible for IP addressing, routing, and the fragmentation and reassembly of IP packets.
KCC	The Knowledge Consistency Checker is a service that automatically generates a replication topology.
latency	The time lag between the beginning of a request for data and the moment it begins to be received. The time necessary for a packet of data to travel across a network.
multimaster replication	A replication model in which any domain controller accepts and replicates directory changes to any other domain controller. This differs from other replication models in which the computer stores the single modifiable copy of the directory and other computers store backup copies.

Term	Description
REPADMIN.EXE	A command-line tool that enables replication consistency to be checked for a KCC recalculation. The switch /showreps displays a list of replication partners. The invocation ID is the database GUID and will show reason for problems.
replication	The process of copying data from a data store or file system to multiple computers to synchronize the data. Active Directory provides multimaster replication of the directory between domain controllers within a given domain. The replicas of the directory on each domain controller are writeable. This allows the update to be applied to any replica of a given domain. The replication service automatically copies the changes from a given replica to all other replicas.
replication latency	Replication takes time. At any given moment, not all the domain controllers in your forest may have equal replicas. The delay between an action and replication throughout your network is referred to as replication latency.
RPC	Remote Procedure Call is a call by one program to a second program on a remote system.
site	A site is one or more well-connected TCP/IP subnets. A site allows administrators to configure Active Directory access and replication topology quickly and easily to take advantage of the physical network. When users log on, Active Directory clients locate Active Directory servers in the same site as the user.
site link	A link between two sites that allows replication to occur. Each site contains the schedule that determines when replication can occur between sites that it connects.
site link bridge	The linking of more than two sites for replication and using the same transport. When site links are bridges, they are transitive (all sites linked for a specific transport implicitly belong to a single site bridge for that transport).
SMTP	The Simple Mail Transfer Protocol is used on the Internet to transfer mail reliably and efficiently. SMTP is independent of the particular transmission subsystem and requires only a reliable, ordered, data stream channel.

Term	Description
TCP/IP	The Transmission Control Protocol/Internet Protocol is a set of protocols that provides communication among diverse networks. Because it accommodates different architectures and operating systems, TCP/IP is the most commonly used Internet protocol.
topology	The relationship among a set of network components. In the context of Active Directory replication, topology refers to the set of connections that domain controllers use to replicate information among themselves.

In Brief

If you want to...	Then do this...
View links	1. Start **Active Directory Sites and Services**. 2. Expand the **Site**, expand the **Servers** container, expand the **Server** and the created connection objects are displayed from **NTDS Settings**.
Create a site link	1. Start **Active Directory Sites and Services**. 2. Right-click the **Inter-Site transport protocol** you want the site link to use, and then choose **New Site Link**. 3. From within **Name**, type the name to be given to the link. 4. Choose two or more sites to connect, and then select **Add**. 5. Configure the site link cost, frequency and availability.
Configure site link cost	1. Start **Active Directory Sites and Services**. 2. Open **Inter-Site Transports** and either the **IP** or **SMTP**. Right-click the site you want to configure the site link cost and then choose **Properties**. 3. From the **Properties** for the site link, from within **Cost**, type in a value. 4. Click **OK**.
Configure replication frequency	1. From the **Properties** for the site link, from within **Replicate Every**, type in the number of minutes. 2. Click **OK**.
Configure site link replication availability	1. From the **Properties** for the site link, choose **Change Schedule**. 2. From **Schedule For**, for the site link, choose the block of time the connection is available to replicate information, and then select **OK**. 3. From Properties, click **OK**.

If you want to...	Then do this...
Create a site link bridge	1. Start **Active Directory Sites and Services**.
	2. Open **Inter-Site Transports** and either the **IP** or **SMTP**. Right-click the site you want to configure the site link cost and then choose **New Site Link Bridge**.
	3. From **New Object-Site Link**, from within **Name**, type a name for the site link bridge.
	4. Choose two or more sites to connect and then select **Add**.
	5. Click **OK.**
Enable transitive site links	1. Start **Active Directory Sites and Services**.
	2. Open **Inter-Site Transports** and either the **IP** or **SMTP**. Right-click the site you want to configure the site link cost and then choose **Properties**.
	3. Choose **General** and then enable **Bridge All Site Links**.
	4. Choose **OK.**

Lesson 7 Activities

Complete the following activities to prepare for the certification exam.

1. Explain how intra-site replication works in Windows 2000.

2. Explain how inter-site replication works in Windows 2000.

3. Explain what the KCC is and what it does.

4. Your Active Directory domain has two domain controllers located on separate segments of the network. The router that connects the two networks fails and the two controllers cannot communicate for 48 hours. When the connectivity between them is restored, describe how much domain information will replicate between the two domains.

5. Define the three-hop rule.

6. Name the tool used to change the replication time for the KCC.

7. If intra-site replication uses RPC, explain what inter-site replication uses.

8. Define the configurations for site links.

9. Explain what a site link bridge is.

10. Explain what multimaster means.

Answers to Lesson 7 Activities

1. The KCC automatically manages replication within a site. A bi-directional ring topology is used intra-site using RPC over TCP/IP without any compression, as domain controllers within a site are thought to be on a fast network.

    The KCC runs every 15 minutes adjusting the topology as needed. As new domain controllers are created, they are automatically placed in the ring. The rings are ordered by the domain controller's GUID to ensure convergence on a single topology as the KCC runs on all domain controllers. There is an exception to the ring rule. There can never be more than three hops between any two domain controllers within the ring; so if there are 7 or more domain controllers, extra links are added to preserve the three-hop rule.

2. Active Directory does not create the links between sites automatically. You create the site links based on the actual network links in your network environment. After your site links are in place, you assign a cost to each site link. This cost helps the KCC determine which site link to make a primary route between sites. Unlike intra-site replication, inter-site replication does not use a notification process. Inter-site replication can be scheduled by the administrator on a per site link basis. Since there is no notice between replication partners, a domain controller does not know which naming context was updated on the source replication partner. The domain controller has to check all existing naming contexts on the source machine.

    While intra-site replication supports only replication based on Remote Procedure Calls (RPCs), Windows 2000 offers the following two methods for inter-site replication: synchronous (scheduled) using RPC over TCP/IP and asynchronous using Simple Mail Transfer Protocol (SMTP).

3. The Knowledge Consistency Checker (KCC) is a built-in service that runs on all domain controllers and automatically establishes connections between individual computers in the same site. These are known as Windows 2000 Directory Service connection objects. An administrator may establish additional connection objects or remove connection objects. At any point, however, where replication within a site becomes impossible or has a single point of failure, the KCC will step in and establish as many new connection objects as necessary to resume Active Directory replication.

4. Only the changes, which have occurred since the last replication, will replicate.

5.   There can never be more than three hops between any two domain controllers within the ring. If there are 7 or more domain controllers, links are added to protect the three-hop rule.

6.   The KCC, which manages the connection objects for inter and intra-site replication by default, runs every 15 minutes. This can be changed with the registry editor. To start the registry editor: from the Start menu, choose Run and type **REGEDIT.EXE**.

7.   Inter-site replication uses two modes of communication: synchronous (scheduled) using RPC over TCP/IP and asynchronous using Simple Mail Transfer Protocol (SMTP).

8.   As part of inter-site replication, you need to configure the following options:

Site link cost—Active Directory always chooses the connection on a per-cost basis, so cheaper connections are used when they are available. The default is 100. The lower the cost the lower the value, and the corresponding higher priority.

Frequency—The frequency provides a value telling Active Directory how many minutes it should wait before any replication is to occur. The replication interval must be at least 15 minutes and no more that 10,080 minutes (1 week).

Availability—This option defines when the site link is available for replication. Because SMTP is asynchronous, it ignores schedules. You do not need to configure SMTP site links unless one of the following situations occur:

• The site links use scheduled connections
• The SMTP queue is not on a schedule
• Information is being directly exchanged from one server to another

All of these options are defined through the Properties window for the site link you are configuring.

9.   Site link bridges are connectors between two site links. If Bridge All Site Links has been enabled, the site link bridges are redundant. They provide the same function as transitive site links.

10.   Multimaster means a directory partition can have many copies that need to be kept consistent between the domain controllers in the same forest. The replication system propagates any changes made on any specific domain controller to all of the other domain controllers in the forest that store the directory partition in which the change occurs.

Lesson 7 Quiz

These questions test your knowledge of features, vocabulary, procedures and syntax.

1. How can you choose between the two inter-site transports?
   A. You would use SMTP as the replication connector if the network connection is unreliable, or domain controllers have no direct network connection but are connected only through a messaging system.
   B. You would use multiple sites and the RPC-over-IP replication connector if reduced network traffic is desired and the connection between domain controllers is reliable.
   C. The SMTP transport creates more network traffic than the RPC site connector does. Use RPCs between sites whenever possible.
   D. You would use only one site if good network connectivity is available and fast client logon is desired.

2. Replication is complex. Which of the following statements are correct?
   A. The fact that one domain controller uses another as a source for replication information is expressed as a connection object in the Active Directory. These define incoming replication only. Once a connection object has been created, it can be used to replicate information from all naming contexts.
   B. You cannot disable the KCC topology generator and manually create the connection objects required for replication.
   C. Intra-site replication, which is replication between domain controllers in different sites, attempts to complete in the fewest CPU cycles possible.
   D. Attribute changes, such as the lockout of user accounts, a change of domain trust passwords, and some changes in the roles of domain controllers, which are considered security-sensitive, are immediately replicated and intra-site partners are notified.

3. Can you identify the correct statements about the factors that influence replication topology?
   A. You replicate data through automatically or manually created network connections.
   B. Site links influence replication topology.
   C. Replication topology controls how and when replication will occur.
   D. Synchronizing your clocks influences replication topology.

4. To ensure that the Active Directory service in the Windows 2000 operating system can replicate properly, a service known as the KCC runs on all domain controllers and automatically establishes connections between individual computers in the same site. What are these called?
   A. Connection objects
   B. Containers
   C. Hierarchical namespace
   D. Organizational Unit

5.   What tasks need to be completed to configure inter-site replication?
      A.   Create site links
      B.   Create the Replication Snap-in
      C.   Configure site links
      D.   Create site link bridges

6.   When you modify the connection objects, what rules apply?
      A.   Replication frequency does not matter. The system sets its own.
      B.   The KCC will never delete a connection object that has been manually created.
      C.   If you create a connection that is identical to one the KCC would create, it will not delete the connection that you created.
      D.   If the replication within a site fails, the KCC will step in and establish any necessary connections to resume Active Directory replication.

7.   Which of the following statements is not true about inter-site replication?
      A.   Replication traffic is compressed to save bandwidth
      B.   Replication partners poll each other for changes on a specified polling interval, during scheduled periods only.
      C.   One domain controller from each domain in a site is designated by the KCC as a bridgehead server.
      D.   Replication uses the remote procedure call (RPC) transport.

8.   Which of the following are advantages that multimaster replication has over single master replications?
      A.   In multimaster replication, if one domain controller becomes unavailable, the other domain controllers can continue to update the directory. In single-master replication, if the primary domain controller becomes inoperable, directory updates cannot take place.
      B.   Servers that are capable of making changes to the directory, which in Windows 2000 are domain controllers, can be distributed across the network and can be located in multiple physical sites.
      C.   Multimaster replication is designed to reduce communication over slow WAN links. An update replicates first to nearby replicas and from there to replicas that are farther away.
      D.   In single-master replication, a destination replica requests information from a source replica.

9.   Which of the following describes site links?
      A.   In a fully routed IP network, you do not need to configure any site link bridges
      B.   The KCC must run on the topology-generating systems.
      C.   All site links for a specific transport implicitly belong to a single site link bridge for that transport.
      D.   By default, all site links that you create are bridged.

10. What role do sites have in replication?
    A. The replicas of the directory on each domain controller are writeable.
    B. Version comparisons of copies of the files to ensure they contain the same data.
    C. When you create a site link, you provide Active Directory with information about what connections are available, which ones are preferred, and how much bandwidth is available.
    D. The replication service automatically copies the changes from a given replica to all other replicas.

Answers to Lesson 7 Quiz

1. Answer A is correct. The SMTP replication connector is used for inter-site transport if the network connection is unreliable or the domain controllers have no messaging system.

    Answer C is correct. You would use RPC connectors as often as possible for inter-site transport as SMTP connectors create more network traffic.

    Answer D is correct. To have the fastest connectivity, use one site.

    Answer B is incorrect. It is a replication recommendation.

2. Answer A is correct. When one domain controller uses another for incoming replication information, that process is expressed as a connection object.

    Answer D is correct. Specific attribute changes that are security-sensitive are replicated immediately.

    Answer B is incorrect. You can disable the KCC topology generator and manually create the connection objects required for replication.

    Answer C is incorrect. Intra-site replication, which is replication between domain controllers in the same site, attempts to complete in the fewest CPU cycles possible.

3. Answer B is correct. Creating a site link between two or more sites is a way to influence replication topology. By creating a site link, you provide Active Directory with information about what connections are available, which ones are preferred and how much bandwidth is available. Active Directory uses this information to choose times and connections for replication that will afford the best performance.

    Answer A is incorrect. You do not replicate through network connections.

    Answer C is incorrect. Replication topology does not control replication.

    Answer D is incorrect. Clock synchronization does not influence replication topology.

4. Answer A is correct. A connection object uses the actual network connections to exchange directory information. Active Directory uses site links as indicators for where it should create connection objects. Without site links, connection objects that use network connections to connect sites will not be created, and domain controllers will be isolated within their sites.

    Answer B is incorrect. A container is like other directory objects in that it has attributes and is part of the Active Directory namespace. However, unlike other objects, it does not usually represent something concrete. It is the container for a group of objects and other containers.

    Answer C is incorrect. A hierarchical namespace, such as the DNS namespace and the Active Directory namespace, are hierarchically structured.

    Answer D is incorrect. An Organizational Unit (OU) is a container object that is an Active Directory administrative partition. OUs can contain users, groups, resources and other OUs.

5. Answers A, C and D are correct. The three tasks you must complete are: create site links, configure site links (site link cost, replication frequency and replication availability) and create site link bridges.

    Answer B is incorrect. There is no snap-in called the Replication snap-in.

6. Answers B, C and D are correct. When you modify the connection objects, the following rules apply:

    • The KCC will never delete a connection object that has been manually created
    • If you create a connection that is identical to one the KCC would create, it will not delete the connection that you created
    • If the replication within a site fails, the KCC will step in and establish any necessary connections to resume Active Directory replication

    Answer A is incorrect. Replication frequency is the duration between replications on a site link and does not apply.

7. Answers A, B and C are correct. They are all true statements about inter-site replication.

    Answer D is incorrect. Intra-site replication uses the Remote Procedure Call (RPC) transport.

8.   Answers A and B are correct. Both are advantages of multimaster over single master replication.

      Answer C is incorrect. Store-and-Forward Replication is designed to reduce communication over slow WAN links. An update replicates first to nearby replicas and from there to replicas that are farther away.

      Answer D is incorrect. In pull replication, a destination replica requests information from a source replica.

9.   Answers A, C and D are correct. By default, all site links that you create are bridged. All site links for a specific transport implicitly belong to a single site link bridge for that transport. In a fully routed IP network, you do not need to configure any site link bridges.

      Answer B is incorrect. The statement that the KCC must run on the topology-generating systems is true about replication paths.

10.   Answer C is correct. When you create a site link, you provide Active Directory with information about what connections are available, which ones are preferred, and how much bandwidth is available.

      Answer A and D are incorrect. Version comparisons of copies of the files to ensure they contain the same data and the replication service automatically copies the changes from a given replica to all other replicas, are part of the definitions of replication.

      Answer B is incorrect. Version comparisons of copies of the files to ensure they contain the same data, is a definition of synchronization.

Management of Operations Masters

In Windows 2000, all domain controllers are considered the same, because Active Directory uses a multiple-master domain model. However, some services cannot function in a multiple master environment. This means changes cannot take place on more than one domain controller at a time. Some domain controllers assume a single-master operations function and are known as operations masters. The single-master domain model is one of the four methods in Windows New Technologies (NT) used to group domains for administrative purposes. A single-master domain model groups user accounts and groups into one domain.

Of the five operations master functions, known as roles, three exist domain wide and two are unique forest wide. For example, if there were 10 domains in your forest, there would be 32 single operations master roles—ten lots of three domains; two forest wide. The domain controllers assigned these roles perform single-master replication.

After completing this lesson, you should have a better understanding of the following topics:

• Operations Masters Management

• Operations Master Role Transfers

Operations Masters Management

Active Directory supports multimaster replication of the Active Directory database between all domain controllers in the domain. Some changes are impractical to perform in multimaster fashion, however, so only one domain controller, called the operations master, accepts requests for such changes. For single-master operations to be performed (Figure 8.1), they are assigned to domain controllers called operations masters.

Figure 8.1 Single Master Domain Model

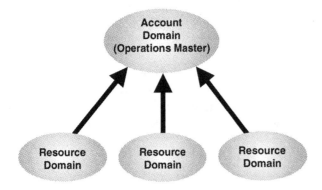

Because the operations master roles can be moved to other domain controllers within the domain or forest, these roles are sometimes referred to as Flexible Single Master Operations (FSMO). In any Active Directory forest, at least five different operations master roles are assigned to the initial domain controller during installation.

In a small Active Directory forest with only one domain and one domain controller, that domain controller will own all of the operations master roles. When you create the first domain in a new forest, all of the single master operations roles are automatically assigned to the first domain controller in that domain.

When you create a new child domain or the root domain of a new domain tree in an existing forest, the first domain controller in the new domain is automatically assigned the following roles:

- Relative IDentifier (RID) master

- Primary Domain Controller (PDC) emulator

- Infrastructure master

Because there can be only one schema master and one domain naming master in the forest, these roles remain in the first domain created in the forest. In a larger network, whether with one or multiple domains, you can re-assign these roles to one or more of the other domain controllers. Some roles must appear in every forest. Other roles must appear in every domain in the forest. By default, as domain controllers are added, the operations master roles are dispersed throughout the forest. Figure 8.2 shows this distribution. In Figure 8.2, Domain A was the first created in the forest and is also known as the forest root domain. It holds both of the forest-wide operations master roles. The first domain controller in each of the other domains is assigned the three domain-specific roles.

Figure 8.2 Operations Master Roles Distribution

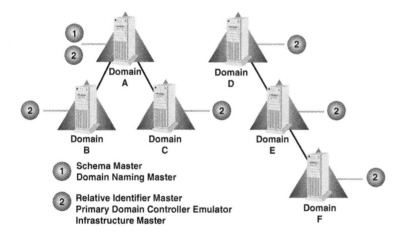

These default operations master locations work for a forest that contains only a few domain controllers in a single site. If you have a forest containing more domain controllers, or a forest that spans multiple sites, you can transfer the default operations master role assignments to other domain controllers in the domain or forest.

The following three domain-wide operations master roles must be unique in each domain. This means there can be only one in each domain in the forest:

RID master—The RID master distributes sequences of RIDs to each domain controller in its domain. Each time a domain controller creates a user, group or computer object, it assigns the object an exclusive Security ID (SID) that the system uses to uniquely identify that object for security permissions and authentication issues. This is similar to the Globally Unique Identifier (GUID) that every object has, but the SID is given only to security-enabled objects and is used only for security authentication and verification purposes.

In a domain, the SIDs must be unique. So that duplicate SIDs cannot be created, the RID master maintains a pool of unique RID values. When a domain controller is added to the network, it is given a number of values from the RID pool for its own use. When a domain controller needs a SID, it takes one from its own RID pool to create a SID with a unique value.

To move an object between domains (using MOVETREE.EXE), you must initiate the move on the domain controller acting as the RID master of the domain that currently contains the object. At any time, there can be only one domain controller acting as the RID master in each domain in the forest.

PDC emulator—The PDC emulator is available for backwards compatibility purposes. One Windows 2000 domain controller acts as a Windows NT PDC. The PDC emulator manages password changes from clients and replicates updates to the Backup Domain Controller (BDC). In Windows 2000 domains operating in native mode, the PDC emulator gets preferential replication of password changes done by other domain controllers in the domain.

If a logon authentication fails at another domain controller because of a bad password, that domain controller forwards the authentication request to the PDC emulator before rejecting the logon attempt. At any time, there can be only one domain controller acting as the PDC emulator in each domain in the forest.

Infrastructure master—The infrastructure master updates all inter-domain references any time an object referenced by another object moves. For example, whenever the members of groups are renamed or changed, the infrastructure master updates the group-to-user references. When you rename or move a member of a group, and that member resides in a different domain from the group, that member may temporarily appear not to be in the group. The infrastructure master of the group's domain is responsible for updating the group so that it knows the new name or location of the member. The infrastructure master distributes the update via multimaster replication.

Unless there is only one domain controller in the domain, you do not assign the infrastructure master role to the domain controller hosting the global catalog. In this situation, the infrastructure master will not function. If all domain controllers in a domain also host the global catalog, including a domain where only one domain controller exists, all domain controllers will have current data and the infrastructure master role is not needed. At any time, there can be only one domain controller acting as the infrastructure master in each domain.

The following two forest-wide operations master roles must be unique in the forest. There can be only one of each throughout the entire forest:

Schema master—The schema master domain controller manages all updates and modifications to the schema. The schema defines each object and its attributes that can be stored in the directory. To update the schema of a forest, you must have access to the schema master. At any time, there can be only one schema master in the entire forest.

Domain naming master—The domain controller holding the domain naming master role controls the addition or removal of domains in the forest. There can be only one domain naming master in the entire forest at any time.

Managing Operations Masters

In an average domain, you assign both the RID master and PDC emulator roles to the same operations master domain controller. In a very large domain, you can reduce the peak load on the PDC emulator master by placing these roles on separate domain controllers, both of which are direct replication partners of the standby operations master domain controller. Generally, you keep the two roles together unless the load on the operations master domain controller justifies separating the roles.

You assign the infrastructure master role to any domain controller in the domain that is not a global catalog host, but is well connected to a global catalog in the same site. If the operations master domain controller meets these requirements, use these criteria unless the load justifies the extra management burden of separating the roles.

Once you have planned all of the domain roles for each domain, you need to consider the forest roles. The schema master and the domain naming master roles should always be assigned to the same domain controller. For best performance, assign them to a domain controller that is well connected to the computers used by the administrator or group responsible for schema updates and the creation of new domains. The load of these operations master roles is very light, so, to simplify management, place these roles on the operations master domain controller of one of the domains in the forest.

To identify the RID master, PDC emulator or infrastructure master roles assignment, follow these steps:

1. From the **Start** menu, choose **Programs, Administrative Tools** and then select **Active Directory Users and Computers**.

2. Right-click **Active Directory Users and Computers** and then choose **Operations Masters**, as in Figure 8.3.

Figure 8.3 Select Operations Master

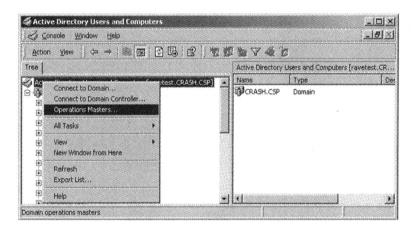

3. From **Operations Master**, choose **RID Pool,** and from **Operations Master**, the name of the RID master will be displayed (Figure 8.4).

Figure 8.4 Operations RID Pool

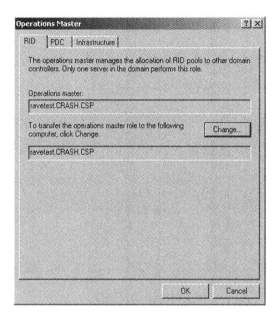

4. Choose **PDC** and, from **Operations Master,** the name of the PDC master will be displayed (Figure 8.5).

Figure 8.5 Operations PDC

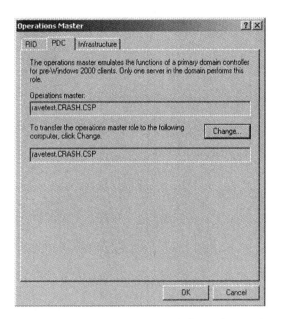

5. Choose **Infrastructure** and, from **Operations Master**, the name of the Infrastructure master will be displayed (Figure 8.6).

Figure 8.6 Operations Infrastructure

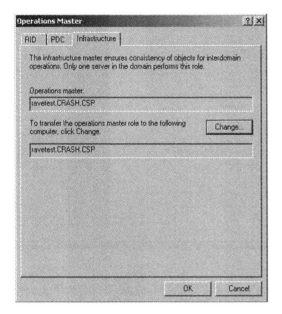

6. Choose **Cancel** to close **Operations Master**.

To identify the domain naming master, follow these steps:

1. From the **Start** menu, choose **Programs, Administrative Tools** and then select **Active Directory Domains and Trusts**.

2. Right-click **Active Directory Domains and Trusts** and then choose **Operations Master**.

3. From **Change Operations Master**, the name of the current domain naming master will be displayed as in Figure 8.7.

Figure 8.7 Operations Domain Naming

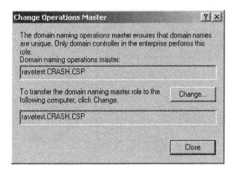

4. Choose **Close** to close **Change Operations Master**.

To identify the schema master, follow these steps:

 Note: The Active Directory Schema snap-in must be installed with the Windows 2000 Administration Tools using Add/Remove programs.

1. From the **Start menu**, choose **Run**.

2. Type **MMC**, and then click **OK**.

3. From the menu bar, choose **Console**, and then select **Add/Remove Snap-In**.

4. Choose **Add**, select **Active Directory Schema** from the list of snap-ins, choose **Add**, **Close**, and then click **OK**.

5. From the console tree, right-click **Active Directory Schema** and choose **Operations Master**.

6. Within Change Schema Master, the name of the current schema master is displayed (Figure 8.8).

Figure 8.8 Schema Master

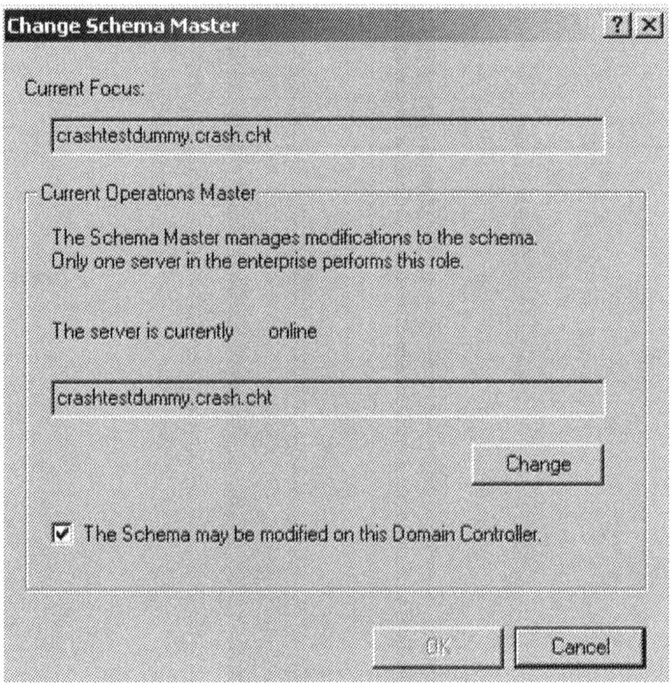

```
Change Schema Master                          ? X

 Current Focus:

  crashtestdummy.crash.cht

 ┌─ Current Operations Master ──────────────────────┐
 │                                                   │
 │  The Schema Master manages modifications to the schema.
 │  Only one server in the enterprise performs this role.
 │                                                   │
 │                                                   │
 │  The server is currently    online               │
 │                                                   │
 │  crashtestdummy.crash.cht                         │
 │                                                   │
 │                                    ┌─────────┐    │
 │                                    │ Change  │    │
 │                                    └─────────┘    │
 │                                                   │
 │  ☑ The Schema may be modified on this Domain Controller.
 └───────────────────────────────────────────────────┘

                        ┌────────┐   ┌────────┐
                        │  OK    │   │ Cancel │
                        └────────┘   └────────┘
```

7. Choose **Cancel** to close the window.

Operations Master Role Transfers

The first domain controller installed in a domain is automatically assigned all the operations master roles. You can change the assignment of operations master roles after setup, but in most cases, this will not be necessary. You will need to be particularly aware of operations master roles if problems develop on an operations master or if you plan to take one out of service. To transfer an operations master role means moving it from one domain controller to another, with the cooperation of the original role holder. Depending upon the operations master role to be transferred, you perform the role transfer using one of the three Active Directory snap-ins, as in Table 8.1.

Table 8.1 Operations Masters and Snap-In Used for Transfer

Role	Snap-in
Schema master	Active Directory Schema
Domain naming master	Active Directory Domains and Trusts
Relative identifier master	Active Directory Users and Computers
PDC emulator	Active Directory Users and Computers
Infrastructure master	Active Directory Users and Computers

You can also use the NTDSUTIL.EXE utility to transfer the operations master roles.

1. From the **Start** menu, choose **Run**, type **cmd** and press the **Enter** key.

2. At the **C:\>** type **ntdsutil.**

3. At **ntdsutil**: type **roles.**

4. At **fsmo maintenance**: type **connections.**

5. At **server connections**: type **connect to server <server name>.**

6. At **server connections**: type **quit.**

7. At **fsmo maintenance**: type **transfer rid master or transfer PDC or transfer infrastruture master or transfer domain naming master or transfer schema master.**

8. Choose **Yes** to the role transfer.

The transfer settings will then be displayed, when complete.

9. At **fsmo maintenance**:type **quit.**

10. At **ntdsutil**: type **quit.**

To use the Windows 2000 Active Directory Users and Computers to transfer the RID operations master, the PDC operations master and the Infrastructure operations master, follow these steps:

1. From the **Start** menu, choose **Programs**, **Administrative Tools** and then select **Active Directory Users and Computers**.

2. Right-click the domain that will become the new RID master, PDC emulator or infrastructure master and then choose **Connect to Domain.**

3. From **Connect To Domain**, type the domain name or choose **Browse** to specify the domain from a list, as in Figure 8.9, and then select **OK**.

Figure 8.9 Change Domain Controller

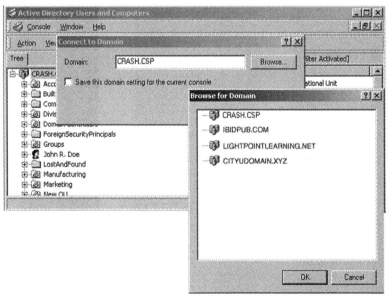

4. Right-click **Active Directory Users and Computers** and then choose **Operations Master**, as in Figure 8.10.

Figure 8.10 Select Operations Master

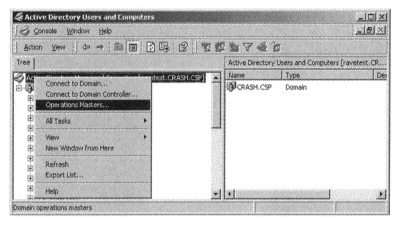

5. From the **RID** property page, choose **Change**. (Figure 8.11).

Figure 8.11 Operations RID Pool

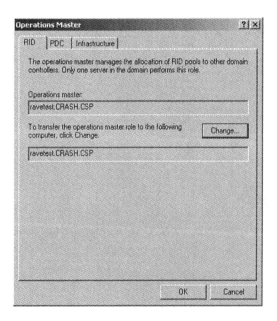

6. Choose **PDC** and then select **Change** (Figure 8.12).

Figure 8.12 Operations PDC

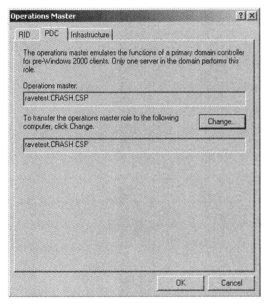

7. Choose **Infrastructure** then select **Change** (Figure 8.13).

Figure 8.13 Operations Infrastructure

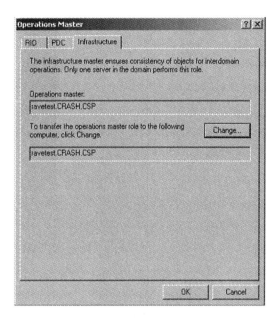

8. Click **OK** to close **Operations Master**.

To transfer the domain naming master, follow these steps:

1. From the **Start** menu, choose **Programs, Administrative Tools** and then select **Active Directory Domains and Trusts**.

2. Right-click the domain controller that will become the new domain naming master and then choose **Connect to Domain Controller**.

3. From Connect to Domain Controller (Figure 8.14), select the computer that will serve as the new Schema Operations Master, or select **Any Writable Domain Controller** to let Active Directory select the new Schema Operations Master, and then click **OK**.

Figure 8.14 Change Domain Controller

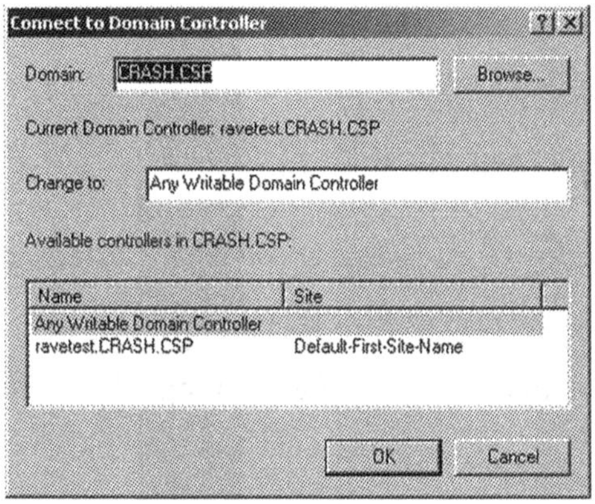

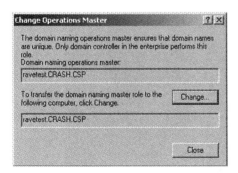

4. Right-click **Active Directory Domains and Trusts** and then choose **Operations Master**.

5. From **Change Operations Master,** choose **Change**, as in Figure 8.15.

Figure 8.15 Change Operations Master

6. Click **Done** to close **Change Operations Master**.

To transfer the schema master, follow these steps:

1. From the **Start menu**, choose **Run**.

2. Type **MMC**, and then click **OK**.

3. From the menu bar, choose **Console**, and then select **Add/Remove Snap-In**.

4. Choose Add, select **Active Directory Schema** from the list of snap-ins, choose **Add, Close,** and then click **OK**.

5. From the console tree, right-click **Active Directory Schema** and choose **Change Domain Controller**.

6. From Change Domain Controller, choose one of the following: **Any DC** to let Active Directory select the new Schema Operations Master, or **Specify Name** and type the name of the new Schema Operations Master (Figure 8.16).

Figure 8.16 Change Domain Controller

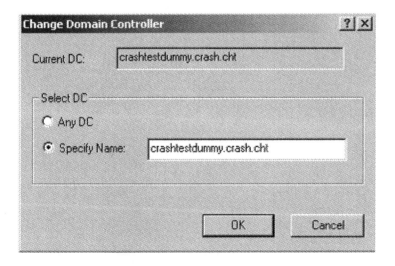

7. **Click** OK.

8. From the console tree, right-click **Active Directory Schema** and choose **Operations Master**.

9. From **Change Schema Master**, choose **Change** (Figure 8.17).

Figure 8.17 Change Operations Master Schema

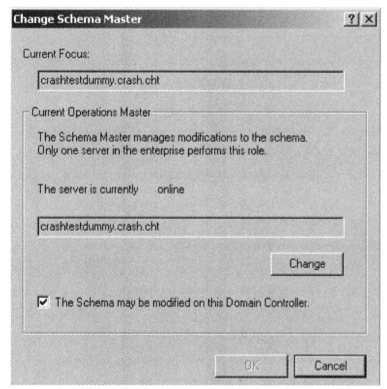

You can also set the registry to allow changes to the Schema by checking the Schema modification box. Also notice if the selected computer is already the schema master.

10. Click **OK** to close the Change Operations Master window.

Vocabulary

Review the following terms in preparation for the certification exam.

Term	Description
BDC	A Backup Domain Controller is a computer running Windows NT Server that receives a copy of the domain's directory database in a Microsoft Windows NT Server domain.
directory	A directory is an online storage location that contains objects that may have various kinds of structures and are related to one another in some way.
domain	In Active Directory, a domain is a boundary for security and administrative purposes. Active Directory data is replicated between domain controllers within a domain.
domain controllers	In a Windows 2000 domain, a domain controller is a computer running Windows 2000 Server that authenticates domain logons and maintains the security policy and the master database for a domain
Domain Naming Master	The Domain Naming Master tracks objects throughout a forest to ensure that they are unique. It also tracks cross references to objects in other directories. There is one per forest.
forests	A group of one or more trees that trust each other. All trees in a forest share a common schema, configuration and global catalog. When a forest contains multiple trees, the trees do not form a contiguous namespace. All the trees in a forest trust each other through transitive bi-directional trust relationships.
FSMO	The Flexible Single Master Operation designates a server that performs one of the following roles: PDC Master, Infrastructure Manager, RID Manager, Schema Manager or Domain Naming Master.
GC	The Global Catalog is built automatically by the Active Directory replication system. The GC contains a partial replica of every Windows 2000 domain in the directory. When given one or more attributes of the target object, the GC enables users and applications to find objects quickly, without knowing what domain the objects occupy. The attributes in the global catalog are those used most frequently in search operations plus those required to locate a full replica of the object.

Term	Description
Infrastructure Master	The Infrastructure Master tracks the object references among domains and maintains a list of the deleted child objects. There is one infrastructure master per domain.
multimaster replication	With multimaster replication, any domain controller accepts and replicates directory changes to any other domain controller. This differs from other replication models in which the computer stores the single modifiable copy of the directory and other computers store backup copies.
Multiple Master Domain Model	A domain model in which there are multiple master user domains and an administrative hierarchy.
NTDSUTIL.EXE	A command line tool for database and FSMO management and is available in the Windows 2000 Resource Kit.
one-way trust	This is a trust relationship where only one of the two domains trusts the other domain. All one-way trusts are non-transitive.
operations master role	The operations masters are domain controllers that have been assigned one or more special roles in an Active Directory domain. The domain controllers assigned these roles perform operations that are single master (not permitted to occur at different places on the network at the same time). The domain controller that controls the particular operation owns the operations master role for that operation. The ownership of these operations master roles can be transferred to other domain controllers.
PDC	A Primary Domain Controller is a computer running Windows NT server that authenticates domain logons and maintains the directory database for a domain in a Microsoft Windows NT Server domain.
PDC Emulator	The Primary Domain Controller Emulator is the first Windows 2000 domain controller created in a domain. Besides replicating domain data to the other Windows 2000 domain controllers, it emulates a primary domain controller for backward compatibility with Windows NT. There is one per domain.

Term	Description
polling	Polling checks for changes in each directory defined in the connection agreement.
RID	The Relative Identifier is part of a security identifier (SID) that identifies an account or group. RIDs are unique to the domain in which an account or group is created.
RID Operations Master	The Relative Identifier Master tracks the assignment of SIDs throughout the domain. There is one per domain.
root domain	The first domain created in Active Directory is the starting point, or root, of the Active Directory. All other domains derive from this initial domain. Only one name can be used for the root domain.
Schema	A schema is a description of the object classes and attributes stored in Active Directory. For each object class, the schema defines what attributes an object class must have, what additional attributes it may have, and what object class can be its parent.
schema master	The schema master is a domain controller assigned to control all updates to the schema within a forest. At any time, there can be only one schema master in the forest.
SID	Security Identifiers are unique, alphanumeric structures for security principles. There is a SID for each user, group or computer. The first part of the SID identifies the domain in which the SID was issued. The second part identifies an account object within the issuing domain—that is, the relative identifier (RID). SIDs are never reused. SIDS are only used by the system and are transparent to the user.
single master domain model	A single master domain model is one of the four methods in Windows NT that you use to group domains for administrative purposes. User accounts and groups are in one domain, known as the account domain. The printers and servers are in resource domains. A one-way trust relationship lets users access the resources in all the account domains.
snap-in	A snap-in is a type of tool you can add to a console supported by Microsoft Management Console (MMC). A stand-alone snap-in can be added by itself, while an extension snap-in can be added to extend the function of another snap-in.

In Brief

If you want to...	Then do this...
Identify the RID master, PDC emulator or the infrastructure master roles assignment	1. From the **Start** menu, choose **Programs**, **Administrative Tools** and then select **Active Directory Users and Computers**.
	2. Right-click **Active Directory Users and Computers** and then choose **Operations Master**.
	3. From **Operations Master**, choose **RID** and the name of the RID master will be displayed.
	4. Choose **PDC** from **Operations Master** and the name of the PDC master will be displayed.
	5. Choose **Infrastructure** from **Operations Master** and the name of the Infrastructure master will be displayed.
	6. Choose **Cancel** to close **Operations Master**.
Identify the domain naming master	1. From the **Start** menu, choose **Programs**, **Administrative Tools** and then **Active Directory Domains and Trusts**.
	2. Right-click **Active Directory Domains and Trusts** and then choose **Operations Master**.
	3. From **Change Operations Master** the name of the current domain naming master will be displayed.
	4. Choose **Close** to close **Change Operations Master**.

If you want to...	Then do this...
Identify the schema master	1. From the **Start** menu, choose **Run** and type **MMC**. 2. From the menu bar of the empty MMC console, choose **Console**, and then select **Add/Remove Snap-in**. 3. Select **Add**, and then choose **Active Directory Schema**. 4. Choose **Close**, and then click **OK**. 5. Right-click **Active Directory Schema** and then choose **Operations Master**. 6. From **Change Operations Master**, the name of the current schema master will be displayed. 7. Choose **Close** to close **Change Operations Master**.
Transfer the RID operations master, the PDC operations master and the infrastructure operations master	1. From the **Start** menu, choose **Programs**, **Administrative Tools** and then select **Active Directory Users and Computers**. 2. Right-click the domain that will become the new RID master, PDC emulator or infrastructure master. Choose **Connect to Domain.** 3. From **Connect To Domain**, type the domain name or choose **Browse** to specify the domain from a list and then select **OK**. 4. Right-click **Active Directory Users and Computers** and then choose **Operations Master**. 5. Choose **RID** and then select **Change**. 6. Choose **PDC** and then select **Change**. 7. Choose **Infrastructure** and then select **Change**. 8. Click **OK** to close **Operations Master**.

If you want to...	Then do this...
Transfer the domain naming master	1. From the **Start** menu, choose **Programs**, **Administrative Tools** and then select **Active Directory Domains and Trusts**.
	2. Right-click the domain controller that will become the new domain naming master and then choose **Connect to Domain**.
	3. From **Connect to Domain**, type the domain name or choose **Browse** to specify the domain from a list, and then select **OK**.
	4. Right-click **Active Directory Domains and Trusts** and then choose **Operations Master**.
	5. From **Change Operations Master** choose **Change**.
	6. Click **OK** to close **Change Operations Master**.
Transfer the schema master	1. From the **Start** menu, choose **Run** and type **MMC**.
	2. From the menu bar of the empty MMC console, choose **Console**, and then select **Add/Remove Snap-in**.
	3. Select **Add**, and then choose **Active Directory Schema**.
	4. Choose **Close**, and then click **OK**.
	5. Right-click **Active Directory Schema** and then choose **Change Domain Controller**.
	6. From **Change Domain Controller**, choose one of the following: **Any DC** to let Active Directory select the new Schema Operations Master, or **Specify Name** and type the **Name** of the new Schema Operations Master.
	7. Choose **OK**.
	8. Right-click **Active Directory Schema** and then choose **Operations Master**.
	9. From **Change Schema Master**, choose **Change**.
	10. Click **OK** to close **Change Operations Master**.

Lesson 8 Activities

Complete the following activities to prepare for the certification exam.

1.   Describe the Schema Master role.

2.   Describe the Domain Naming Master role.

3.   Describe the Relative ID Master role.

4.   Describe the PDC Emulator role.

5.   Describe the Infrastructure Master role.

6.   Define an Operations Master.

7.   Explain what a single master domain model is.

8.   Explain how the RID operations master handles SIDs.

9.   Describe how you change the RID master FSMO.

10.   Describe the tools used to transfer the Operations Masters.

Answers to Lesson 8 Activities

1. The Schema Master maintains the master copy of the schema. There is one per forest.

2. The Domain Naming Master tracks object names throughout the forest to ensure they are unique. It also tracks the cross references to objects in other directories. There is one per forest.

3. The RID Master tracks the assignments of SIDs throughout the domain. There is one per domain.

4. The PDC Emulator, emulates a primary domain controller for backwards compatibility with Windows NT. There is one per domain.

5. The Infrastructure Master tracks the object references among domains and maintains a list of deleted child objects. There is one per domain.

6. An Operations Master is a domain controller that has been assigned one or more special roles in an Active Directory domain. The domain controllers assigned these roles perform operations that are single master (not permitted to occur at different places on the network at the same time). The domain controller that controls the particular operation owns the operations master role for that operation. The ownership of these operations master roles can be transferred to other domain controllers.

7. A single master domain model is one of the four methods in Windows NT that you use to group domains for administrative purposes. User accounts and groups are in one domain, known as the account domain. The printers and servers are in resource domains. A one-way trust relationship lets users access the resources in all the account domains.

8. Each time a domain controller creates a user, group or computer object, it assigns the object an exclusive Security ID (SID) that the system uses to uniquely identify that object for security permissions and authentication issues. This is similar to the Globally Unique Identifier (GUID) that every object has, but the SID is given only to security-enabled objects and is used only for security authentication and verification purposes. In a domain, the SIDs must be unique. So that duplicate SIDs cannot be created, the RID master maintains a pool of unique RID values. When a domain controller is added to the network, it is given a number of values from the RID pool for its own use. When a domain controller needs a SID, it takes one from its own RID pool to create a SID with a unique value.

9.   To modify the role you use the Active Directory Users and Computers MMC snap-in on the Domain Controller.

In the left hand pane right-click on the domain and select **Connect to Domain Controller**.

1. Select the domain controller you wish to make the FSMO role owner and choose **OK**.

2. Right click on the domain again, select **Operations Masters** from the context menu and select **RID Pool**.

3. The current machine holding the RID master FSMO role is displayed.

4. To change it, choose **Change**.

You can also do this using the NTDSUTIL.EXE utility.

10.   For the schema master, you use the Active Directory Schema.
For the domain naming master, you use the Active Directory Domains and Trusts.
For the relative identifier master, PDC emulator and infrastructure master, you use the Active Directory Users and Computers snap-ins.
You can also use the NTDSUTIL.EXE to transfer the roles from the command line.

Lesson 8 Quiz

These questions test your knowledge of features, vocabulary, procedures, and syntax.

1. Which operations master roles are forest wide?
   A. Schema master, domain naming master, RID master, PDC emulator and infrastructure manager
   B. RID master, PDC emulator, infrastructure manager
   C. Schema master, domain naming master
   D. RID master, domain naming master

2. You have a small forest with one domain and one domain controller. Which of the operations masters are on that controller?
   A. All of the operations masters
   B. Only the forest wide operations masters
   C. Only the domain wide operations masters
   D. Only the schema master

3. You create a new child domain in your existing forest. What roles are automatically assigned to the first domain controller in the new domain?
   A. The schema master and the domain naming master
   B. The RID master, the PDC emulator, infrastructure master
   C. The domain wide operations masters
   D. The forest wide operations masters

4. The schema master controls all updates and modifications to the schema. How do you access it?
   A. From the Active Directory Schema snap-in; however it is not available by default and must be installed.
   B. You cannot modify the schema master.
   C. You use Active Directory Users and Computers.
   D. You create a custom MMC and add the Active Directory Schema snap-in to it.

5. You are unsure which of your domain controllers has the PDC emulator master role assignment. What do you do to find out where it is?
   A. Open the Active Directory Schema snap-in, right-click Active Directory Schema and choose Operations Masters.
   B. You open the Active directory Users and Computers, choose Operations Masters, and then select PDC.
   C. From the Start menu, choose Run and enter MMC. Choose OK. From the Console menu choose add remove snap-in.
   D. You open the Sites and Services, choose PDC and then select display.

6.   Why would you transfer an operations master?
      A.   You can change the assignment of operations master roles after setup, but in most
            cases, this will not be necessary.
      B.   If problems develop on an operations master.
      C.   You plan to take the controller that contains one out of service.
      D.   To make system administration easier.

7.   You are planning a forest for a large organization, what do you need to take into
      consideration for the operations master roles?
      A.   Assign the infrastructure master role to the domain controller hosting the global
            catalog.
      B.   The schema master and the domain naming master roles should always be
            assigned to the same domain controller.
      C.   You assign both the RID master and PDC emulator roles to the same operations
            master domain controller.
      D.   You can assign the operations master roles to any domain controller that you
            want.

8.   Which of the following describes the PDC Emulator?
      A.   As any domain controller, it can validate an NT 4.0 client logon.
      B.   It handles password changes for Windows NT 4.0 clients and to Windows NT
            Backup Domain Controllers (BDC).
      C.   If logon is rejected by a domain controller, the login is then passed to it to make
            certain the user's password hasn't changed.
      D.   It looks after inter-domain references any time an object referenced by another
            object moves.

9.   You have a forest with 14 domains. How many operations masters will you have?
      A.   14 lots of 3, plus 2
      B.   14 lots of 5
      C.   30
      D.   44

10.   Which of the following statements describe the infrastructure master?
      A.   It is responsible for updating all inter-domain references any time an object
            referenced by another object moves.
      B.   In a domain, it is responsible for updating the group so that it knows the new
            name or location of the member.
      C.   It distributes the updates using multimaster replication.
      D.   If all domain controllers in a domain also host the global catalog, all domain
            controllers have current data and therefore it is not needed.

Answers to Lesson 8 Quiz

1.   Answer C is correct. The schema master and the domain naming master are the two that are forest wide.

      Answer A is incorrect. It is a list of all the operations masters.

      Answer B is incorrect. It is a list of the domain wide operations master roles.

      Answer D is incorrect. The RID master is a domain wide role and the domain naming master is a forest wide operations master role.

2.   Answer A is correct. When you create the first domain in a new forest, all of the operations master roles are automatically assigned to the first domain controller in that domain.

      Answers B and C are incorrect. As there is only the one domain controller in the forest, by default it will contain all of the operations masters.

      Answer D is incorrect.

3.   Answers B and C are correct. When you create a new child domain, the domain wide operations masters, RID master, PDC emulator and infrastructure manager are automatically assigned to the new domain controller.

      Answers A and D are incorrect. The Schema master and the domain naming master are forest wide roles and they only occur in one domain controller in a forest by default.

4.   Answers A and D are correct. Access is through the Active Directory Schema snap-in, however it is not available by default and must be installed. You create a custom MMC and add the Active Directory Schema snap-in to it.

      Answer B is incorrect. The schema master can be modified.

      Answer C is incorrect. However, Active Directory Users and Computers can be used to transfer the RID master, PDC emulator and infrastructure managers.

5.   Answer B is correct. You Open the Active directory Users and Computers, select Operations Masters, and then choose PDC. The name of the PDC emulator is displayed.

      Answer A is incorrect. The procedure identifies the schema master.

      Answer C is incorrect. The procedure described adds or removes an extension from a snap-in.

      Answer D is incorrect. The procedure is made up.

6.   Answers A, B and C are correct. You will need to be particularly aware of operations masters roles if problems develop on an operations master or if you plan to take one out of service. To transfer an operations master role means moving it from one domain controller to another, with the cooperation of the original role holder.

      Answer D is incorrect. You can change the assignment of operations master roles after setup, but in most cases, this will not be necessary.

7.   Answer B is correct. The schema master and the domain naming master roles should always be assigned to the same domain controller.

      Answer C is partly correct. In an average domain, you assign both the RID master and PDC emulator roles to the same operations master domain controller. In a very large domain, you can reduce the peak load on the PDC emulator master by placing these roles on separate domain controllers.

      Answer A is incorrect. Unless there is only one domain controller in the domain, you do not assign the infrastructure master role to the domain controller hosting the global catalog.

      Answer D is incorrect. All of the above must be taken into consideration.

8.   Answers A, B and C are correct. As any domain controller can validate an NT 4.0 client logon. The PDC emulator handles password changes for Windows NT 4.0 clients and Windows NT BDCs. If a logon is rejected by a domain controller, the login is then passed to the PDC Emulator to make certain the user's password hasn't changed.

      Answer D is incorrect. The infrastructure manager looks after inter-domain references any time an object referenced by another object moves.

9.   Answers A and D are correct. There are 14 domains with 3 domain-wide operations master roles plus two forest-wide operations master roles for a total of 44 operations masters.

      Answers B and C are incorrect. They are incorrect totals.

10.   Answers A, B, C and D are correct. The infrastructure master is responsible for updating all inter-domain references any time an object referenced by another object moves. When you rename or move a member of a group, the infrastructure master of the group's domain is responsible for updating the group so that it knows the new name or location of the member. The infrastructure master distributes the update using multimaster replication. If all domain controllers in a domain also host the global catalog (including the situation where only one domain controller exists), all domain controllers have current data and therefore the infrastructure master role is not needed.

Lesson 9

Active Directory Database Management

The directory in Active Directory is composed of specialized databases that help administrators organize and manage everything on their network and help end users find these network resources. The Active Directory database is dynamic and flexible and requires management. Windows 2000 has a variety of tools available to aid administrators in Active Directory database management.

After completing this lesson, you should have a better understanding of the following topics:

- Active Directory Database Management

- Active Directory Database Backups

- Active Directory Database Management Restoration

- System Failure Recovery

Active Directory Database Management

Active Directory's database engine is called the Extensible Storage Engine (ESE). The following primary files make up the Active Directory Database:

- NTDS.DIT (the database file)

- Log files (sequential records of each change to the database)

Because Active Directory is a distributed database, the ESE enables the database to grow to 16 terabytes. Theoretically, a 16-terabyte database can hold more than 10 million objects.

Important to maintaining your Active Directory database are the following functions:

- Recognizing the components of the Active Directory and where they are stored on your system

- Garbage collection—or automatic database cleanup

- Defragmenting the database

- Backing up and restoring the database

Maintaining an Active Directory Database

The Active Directory database's NTDS.DIT file is also called the data store. Only the Microsoft Jet Database Engine can manipulate information inside the data store. However, you can administer the NTDS.DIT using NTDSUTIL, a command-line tool for database management. With the NTDSUTIL utility, you can take the NTDS.DIT file off-line for replacement if it has become corrupted.

There are two NTDS.DIT files. At C:\WINNT\SYSTEM32 the default template is installed for the Active Directory database. During installation, this file is copied to the C:\WINNT\NTDS directory. This copied file is used to start the Active Directory. Other domain controllers also write their updates to this file. You can specify the location of the database files and the log files used to keep track of transactions to the database using the Active Directory Installation Wizard, as shown in Figure 9.1.

Figure 9.1 Database and Log Locations

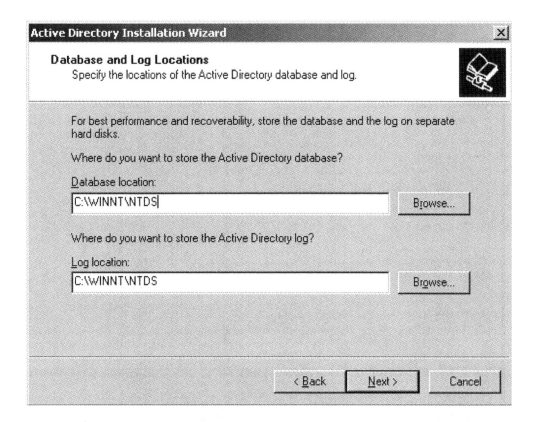

In case of a system crash or database corruption, the ESE uses the transactions from the logs to complete the restore of the Active Directory database after restoring the database from a backup.

Active Directory can record either circular or sequential logs. At specified intervals, circular logs overwrite transactions recorded. In sequential logging, the transactions are never overwritten. They grow until they reach a specified size. In the event that a database becomes corrupt, sequential logging can provide an extra measure of protection. When you restore a database from a sequential log file, you have a continuous record of transactions.

Garbage collection is the Active Directory's automatic database cleanup. This happens every 12 hours. Garbage collection takes care of the following procedures:

- Deleting old log files

- Deleting tombstones—objects that you have marked for deletion in the database

- Defragmenting the database

Defragmentation of the database is a process that rearranges the pages of a file and compacts them. The process is similar to defragmenting the hard drive of a PC. Defragmentation can take place on-line or off-line. On-line defragmentation rearranges the data; however, no space freed up by the defragmentation is released back to the system. To defragment the system off-line you must be in the Directory Repair Service mode.

To enter the Directory Services Repair mode, follow these steps:

1. Press **F8** during the server's boot sequence.

2. From the list of boot options, use the arrow keys to choose **Directory Services Restore Mode (Windows 2000 domain controllers only)**, and then press **ENTER**.

Off-line defragmentation creates a new, more compact copy of the database in a different directory. You can archive the old database file to a separate directory and replace it with the new compacted database.

 Warning: Keep a copy of the old database until you are sure the compacted database loads correctly.

Active Directory Database Backups

The Backup utility helps protect your data from unintentional loss if your system encounters a hardware or storage media failure. For example, you can use Backup to create an identical copy of the data on your hard disk and store the copy on another storage device such as a hard disk or tape. If the original data is accidentally erased or overwritten, or becomes inaccessible because of a hard disk malfunction, you can easily restore the data from the archived copy.

Using Backup, you can:

- Archive selected files and folders on your hard disk

- Restore the archived files and folders to your hard disk or any other disk you can access

- Create an Emergency Repair Disk (ERD) that will help you repair system files if they are corrupted or accidentally erased

- Make a copy of any remote storage data and any data stored in mounted drives

- Make a copy of your computer's System State, which includes the registry, the Active Directory database, the COM+ Class Registration database, system boot files and the Certificate Services database

- Schedule regular backups to keep your archived data up-to-date

Before you backup the Active Directory, you need to ensure users have closed their files, as the Backup Wizard will not backup files locked by applications.

If you use a removable media device you also need to make sure of the following points:

- The device is attached to a computer on the network and is turned on

- The media is listed on the Windows 2000 Hardware Compatibility List (HCL)

- The media is loaded into the device

Backing Up the Active Directory

After you have completed the preliminary tasks, you can perform the backup using the Backup Wizard. To start the Backup Wizard, follow these steps:

1. From the **Start menu**, choose **Programs**, **Accessories**, **System Tools**, and then choose **Backup**.

2. **Welcome to the Windows 2000 Backup and Recovery Tools** opens, as in Figure 9.2.

Figure 9.2 Welcome to the Windows 2000 Backup and Recovery Tools

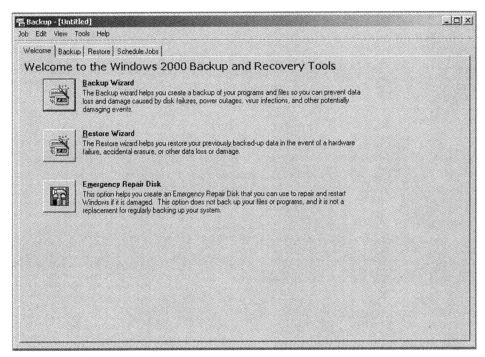

3. Choose **Backup Wizard** and then select **Next** to begin the Wizard.

4. Proceed through **What to Backup**, **Where to Store the Backup** and **Advanced Backup**, choosing the appropriate selections from each screen.

5. From **Completing The Backup Wizard**, choose **Finish**.

The first step of using the Backup Wizard is to backup the Active Directory System State data, as in Figure 9.3.

Figure 9.3 Backup Wizard What to Backup

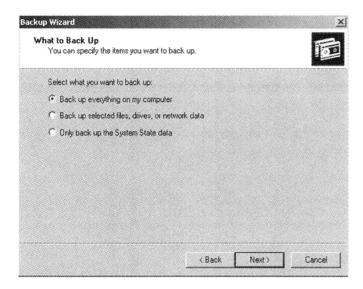

In Windows 2000, you can backup and restore the following system components:

- Registry

- COM+ Class Registration database

- Boot files, including the system files

- Certificate Services database

- Active Directory directory service

- SYSVOL directory

- Cluster service information

When you choose to backup System State data, all of the System State data that is relevant to your computer is backed up. System Data can only be backed up on a local computer.

Note: You cannot choose to backup the individual components of the System State data, due to dependencies among System State components.

After you have chosen to Backup the System State data and selected **Next,** You will need to provide information about the backup media, as in Figure 9.4.

Figure 9.4 Backup Wizard Where to Store the Backup

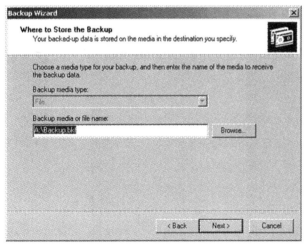

The information in Table 9.1 describes the information required for the backup media options.

Table 9.1 Options for Backup Media

Option	Description
Backup Media Type	This option refers to any medium you wish to use, such as a file or tape. The file can be created on any disk-based medium.
Backup Media or File Name	This option refers to the location where Windows Backup will store the data. For a file, type the path and name, and for a tape, type the tape name.

The Backup Wizard displays the wizard settings after you have entered the media information. You can then do one of the following actions:

Start the Backup—By choosing Finish, the Backup Wizard will display the status information about the backup.

Specify advanced backup options—By choosing Advanced you can specify advanced backup settings.

Selecting advanced backup options allows you to change the settings for the current backup. The advanced settings are described in Table 9.2.

Table 9.2 Advanced Backup Settings

Advanced Settings Page	Advanced Option	Description
Type of Backup	Choose The Type Of Backup Operation To Perform	A list is displayed, from which you can choose the backup type to be used for this backup. Choose one of the following: **Copy backup**—A copy backup copies all selected files but does not mark each file as having been backed up. **Daily backup**—A daily backup copies all of the selected files modified the day the daily backup is completed. **Differential backup**—A differential backup copies the files created or changed since the last normal or incremental backup. **Incremental backup**—An incremental backup backs up only those files created or changed since the last normal or incremental backup. **Normal backup**—A normal backup copies all selected files and marks each file as having been backed up (in other words, the archive attribute is cleared). With normal backups, you need only the most recent copy of the backup file or tape to restore all of the files. You usually perform a normal backup the first time you create a backup set.
	Backup Migrated Remote Storage Data	Enabling this selection will backup the data moved to remote storage.

Advanced Settings Page	Advanced Option	Description
How to backup	Verify Data After Backup	Enabling this option, Windows Backup will confirm the files are correctly backed up. This option is recommended.
	Use Hardware Compression, If Available	Enabling this option, Backup will use hardware compression for those devices that support it.
Media Options	If The Archive Media already Contains Backups	Specify these options if the backup should replace or append the existing backup on the backup media. Choose Append This Backup To Media to store multiple backups on a storage device. Choose Replace The Data On The Media With This Backup if you wish to save only the most recent backup and do not need to save the previous backups.
	Allow Only The Owner And The Administrator Access To The Backup Data And To Any Backups Appended To This Media	Enabling this option allows you to restrict who has access to the backed up file or tape. This option is only available if you have selected replacing existing backups. If you need to backup the registry in Active Directory, by selecting this option you can prevent others from getting copies of the data.
Backup Label	Backup Label	Type in a name description for the backup log. The default is Set Created Data at Time.
When To Backup	When To Backup	Using these options, you can specify Now or Later. Later will also let you specify a job name and start date.
	Job Name	Type in a name for the backup job.
	Start Date	Type in a date to start the backup job.
	Set Schedule	Allows you to set up a backup schedule.

You can also run a backup without using the Backup Wizard. To run a backup, follow these steps:

1. From the **Start** menu, choose **Programs, Accessories, System Tools** and then choose **Backup.**

2. **Welcome to the Windows 2000 Backup and Recovery Tools** will open, as seen in Figure 9.5.

Figure 9.5 Welcome to the Windows 2000 Backup and Recovery Tools

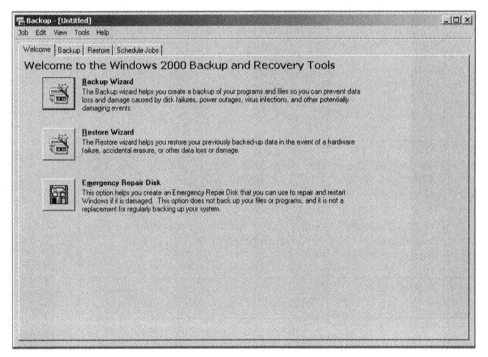

3. Choose the **Backup** tab and enable **System State**, as in Figure 9.6.

Figure 9.6 Backup

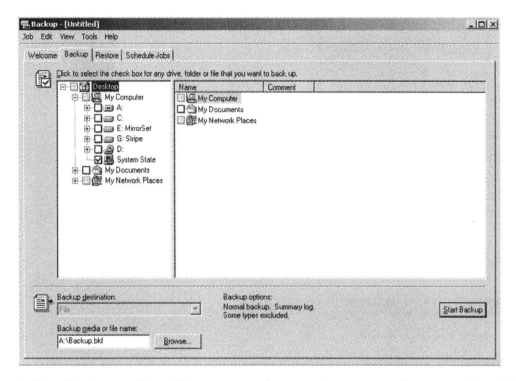

4. From **Backup media or file name**, type the appropriate response for your needs and then choose **Start Backup**.

5. Backup will give you the option to append or replace the media, as in Figure 9.7.

Figure 9.7 Backup Job Information

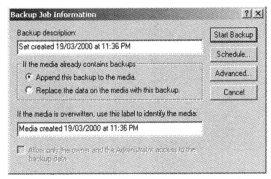

6. You can also configure some **Advanced** options and schedule the backup, as in Figure 9.8.

Figure 9.8 Advanced Backup Options

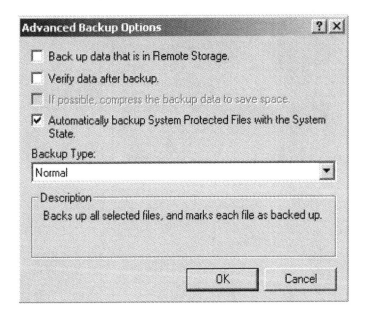

Note: The backup process creates a backup log. This text file is stored on the hard disk of the computer where you ran Windows Backup.

Active Directory Database Management Restoration

The System State data is a collection of the distributed services, such as the directory service in Active Directory. You are backing up all Active Directory data that exists on a domain controller when you backup the System State data on that server. To restore these distributed services to that server, you must restore the System State data. On the other hand, if you have more than one domain controller, and your Active Directory is replicated to any of the other servers, you will need to perform what is called an authoritative restore in order to ensure that your restored data gets replicated to all of your servers.

Backup operates in nonauthoritative restore mode during a normal restore operation. Any data you restore, including Active Directory objects, will have their original update sequence number. Because Active Directory uses this number to replicate changes among the servers in your organization, any data that is restored nonauthoritatively will appear to the Active Directory as old data. This means the data will never be replicated to your other servers. Through replication, Active Directory will update the data you have restored with newer data from your other servers. Authoritative restore solves this problem.

Note: There are two ways to restore the Active Directory: authoritive and nonauthoritative.

Restoring an Active Directory Database

If you are restoring the System State data to a domain controller, you must decide to do an authoritive or a nonauthoritative restore. The default for a domain controller is nonauthoritative.

To do a nonauthoritative restore of the System State data on a domain controller, you must start your computer in the Directory Services Restore Mode. In this mode, you can restore the SYSVOL directory files and the Active Directory Services database. You can only restore the System State data on a local computer.

Warning: If you restore the System State data and do not specify an alternative location for the restored data, Backup will overwrite the current System State data with the backed up System State data.

To nonauthoritatively restore Active Directory, follow these steps:

1. Reboot the computer.

2. During **Startup**, at the point where the operating system is selected, press **F8**.

3. Ensure the domain controller is off line—from the **Windows 2000 Advanced Options** menu, as in Figure 9.9, chooose **Directory Services Restore Mode** and then select **Enter**.

Figure 9.9 Windows 2000 Advanced Options

```
Windows 2000 Advanced Options Menu
Please select an option:

Safe Mode
Safe Mode with Networking
Safe Mode with Command Prompt

Enable Boot Logging
Enable VGA Mode
Last Known Good Configuration
Directory Services Restore Mode (Windows 2000 domain controllers only)
Debugging Mode

Boot Normally
Return to OS Choices Menu

Use ↑ and ↓ to move the highlight to your choice.
Press Enter to close.
```

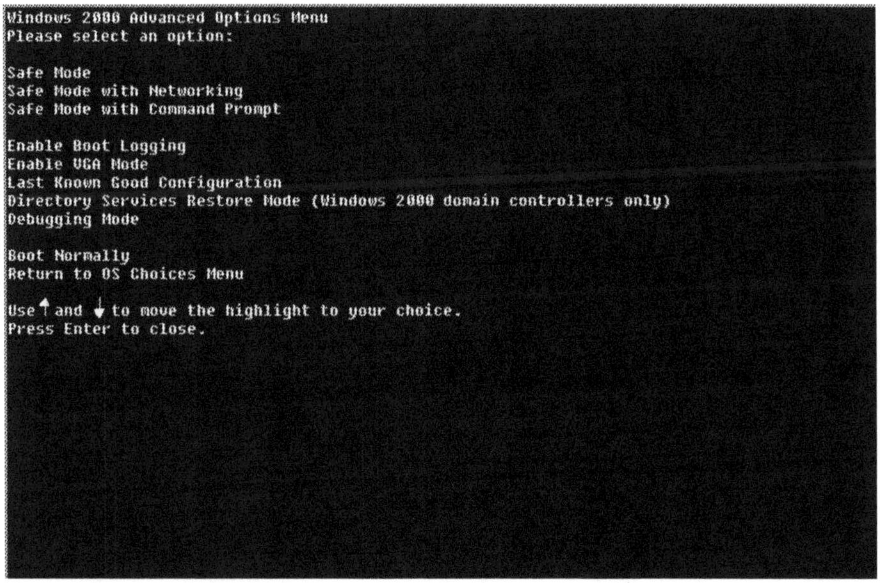

4. From **Please Select The Operating System To Start**, choose **Windows 2000 Server** and then select **Enter**.

5. Log on as **Administrator**.

 Note: When you restart the computer in Directory Services Restore mode, you must log on as Administrator by using a valid Security Accounts Manager (SAM) account name and password, not the Active Directory Administrator's name and password. This is because Active Directory is offline and account verification cannot occur. The SAM account database is used to control access while Active Directory is offline.

6. When the message displays informing you that Windows is running in Safe Mode, as seen in Figure 9.10, choose **OK**.

Figure 9.10 Safe Mode

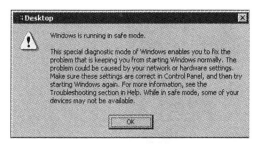

1. From the **Start** menu, choose **Programs, Accessories, System Tools** and then select **Backup**.

2. From **Welcome to The Windows 2000 Backup And Recovery Tools**, choose **Restore Wizard** and then select **Next**.

3. From **Restore Wizard What to Restore** (Figure 9.11), expand the media type that contains the data you wish to restore or choose **Import File**.

Figure 9.11 Restore Wizard What to Restore

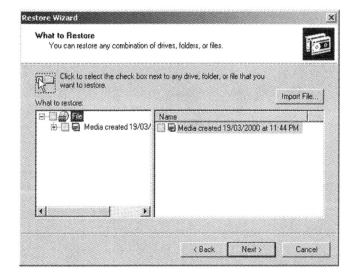

4. Expand the appropriate media until the data you want to restore is visible.

 Note: You can choose to restore a backup set or specific files and folders.

---

5. Choose **Finish** to have the **Restore Wizard** display the status information about the backup or **Advanced** to specify advanced restore settings.

Authoritative Restore of Active Directory

An authoritative restore occurs after a nonauthoritative restore. It chooses the complete directory, a subtree or individual objects to be recognized as authoritative with respect to the domain controllers in the forest. The NTDSUTIL utility allows you to mark objects as authoritative so that as they are replicated they update the existing copies of the object throughout the forest.

To authoritatively restore Active Directory, follow these steps:

1. Carry out the nonauthoritative restore and restart the computer.

2. During **Startup**, at the point where the operating system is selected, press **F8**.

3. Ensure the domain controller is off line. From the **Windows 2000 Advance Options** menu, choose **Directory Services Restore Mode** and then select **Enter**.

4. From **Please Select The Operating System To Start**, choose **Windows 2000 Server** and then select **Enter**.

5. Log on as **Administrator**.

6. When the message informing you that Windows is running in Safe Mode displays, choose **OK**.

7. From the **Start** menu, choose **Programs, Accessories** and then select **Command Prompt**.

8. At the command prompt, type **ntdsutil** and then choose **Enter**.

9. At the **NTDSUTIL** prompt, type **authoritative restore** and then choose **Enter**.

10. When the **Authoritative Restore** prompt displays, type **restore database** and choose **Enter** to authoritatively restore the entire directory or type **restore subtree <subtree distinguished name>** and choose **Enter** to authoritatively restore a portion of the subtree, such as an OU.

For example, to restore the Learning1 OU in the Lightpoint.net domain, the command would be: restore subtree OU=Learning1, DC=Lightpoint DC=NET

11. To exit the **NTDSUTIL** utlity, type **quit**, choose **Enter** and close the command prompt window.1

12. Restart the domain controller in normal mode and connect the restored domain controller to the network.

Normal replication begins when the domain controller is back online and connected to the network. Replication will bring the restored domain controller up to date with any of the changes that are not overridden by the authoritative restore. Replication will also propagate the authoritatively restored objects to the rest of the domain controllers.

System Failure Recovery

A computer failure is any incident that causes a computer to be unable to start or continue running. The causes of computer failures range from malfunctioning hardware to a complete system loss from fire or other similar events. When Windows2000 encounters such an event, it might report a STOP error, and display the information necessary for you and a Microsoft Product Support Services engineer to locate and identify problem areas.

Failure recovery is restoring a computer so you can log on and access system resources after a computer failure has occurred. In Windows 2000, you have the following options to help you identify and recover from computer failures:

Safe mode—You use safe mode startup options to start the system with only the minimum of necessary services. The safe mode options, including Last Known Good Configuration, are particularly helpful if a newly installed device driver is causing problems with the system starting (Figure 9.12).

Figure 9.12 Safe Mode Startup

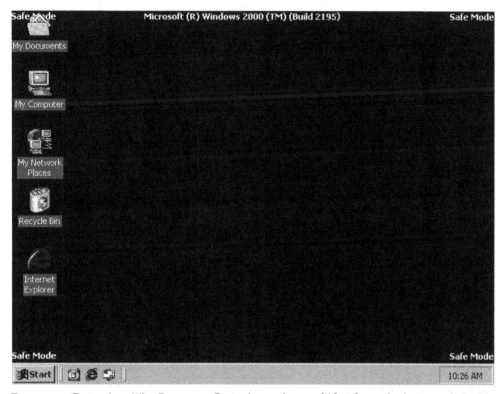

Recovery Console—The Recovery Console can be used if safe mode does not help. To start the system, use the Setup Compact Disc (CD) or floppy disks you have created from the CD. You then access the Recovery Console, a command-line interface. From this interface, you can carry out tasks, such as starting and stopping services and accessing the local drive (including drives formatted with the NT file system (NTFS)).

Warning: The Recovery Console is a powerful command. It is recommended only for advanced users or administrators.

Emergency Repair Disk—If safe mode and the Recovery Console cannot be used or is not workable in your situation, and if you have made appropriate advance preparations, you can try to repair your system with the ERD. You use the ERD to repair core system files (Figure 9.13).

Figure 9.13 Emergency Repair Disk

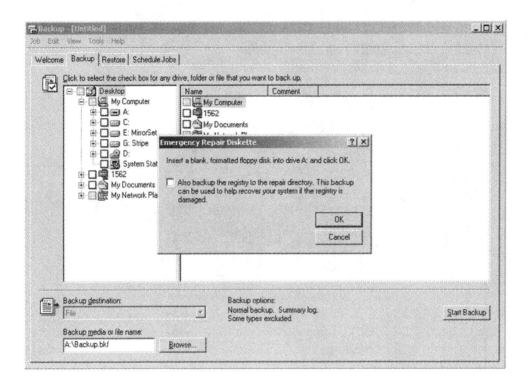

Recovering from a System Failure

You can start and stop services, read and write data on a local drive, copy data from a floppy disk or CD, format drives, fix the boot sector or master boot record, and perform other administrative tasks, using the Recovery Console. It is useful if you need to repair your system by copying a file from a floppy disk or CD-ROM to your hard drive, or to reconfigure a service that is preventing your computer from starting properly.

To start the Recovery Console, follow these steps:

1. Put the Windows 2000 Setup CD, or the first floppy disk you created from the CD, in the appropriate drive: For systems that cannot start (boot) from the CD drive, you must use a floppy disk. For systems that can start (boot) from the CD drive, you can use either the CD or a floppy disk.

2. Restart the computer and, if you are using floppy disks, respond to the prompts requesting each floppy disk.

3. When the text-based part of **Setup** begins, follow the prompts, choosing the **repair or recover** option by pressing **R**.

4. When prompted, choose the **Recovery Console** by pressing **C**.

5. Follow the instructions for reinserting one or more of the floppy disks you created for starting the system.

6. If you have a dual-boot or multiple-boot system, choose the Windows 2000 installation that you need to access from the **Recovery Console**.

7. When prompted, type the **Administrator password**, as in Figure 9.14.

Figure 9.14 Recovery Console

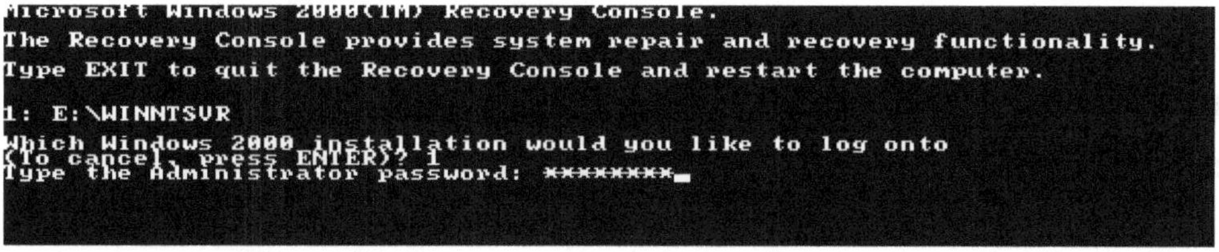

```
Microsoft Windows 2000(TM) Recovery Console.
The Recovery Console provides system repair and recovery functionality.
Type EXIT to quit the Recovery Console and restart the computer.

1: E:\WINNTSVR
Which Windows 2000 installation would you like to log onto
(To cancel, press ENTER)? 1
Type the Administrator password: ********_
```

8. The **Recovery Console** gives you basic access to your file system (Figure 9.15). At the system prompt, type Recovery Console commands: **help** for a list of commands or **help commandname** for help on a specific command.

Figure 9.15 Basic Access

```
The volume in drive E has no label
The volume Serial Number is 5cd1-0480
Directory of E:\WINNTSVR
12/08/99   05:04p    <da------>     0  .
11/11/99   11:43a    <da------>     0  ..
07/10/99   07:00a    <da------>     0  addins
09/10/99   01:00a    <da------>     0  Application Compatibility Scripts
04/10/99   02:10p    <-a------>  1272  Blue Lace 16.bmp
05/10/99   06:00a    <-a------> 83844  certocm.log
09/10/99   08:00a    <-d------>  2994  clock.avi
08/10/99   05:00p    <-a------>     0  CLUSTER
09/10/99   01:00a    <-a------> 17062  Coffee Bean.bmp
11/11/99   11:43a    <-a------>  1398  commcomp.log
11/11/99   12:14p    <-a------> 58896  comsetup.log
07/10/99   07:00a    <da------>     0  Config
11/11/99   11:43a    <da------>     0  Connection Wizard
11/11/99   12:14p    <da------>     0  Cursors
12/08/99   05:04p    <da------>     0  Debug
11/11/99   11:43a    <-a------>  2880  Del_1.isu
07/10/99   07:00a    <-a------>  5592  Del_2.isu
09/10/99   01:00a    <-a-h---->   271  deltsul.exe
12/08/99   02:12p    <-a------>   262  desktop.ini
07/10/99   02:00p    <-a------>   744  dhcpnt.log
11/11/99   02:00p    <-a------>   840  dmi32c.log
12/08/99   05:00p    <-a------>   666  domprac.log
                                       domprac.log
More:    ENTER=Scroll (Line)     SPACE=Scroll (Page)     ESC=Stop
```

9. To exit **Recovery Console**, type **Exit**.

The ERD helps you to recover or repair a system that cannot load Windows 2000. Using the ERD, you repair problems with system files and the partition boot sector. This can happen when your hard disk fails or when some of your system files are corrupted or accidentally deleted. System files are the files used to load, configure and run the operating system. If any system files are missing or corrupted, you can use the ERD to repair those files. The partition boot sector holds information about the file system structure and instructions for loading the operating system. If you have a dual-boot system, the ERD contains information about the settings that specify which operating system to start and how to start it.

You should regularly update your ERD to record your latest system settings. The ERD is designed for restarting your computer or repairing system files—it does not back up any of your files or programs.

Tip: The copy of the registry that the ERD contains is the original registry from your initial Setup; therefore, you should not use the ERD to repair registry problems.

To create an ERD, follow these steps:

1. From the **Start** menu, choose **Programs**, **Accessories**, **System Tools**, and then select **Backup**.

2. From the **welcome** property page, choose **Create an Emergency Repair Disk**.

3. When prompted, insert a blank, formatted 1.44-MB disk in your floppy disk drive, and then choose **OK**.

4. When the process is complete, remove the disk, label it "Emergency Repair Disk," and then store it in a safe location.

To restore your settings from the ERD, you will need your Windows 2000 CD, the Windows 2000 Setup disks and the ERD. During the restoration process, you can select F1 for more information about your options. Because any missing or corrupted files are replaced with files from the Windows 2000 CD, any changes you made to the system after the original installation are lost.

To restore your settings from the ERD, follow these steps:

1. Use the Windows 2000 Setup disks or the Windows 2000 CD to start your computer.

2. After Setup finishes copying files from the Setup disks, the system restarts, and text-based installation mode starts.

3. When the text-based part of **Setup** begins, follow the prompts, choosing the **repair or recover** option by pressing **R**.

4. When prompted to enter the type of **repair or recovery option** required, press **R** to repair a damaged Windows 2000 installation.

5. Choose either **Fast repair** or **Manual repair**. Choose **F** for Fast repair if you want Setup to automatically attempt to repair system files, the partition boot sector, and the startup environment. Press **M** for Manual repair if you want Setup to selectively repair system files, the partition boot sector, or the startup environment. Manual repair does not repair the registry.

6. Follow the instructions as they appear and insert the ERD when prompted.

When the repair process is complete, your computer restarts and Windows 2000 is launched.

Vocabulary

Review the following terms in preparation for the certification exam.

Term	Description
attribute	An attribute is a parameter describing an object. Objects consist of optional and required attributes.
backup	A backup is a duplicate copy of a program, a disk, or data, created for archiving purposes or for ensuring that valuable files cannot be lost if the active copy is destroyed or damaged.
boot files	Boot files are the system files needed to start Windows 2000.
CD	CD is an acronym for Compact Disc. This form of information storage is characterized by high capacity and the use of laser optics rather than magnetic means for reading data.
circular logging	Log files record system events or transactions. A circular log file overwrites existing entries after the log reaches a specified size or age.
Cluster Database	The Cluster Database is the essential software component that controls all aspects of server cluster operation. Each node in a server cluster runs one instance of the Cluster service.
defragmentation	In Active Directory, defragmentation rearranges how the data is written in the directory database file to compact it.
ERD	An Emergency Repair Disk is created by the Backup utility. It contains information about your current Windows system settings. This disk can be used to repair your computer if it will not start or if your system files are damaged or erased.
ESE	The Extensible Storage Engine stores all Active Directory objects. It reserves storage only for space that is used. When more attributes are added, more storage is dynamically allocated. The ESE stores multiple-value attributes and properties and communicates directly with individual records in the directory data store based on the object's relative distinguished name attribute.
garbage collection	Garbage collection is Active Directory's automated database cleanup. By default, this happens every 12 hours and deletes old log files, tombstones and defragments the database file.

Term	Description
log file	A log file stores messages generated by an application, service or operating system. These messages track the operations performed. Log files are usually plain text (ASCII) files and often have a .log extension. In Backup, the log file contains a record of the date the tapes were created and the names of files and directories successfully backed up and restored.
Microsoft Jet Database engine	The Microsoft Jet database engine is a database management system that retrieves data from and stores data in user and system databases.
NTDSUTIL	The NTDSUTIL utility is a command line tool for managing the Active Directory database and Operations Master objects.
NTFS	New Technologies File System is a file system that is designed for Windows 2000 and supports many features, such as file system security, Unicode, recoverability and long file names. It also stores an Access Control List (ACL) with every file and folder.
Recovery Console	Using the Recovery Console, a command line tool, you can start and stop services, read and write data on a local drive, copy data from a floppy disk or CD, format drives, fix the boot sector or master boot record, and perform other administrative tasks.
registry	The registry in Windows 2000 is a database repository for information about a computer's configuration. The registry contains information that Windows 2000 continually references during operation. The registry is organized hierarchically as a tree and is made up of keys and their sub-keys, hives, and value entries.
replication	Replication is the exchange of database information between the controllers and domains. This periodic exchange ensures that all of the domain controllers within a domain contain consistent information.
safe mode	When you start Windows 2000 in safe mode, it starts without the network components and it loads only the basic drivers. This mode is used for troubleshooting the computer.

Term	Description
SAM	Security Accounts Manager is a Windows 2000 service used during the login process that maintains user information.
sequential logging	A sequential log is one that records transactions and events in the order that they happen. Unlike a circular log file, information in a sequential log is not overwritten when it reaches a specific size or age. Once it fills, it creates a new file.
system files	Files used by Windows to load, configure and run the operating system. Generally, system files must never be deleted or moved.
System State	For all Windows 2000 operating systems, the System State data includes the registry, the system boot files and the Certificate Services database (if the server is operating as a certificate server). If the server is a domain controller, the System State data also includes the Active Directory directory services database and the SYSVOL directory.
SYSVOL	SYSVOL is a shared directory that stores the server copy of the domain's public files, which are replicated among all domain controllers in the domain.
tombstone	Objects with a tombstone remain in the database for the life of the tombstone (the default is 60 days) and are invisible to client requests. This process allows enough time for the tombstone to replicate to all of the domain controllers in the network. During garbage collection, objects that have gone past the tombstone lifetime are physically removed from the database.
WINS	The Microsoft Windows Internet Naming Service dynamically maps IP addresses to computer names (NetBIOS names). This lets users access resources by name instead of forcing them to use difficult to remember and hard to recognize IP addresses. WINS servers support clients running Windows NT and earlier Windows operating systems.

In Brief

If you want to...	Then do this...
Enter the Directory Services Restore mode	1. Press **F8** during the server's boot sequence. 2. To enter the **Directory Services Restore** mode, choose **Directory Services Restore** mode from the list.
Start the Backup Wizard	1. From the **Start** menu, choose **Programs, Accessories, System Tools** and then select **Backup**. **2. Welcome to the Windows 2000 Backup and Recovery Tools** opens. 3. Choose **Backup Wizard** and then select **Next** to begin the Wizard. 4. Proceed through **What to Backup, Where to Store the Backup** and **Advanced Backup**. On each screen choose the appropriate selections. 5. From **Completing The Backup Wizard**, choose **Finish**.
Do a backup without using the Backup Wizard	1. From the **Start** menu, choose **Programs, Accessories, System Tools** and then select **Backup**. **2. Welcome to the Windows 2000 Backup and Recovery Tools** opens. 3. Choose the **Backup** property page , and then select the folders and files you want to backup. 4. From within **Backup media or file name**, type the appropriate response for your needs and then choose **Start Backup**. 5. Backup will give you the option to append or replace the media.

If you want to...	Then do this...
Start the Recovery Console	1. Put the Windows 2000 Setup CD, or the first floppy disk you created from the CD, in the appropriate drive. For systems that cannot start (boot) from the CD drive, you must use a floppy disk. For systems that can start (boot) from the CD drive, you can use either the CD or a floppy disk.
	2. Restart the computer. If you are using floppy disks, respond to the prompts that request each floppy disk.
	3. When the text-based part of **Setup** begins, choose the **repair or recover** option by pressing **R**.
	4. When prompted, choose the **Recovery Console** by pressing **C**.
	5. Follow the instructions for reinserting one or more of the floppy disks you created for starting the system.
	6. If you have a dual-boot or multiple-boot system, select the Windows 2000 installation that you need to access from the **Recovery Console**.
	7. When prompted, type the Administrator password.
	8. The **Recovery Console** gives you basic access to your file system.
	9. At the system prompt, type Recovery Console commands: **help** for a list of commands or **help commandname** for help on a specific command.
	10. To exit the Recovery Console and restart the computer, type **Exit**.

Lesson 9 Activities

Complete the following activities to prepare for the certification exam.

1. You need to restart your computer in the Directory Services Restore mode. Describe how you logon and the reason why.

2. You have run a script to modify a large number of user accounts in your domain. After the script is finished, you discover the wrong attributes were modified. When you restore the domain controller from a backup, you find that the attributes are still modified. Describe what you should do.

3. Describe the five types of backup options available.

4. Your computer fails to boot up into the Windows 2000 desktop. Describe the system failure options available.

5. Before backing up, some preliminary tasks need to take place. Explain these tasks.

6. List the functions for maintaining the Active Directory.

7. Describe the NTDS.DIT file and where it is stored.

8. Describe database defragmentation.

9. Define the Windows 2000 failure recovery options.

10. Explain an ERD.

Answers to Lesson 9 Activities

1.   When you restart the computer in Directory Services Restore mode, you must log on as Administrator by using a valid SAM account name and password, not the Active Directory Administrator's name and password. This is because Active Directory is offline and account verification cannot occur. The SAM account database is used to control access while Active Directory is offline.

2.   You will need to take the domain controller off-line and repeat the non-authoritative restore. Then, perform an authoritative restore before bringing the domain controller back online.

3.   **Copy backup**—A copy backup copies all selected files but does not mark each file as having been backed up.

    Daily backup—A daily backup copies all of the selected files modified the day the daily backup is completed.

    Differential backup—A differential backup copies the files created or changed since the last normal or incremental backup.

    Incremental backup—An incremental backup backs up only those files created or changed since the last normal or incremental backup.

    Normal backup—A normal backup copies all selected files and marks each file as having been backed up (in other words, the archive attribute is cleared). With normal backups, you need only the most recent copy of the backup file or tape to restore all of the files. You usually perform a normal backup the first time you create a backup set.

4.   **Safe mode**—You use safe mode startup options to start the system with only the minimum of necessary services. The safe mode options, including Last Known Good Configuration, are particularly helpful if a newly installed device driver is causing problems with the system starting.

    Recovery Console—The Recovery Console can be used if safe mode does not help. To start the system, you use the Setup CD or floppy disks you have created from the CD. You then access the Recovery Console, a command-line interface. From this interface, you can carry out tasks, such as starting and stopping services and accessing the local drive (including drives formatted with the NTFS file system).

    Emergency Repair Disk—If safe mode and the Recovery Console cannot be used or are not workable in your situation, and if you have made appropriate advance preparations, you can try to repair your system with the ERD. You use the ERD to repair core system files.

5. Before you backup the Active Directory, you need to ensure users have closed their files, as the Backup Wizard will not backup files locked by applications. If you use a removable media device you also need to make sure of the following:

   • The device is attached to a computer on the network and is turned on

   • The media is listed on the Windows 2000 Hardware Compatibility List (HCL)

   • The media is loaded into the device

6. Important to maintaining your Active Directory Database are the following functions:

   • Recognizing the components of the Active Directory and where they are stored on your system

   • Garbage collection—or automatic database cleanup

   • Defragmenting the database

   • Backing up and restoring the database

7. There are two NTDS.DIT files. At C:\WINNT\SYSTEM32 the default template is installed for the Active Directory database. During installation, this file is copied to the C:\WINNT\NTDS directory. This copied file is used to start the Active Directory. Other domain controllers also write their updates to this file. You can specify the location of the database files and the log files used to keep track of transactions to the database using the Active Directory Installation Wizard.

8. Defragmentation of the database rearranges the pages of a file and compacts them. The process is similar to defragmenting the hard drive of a computer. Defragmentation can take place on-line or off-line. On-line defragmentation rearranges the data; however, no space freed up by the defragmentation is released back to the system. To defragment the system off-line you must be in the Directory Repair Service mode.

9. Failure recovery is restoring a computer so you can log on and access system resources after a computer failure has occurred. In Windows 2000 you have the following options to help you identify and recover from computer failures:

   Safe mode—You use safe mode startup options to start the system with only the minimum of necessary services.

   Recovery Console—The Recovery Console can be used if safe mode does not help. To start the system, use the Setup Compact Disc (CD) or floppy disks you have created from the CD. You then access the Recovery Console, a command-line interface. From this interface, you can carry out tasks, such as starting and stopping services and accessing the local drive (including drives formatted with the NTFS file system).

   Emergency Repair Disk—If safe mode and the Recovery Console cannot be used or are not workable in your situation, and if you have made appropriate advance preparations, you can try to repair your system with the ERD. You use the ERD to repair core system files.

10.   The ERD helps you to recover or repair a system that cannot load Windows 2000. Using the ERD, you repair problems with system files and the partition boot sector. This can happen when your hard disk fails or when some of your system files are corrupted or accidentally deleted. If you have a dual-boot system, the ERD contains information about the settings that specify which operating system to start and how to start it.

You should regularly update your ERD to record your latest system settings. The ERD is designed for restarting your computer or repairing system files. It does not back up any of your files or programs.

Lesson 9 Quiz

These questions test your knowledge of features, vocabulary, procedures and syntax.

1. Which of the following fits this definition? After this procedure, any component of the System State that is replicated with another domain controller will be brought up to date by replication after you restore the data.
   A. An advanced restore option
   B. A nonauthoritative restore
   C. The NTDSUTIL utility
   D. An authoritative restore

2. The Active Directory database is also known as the data store. What is the name of this file?
   A. NTDS
   B. NTDSUTIL.Exe
   C. NTDS.DIT
   D. C:\WINNT\NTDS\NTDS.DIT

3. Which of the following is part of the System State data?
   A. Registry
   B. SYSVOL Directory
   C. Schema Master
   D. Active Directory database

4. Which of the following objects make up the data store?
   A. NTDS.DIT, log files
   B. SYSVOL, registry
   C. NTDS.DIT, boot files, SYSVOL
   D. Log files, tombstones, NTDS.DIT

5. Garbage Collection is Active Directory's automatic database cleanup. What does it do?
   A. Deletes old log files
   B. Deletes tombstones
   C. Runs every 12 hours
   D. Defrags the database

6. Which of the following statements is correct?
   A. You can backup the individual components of the System State data, because there are no dependencies among System State components.
   B. When you choose to backup System State data, all of the System State data that is relevant to your computer is backed up.
   C. When you choose to backup System State data, only the System State data you select for your computer is backed up.
   D. You cannot choose to backup the individual components of the System State data, due to dependencies among System State components.

7. What function does NTDSUTIL perform in backup and restore?
   A. NTDSUTIL allows you to transfer roles from one server to another.
   B. NTDSUTIL allows you to take the database offline so you can replace the entire database if it has become corrupt.
   C. NTDSUTIL allows you to mark objects as authoritative.
   D. NTDSUTIL is the data store.

8. What features will allow you to repair a system that will not start or load Windows 2000?
   A. Safe Mode
   B. ERD
   C. Recovery Console
   D. NTDSUTIL

9. What is the difference between circular logging and sequential logging?
   A. Sequential logs overwrite their files after a specified period, circular logging collects data until it reaches a specified limit and then it starts a new file.
   B. Circular logging defines a comma-delimited log file, sequential logging defines a sequential, binary-format log file.
   C. For the most part, they track the same information. The differences among them are depth of detail, type of display, and analytical uses.
   D. Circular logs overwrite their files after a specified period, sequential logging collects data until it reaches a specified limit and then it starts a new file.

10. What functions are important to maintaining your Active Directory database?
    A. Recognizing the components of the Active Directory and where they are stored on your system.
    B. Garbage collection—or automatic database cleanup.
    C. Defragmenting the database.
    D. Backing up and restoring the database.

Answers to Lesson 9 Quiz

1. Answer B is correct. After a nonauthoritative restore, any component of the System State that is replicated with another domain controller will be brought up to date by replication after you restore the data.

    Answer A is incorrect. The advanced restore options affect how the file is restored, not what happens to the file after it is restored.

    Answer C is incorrect. The NTDSUTIL is a command line tool for database and FSMO management and is used when performing an authoritative restore.

    Answer D is incorrect. If you do not want to replicate the changes that have been made subsequent to the last backup, you perform a nonauthoritative restore.

2. Answer C is correct. The name of the Active Directory database file is NTDS.DIT.

    Answer D is correct. C:\WINNT\NTDS\NTDS.DIT also describes the path location.

    Answer A is incorrect. NTDS is not enough information to identify the database name.

    Answer B is incorrect. NTDSUTIL.EXE is the name of the utility you use to manage the database.

3. Answers A, B and D are correct. Your computer's System State data includes the registry, the Active Directory database, the COM+ Class Registration database, system boot files and the Certificate Services database.

    Answer C is incorrect. The Schema Master is an Operations Master.

4. Answer A is correct. The primary files that make up the data store are NTDS.DIT and the log files.

    Answer B is incorrect. The SYSVOL and registry are part of the System State data.

    Answer C is incorrect. SYSVOL and boot files are part of the System State data.

    Answer D is incorrect. Tombstones are objects that have been marked for deletion.

5.   Answers A, B, C and D are correct. Garbage collection is the Active Directory's automatic database cleanup. This happens every 12 hours. Garbage collection takes care of the following: deleting old log files, deleting tombstones and defragmenting the database.

6.   Answers B and D are correct. When you choose to backup System State data, all of the System State data that is relevant to your computer is backed up. You cannot choose to backup the individual components of the System State data, due to dependencies among System State components.

Answers A and C are incorrect. They are the opposite of the correct answers.

7.   Answer B is correct. NTDSUTIL allows you to take the database offline so you can replace the entire database if it has become corrupt. You can then replace it with a backup copy.

Answer C is correct. NTDSUTIL allows you to mark objects as authoritative, ensuring that any replicated or distributed data that you have restored is properly distributed through your network after a restore.

Answer A is incorrect. NTDSUTIL is used to transfer Operations Master roles but it does not answer the question "What function does NTDSUTIL perform in backup and restore"?

Answer D is incorrect. NTDS.DIT is the data store or the Active Directory database.

8.   Answers A, B and C are correct. Features that allow you to repair a system that will not start or will not load Windows2000 are Safe Mode, ERD and the Recovery Console.

Answer D is incorrect. The NTDSUTIL utility is a command line tool for managing the Active Directory database and Operations Master objects.

9.   Answer D is correct. Circular logs overwrite their files after a specified period, sequential logging collects data until it reaches a specified limit and then it starts a new file.

Answer A is incorrect. Circular logging and sequential logging are reversed.

Answer B is incorrect. Text File—CSV defines a comma-delimited log file, Text File–TSV defines a sequential, binary-format log file.

Answer C is incorrect. What is described are protocol logs. Protocol logs track the commands an SMTP virtual server receives from SMTP clients.

10.   Answers A, B C and D are all correct. All are important to maintaining your Active Directory database.

Active Directory Management Scenario

An organization's information infrastructure needs to adapt to rapidly changing global business conditions. In this scenario, we will walk through an Active Directory implementation for a worldwide organization called IBID Publishing. The Enterprise Center develops markets and implements educational software. A major function of an organization's information infrastructure is to handle information about people, including all of the attributes that represent their network identity, such as title, position, rights and privileges to company resources, as well as personnel information including salary, benefits, and other personal information.

The Active Directory service of the Windows 2000 operating system brings order to diverse directory server hierarchies, or namespaces. Namespace is the logical naming of domainsibid.com and their trust relationships, including their supporting infrastructure. Active Directory is an enterprise-class directory that uses the namespace equivalent to the Internet, providing a single point of administration and replication, a hierarchical view of the directory, extensibility, scalability, distributed security and multimaster replication.

After completing this lesson, you should have a better understanding of Active Directory Implementation and Administration.

Active Directory Implementation and Administration

 Note: The names provided in this section are for illustration purposes only and do not reflect actual names or companies.

In today's businesses, information about people, applications and other network resources is often scattered throughout the organization in different systems. As companies continually increase the number of applications and platforms they use, the management task becomes increasingly complex. Companies begin to manage duplicate information in many different places, leading to an information control nightmare. Although Active Directory has many advantages for organizations of all sizes, it would be difficult for us to discuss the different plans.

Active Directory simplifies administration of networks by delegating authority and centralizing directory information. There is a difference between the Windows New Technology (NT) domainibid.com system and the Windows 2000 Active Directory service. In the past, IBID Publishing created separate user domainsibid.com to delegate administration of particular groups of users in the organization. Using Windows 2000, IBID Publishing can now delegate fine-grained administrative authority at the Organizational Unit (OU) level.

In addition, with the Windows NT 4.0 operating system, domains with a large number of objects (more than approximately 40,000) had to be divided into smaller domains to house the scalability limitations of the domain accounts database. In practice, you could not put that many objects in a domain. Logon times would be so slow, users would time out, and the system would freeze up. In Windows 2000, this constraint has been removed. A single domain can hold millions of objects. Administrators must understand these differences and plan their Active Directory-based structure accordingly.

In this lesson, we will review the namespace design and deployment activities associated with the implementation of the Active Directory. The infrastructure elements we will cover include the Windows 2000 Active Directory and Domain Name System (DNS) namespaces, forests, domainsibid.com, administrative structure and organizational units, sites, domainibid.com controller placement and specifications.

Implementing and Administering Active Directory in an Enterprise Environment

Having a well thought-out Active Directory implementation plan is essential to a cost-effective and tranquil deployment. Investing time in the planning phase will help you avoid spending time and money reworking structures that you have already put in place.

While you create your own plan, the following are some considerations that will help you with your deployment:

• Learn the key Active Directory concepts that influence structure planning, and adjust the suggested planning steps to best suit your organization

• Identify the people in your organization who should participate in structure planning

• Understand how existing business practices might need to change or evolve to take full advantage of Active Directory

• Understand the flexibility of the structures you create, and realize which of your choices will be easy or hard to change in the future

The scope of this lesson does not include complete details of an Active Directory deployment. However, Figure 10.1 shows the primary steps in designing the Active Directory structure.

Figure 10.1 Planning Flow Chart

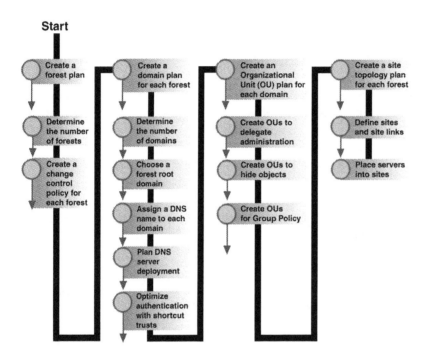

The Active Directory Service

Active Directory defines the scope and manages the administration for an assembly of resources on a network, such as users, computers, printers and groups. The network and its objects are organized by forests, domainsibid.com, trust relationships, organizational units and sites. In addition to handling the administrative directory services, the Windows 2000 Active Directory service will be used by IBID Publishing to fulfill a range of naming, name resolution, administrative, registration and query needs. Figure 10.2 shows the Active Directory's overall function in IBID Publishing Publishing's system.

Figure 10.2 Active Directory Service

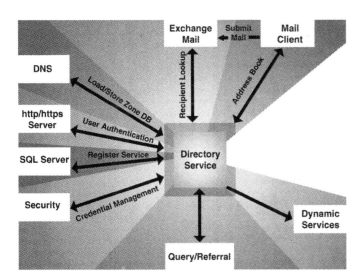

Directory Service Architecture

Active Directory's data store is logically centralized but physically distributed. Because all domainsibid.com store forest-wide configuration and schema information, if the information requested is not stored locally, each domainibid.com can reference objects stored in any other domain. Active Directory provides a hierarchical namespace of objects in accordance with the following description:

- The Distinguished Name (DN) of each directory object uniquely identifies it in the database

- The object's DN is made up of its Relative Distinguished Name (RDN) and the chain of successive parent objects

- The database stores the RDN for each object and a reference to the parent object

- The database layer follows these parent references and concatenates the successive RDNs to form the DN of the object

Active Directory functionality, as shown in Figure 10.3, is a layered architecture representing the server procedures that provide directory services to the client applications and the protocols used.

Figure 10.3 Layers and Interface Agents

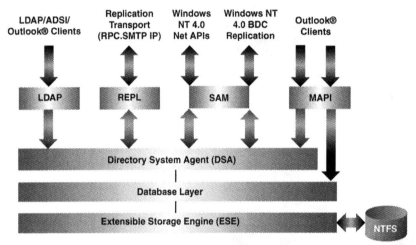

IBID Publishing designed their Active Directory service to provide the following benefits:

Replication—Active Directory uses multimaster replication, so that the directory can be updated at any domainibid.com controller. If a domain controller within a domain stops or fails, the other domain controllers in that domain can provide directory access because they contain the same directory information.

For IBID Publishing, this means that key services always have access.

Security—Key security features included with Active Directory are the management of user and computer authentication and access control. Active Directory centralizes this by using Kerberos authentication. Not only can access control be defined on each object, but also on each property of each object in the directory.

This fine-grained delegation of authority at the OU level will allow IBID Publishing to improve both security and operational efficiency, particularly in handling frequent organizational change.

Interoperability—The Active Directory uses standard directory access protocols, such as Lightweight Directory Access Protocol (LDAP). Because of this, it can work with other directory services employing these protocols. A number of Application Programming Interfaces (APIs), such as Active Directory Service Interfaces (ADSIs), offer developers access to these protocols.

Integration with DNS—DNS translates human-readable computer names, such as mycomputer.enterprise.center.com to numeric Internet Protocol (IP) addresses. Through this functionality, clients and servers in Transmission Control Protocol/Internet Protocol (TCP/IP) networks are able to identify and connect to each other. DNS is Active Directory's name location service.

IBID Publishing will use the Dynamic DNS service included in Windows 2000 Advanced Server to reduce network administrative complexity and redundant DNS infrastructure.

Policy-based administration—Group Policies are configuration settings that are applied to users or computers. All Group Policy settings are contained in Group Policy Objects (GPOs). GPOs can be applied to sites, domainsibid.com or OUs.

IBID Publishing will use GPO settings to define user access to domainibid.com resources, such as applications, and how these domain resources are configured for use.

Scalability—Multiple domainsibid.com can be combined into a domainibid.com tree and multiple domain trees can be combined into a forest. Active Directory can include a number of domains, each with multiple Domain Controllers (DCs).

This kind of scalability will enable IBID Publishing to size the directory to meet any network requirements.

Extensibility—The schema contains a definition of each object class, and each object class's attributes that can be stored in the directory. The Active Directory schema is extensible. This means administrators can add new classes of objects to the schema and add new attributes to existing classes of objects.

For example, IBID Publishing could add a Purchasing Permission attribute to a user object and, as part of each user's attribute set, the user's purchasing limit would be accessible.

IBID Publishing Organizational Structure

The primary business of IBID Publishing is educational software design, development and deployment. IBID Publishing's testing division plays a strategic role in testing and deploying Enterprise Center software before release to other customers. This division exists as a complete entity separate from, but mirroring many of, the aspects in their corporate Active Directory structure. This means that they can set up their Windows 2000 system in the testing division and migrate each portion as it is tested into the rest of the corporate structure.

IBID Publishing comprises approximately 500 staff positions worldwide, another 9,000 users on a part-time or full-time basis, 3000 desktops and 250 servers that span 75 sites in 14 countries.

Like other international organizations, IBID Publishing is organized into functional groups. This includes Information Technology (IT), Accounting, Human Resources, Product Development, Marketing, Testing and Administration. Four IT groups are involved in the Windows 2000 domain namespace design and deployment. The deployment team also includes members from other areas of the company, such as product development and product support services. Common in most IT companies are internal reorganizations. During the course of the Windows 2000 deployment, IBID Publishing could undergo several reorganizations.

Namespace Design Environment

The project team is responsible for defining and coordinating the delivery of deployment tasks so that project goals and milestones are achieved in a timely fashion. The Active Directory service must be in place before setting up other features and products depending on it. The first task is to design and deploy the Windows 2000 domain and account infrastructure components. Elements are organized into OUs within a domainibid.com. Domains link together to form trees, and trees join to create a forest.

Pilot Testing

During pilot testing of Windows 2000 Advanced Server, IBID Publishing built an Active Directory-based environment for learning purposes as part of their testing lab. One thousand users from IBID Publishing business units and product groups were moved into the pilot environment to authenticate against Windows 2000. This pilot environment allowed for testing of all aspects of Windows 2000 throughout deployment and provided a test environment for the development of new products and services.

Namespace Design Goals

The IBID Publishing plan for Active Directory needs to be general and flexible. Some overall objectives of deployment include the following:

• The deployment of the design must be achievable in a defined time period, including periodic revisions to include new features

- Existing IT services and user functionality must be maintained

- The design must isolate particular environments, such as production environments from testing environments, by using separate forests

- Support of evolutionary migration paths and existing Windows NT 4.0 controllers may need to be preserved

- The design must facilitate domainibid.com consolidation of existing Windows NT 4.0 resource domainsibid.com into OUs in geographically-based Windows 2000 child domains

- Use the security granularity of Active Directory for greater administrative flexibility and to provide delegated resource control

- Mapping to the DNS namespace, the design must incorporate most of the domainsibid.com into the existing organization's corporate root DNS namespace

- Domain names can be based on geographical regions or data center boundaries, reducing the impact of business unit reorganizations on the namespace

- Consider future developments and expansions to the network

Namespace Design Process

With these goals in mind, the team has developed the following four-step plan for Active Directory deployment, starting with the namespace design.

Create a Forest Plan:

- Determine the number of forests

- Create a change control policy for each forest

Create a Domain Plan for each forest:

- Determine the number of domainsibid.com

- Choose a forest root domain

- Assign a DNS name to each domainibid.com

- Plan DNS server deployment

- Optimize authentication with shortcut trusts

Create an OU plan for each forest:

- Create OUs to delegate administration

- Create OUs to hide objects

- Create OUs for Group Policy

Create a Site Topology/Server Placement plan for each forest:

- Define sites and site links

- Size/place servers into sites

Creating the Forest Plan

Although a single domainibid.com is the easiest to deploy, IBID Publishing determined that they needed a number of domainsibid.com. The domains can be arranged into a tree or forest.

 Note: Domains in trees and forests contain the same configuration, schema and global catalog. As the domainsibid.com are placed into trees or forests, the two-way transitive trust relationship allows them to share resources.

In Windows 2000 Active Directory, domainsibid.com are named DNS names, but before beginning to use DNS, IBID Publishing must plan their DNS namespace. Some decisions need to be made, including the following:

- A DNS name has been previously chosen and in use on the Internet (enterprisecenter.com)

- The company's internal Active Directory namespace will be different from the external namespace (sysadmin.ec.com)

Forest Structure

From the physical view, a forest is a distributed database and domainsibid.com define specific divisions of the database. From the logical view, a forest is a collection of domains and domainibid.com trees defining the replication and security boundaries of Windows 2000.

 Note: The Active Directory cannot be larger than the forest.

Domains in a forest are automatically connected by bi-directional transitive trust relationships. However, you can establish one-way only, non-transitive trusts between domainsibid.com in different forests. Accordingly, when access between domains must be isolated, each domainibid.com must reside in a separate forest.

For example, IBID Publishing product groups, such as the Educational Programs development group and the testing group, have environments requiring regular server infrastructure changes and re-configurations. These dynamic environments are required to support the product development process and ongoing product testing activities. The development process requires frequent changes to the schema design of the Active Directory service.

Schema changes have an effect on the entire forest so the development group and the testing group need their own isolated forests for the greatest flexibility and to isolate frequent schema changes from the production environment. The Active Directory is used to administer the high-level forest configuration, user accounts and system access.

The sysadmin.ibid.com forest is the primary container of IBID Publishing's corporate domainibid.com user accounts, groups and corporate resources. The root of the forest is the sysadmin.ibid.com domain. A top-level placeholder, this domain holds a limited number of administrative accounts and resources that need to be available to the whole organization.

Domains inside the sysadmin.ibid.com forest have numerous external trusts to child domains in different development forests. The prefix (DC=sysadmin) is added to ibid.com in order to differentiate the intranet from the Internet namespace (ibidpublishing.com).

All domainsibid.com in a forest share a common schema and configuration information. Therefore, domains in each forest make up the administrative, security and replication boundaries for a collection of objects, such as users, groups and computers, relevant to a particular group of users. Figure 10.4 shows a view of IBID Publishing's Windows 2000 forest.

Figure 10.4 High-Level Forest Structure

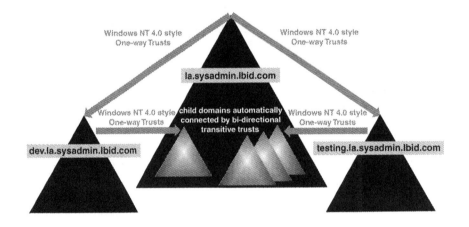

Domain Structure

Domains are the core unit of a logical structure in Active Directory. They correspond to a logical partition for both security and directory replication within Active Directory. Every domainibid.com must have at least one domain controller. Each domain has a common schema and forest configuration that all of the domain controllers in a forest share with the other controllers in the forest. A single domain can span multiple physical locations or sites. To do this, Active Directory uses a multimaster peer-controller model.

All of the domain controllers that are authoritative for a domain receive changes and propagate those changes, allowing inter-site replication to occur within a domain. All domainsibid.com within an Active Directory tree share a common directory schema, configuration information and global catalog.

IBID Publishing's Windows NT 4.0 logical domainibid.com model was made up of seven Master Domains (MDs) that each trusted the other MDs, and 200 resource domainsibid.com, which, in turn, trust each of the seven MDS, as shown in Figure 10.5. In IBID Publishing's network, resource domains are units of delegated administration. This kind of environment is complex to manage, as it creates a huge web of trust relationships that must be managed by the administrators.

Figure 10.5 Windows NT 4.0 Domain Structure

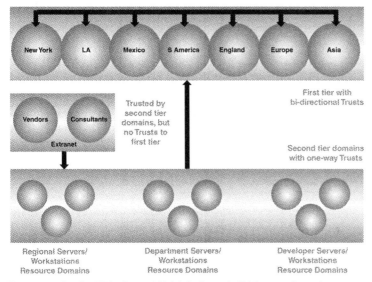

For users in the Windows NT 4.0 domainibid.com, locating resources was difficult. A user needed to know the location of a particular resource, such as a printer, to find and use it. Name resolution service was done primarily through the Microsoft Windows Internet Naming Service (WINS). WINS dynamically maps IP addresses to computer names or Network Basic Input/Output System (NetBIOS) names. This lets users access resources by name instead of forcing them to use difficult to remember and hard to recognize IP addresses.

WINS servers support clients running Windows NT and earlier Windows operating systems. As WINS is non-hierarchal, the WINS servers for the network would be heavily accessed each time a resource location was unknown. Replication traffic for WINS service is heavy, as a change in one WINS database needs to be replicated worldwide.

With Active Directory, the new domainibid.com hierarchy will allow users to search multiple domainsibid.com with one query to the Active Directory Global Catalog (GC) service. The GC is a searchable index that enables users to search for network objects without knowing their domain locations. The GC is a partial replica of the Active Directory. Finding a resource in Active Directory is much easier; a user effectively queries against all domains at once and does not need to know the location of the resource. Built automatically by the Active Directory replication system, the attributes in the GC catalog are those used most frequently in search operations and those required to locate a full replica of the object.

In theory, if IBID Publishing's network were linked by permanent connections with ample bandwidth, there would be no architectural need for more than one domainibid.com. Nevertheless, adding domainsibid.com can solve both architectural and political issues. As user logon authentication and access is largely controlled at the domain level, adding additional domains will decentralize the control of the network.

In this design, the old Windows NT 4.0 geographical MDs become child domains of sysadmin.ibid.com in the Windows 2000 forest. A number of domainsibid.com have been consolidated, as shown in Figure 10.6.

Figure 10.6 Windows 2000 Domain Structure

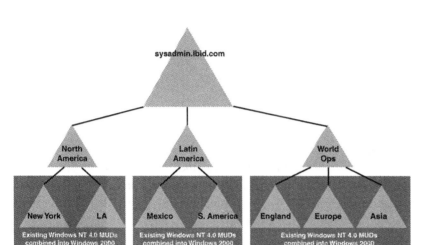

The new domainibid.com design eliminates resource domainsibid.com, collapsing them into OUs. Because Windows 2000 automatically establishes trust relationships between domains, trust management is easier. Trusts between domains in the same forest are transitive and hierarchical. If domain A trusts domain B and domain B trusts domain C, domain A also trusts domain C. The vast majority of the trust relationships Enterprise Center had to manage manually are eliminated, network traffic is reduced and fewer domain controllers are needed.

For example, in the North American child domain MD consolidation process:

- Departmental global groups can be eliminated

- A number of local groups can be eliminated

- A large number of resource domainibid.com trusts that were individually managed under Windows NT 4.0 can be eliminated

- Authentication across the Wide Area Network (WAN) will be improved

- Centralized OU management can be enabled

- GPO creation and management will be enabled

- The number of domainibid.com controllers would be reduced

The new design gives finer control of delegated authority by moving a great number of objects into OUs instead of resource domainsibid.com.

DNS Structure

DNS is a hierarchal, distributed database consisting of resource records containing a DNS name, record type and data values associated with that record type. It is an industry standard name resolution service. DNS can translate an IP address into a domainibid.com name. For example, a numeric address like 232.452.120.54 can become something like sysadmin.ibid.com. Figure 10.7 describes how DNS finds the IP address of a computer based on its name.

Figure 10.7 DNS Location

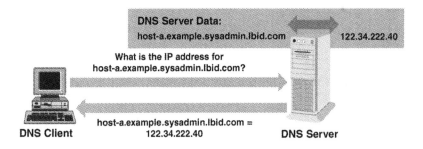

The Active Directory service can use any DNS server that backs its dynamic update protocols and the Service Resource Record (SRV). SRV is used in a zone to register and locate well-known TCP/IP services. The SRV resource record is used in

Windows 2000 to locate domainibid.com controllers for Active Directory Service. WINS name resolution is still supported, primarily for legacy clients.

Windows 2000 domain names are DNS names. This decreases WAN traffic for DNS queries for resources found within the given domainibid.com and allows intranet users to find resources with the same simple naming convention. For example, the fictional JamesSmith@ec.com is both a user name in the la.sysadmin.ibid.com domain and an Internet e-mail address. Figure 10.8 shows a comparison between the DNS and Active Directory namespace.

Figure 10.8 Comparing DNS and Active Directory Namespace Roots

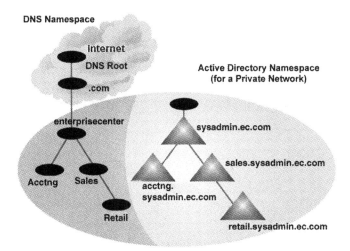

IBID Publishing's implementation of DNS in Windows 2000 can use the Active Directory service instead of the standard DNS structure as its data storage and replication engine. This implementation will give them the following benefits:

- Only the changes to the database need to be replicated instead of the entire database

- Active Directory replication is secure

- Because integrated DNS replication is performed by the Active Directory service, there is no need to support a separate topology for replication for DNS servers

- Because Active Directory replication is multimaster rather than the single master available with DNS, information is propagated to all controllers in the domainsibid.com

When DNS is integrated into Active Directory service, the replication engine always synchronizes the DNS zone information. Each new domainibid.com controller handles its DNS registration and updates without administrative intervention because IBID Publishing deploys Windows 2000 throughout the organization.

The following goals were established for IBID Publishing's DNS design:

- Implement the intranet namespace (sysadmin.ibid.com) internally to differentiate between intranet resources and Internet resources (ibidpublishing.com)

- Ease the transition from names used by WINS to the Fully Qualified Domain Names (FQDN) used by DNS

- Make efficient use of the network bandwidth to provide precise and timely name resolution responses to the users

- Minimize the administrative overhead by using DNS where appropriate and placing all legacy systems in the legacy zone (dns.ibid.com)

Preliminary testing indicated that IBID Publishing could use the integration of DNS in Windows 2000 and design each domainibid.com controller to provide DNS services as well. On their organization's network, DNS is set up to run in DS integrated mode for all zones. DNS registration is automatic, as each new domain controller is added into the namespace, as shown in Figure 10.9.

Figure 10.9 DNS Updates the Database when Addresses Change

The logon name for clients running earlier versions of the Microsoft operating systems is the NetBIOS domainibid.com name concatenated with the Security Accounts Manager (SAM) account name. For example: IBID Publishing\johns. A Windows 2000 machine can be identified by a NetBIOS name, for backwards compatibility, and by a full DNS computer name that is a concatenation of the host name and primary DNS suffix. By default, the primary DNS suffix of a computer is set to the DNS domain name of the Active Directory service to which it is joined.

The following table describes the correlation between the Windows NT 4.0 domainsibid.com, the NetBIOS name that legacy Windows-based users will see and the DNS name all of the Windows 2000 users will see.

IBID Publishing used the NetBIOS name of each upgraded domainibid.com as the leftmost label in the DNS name of the domain, as shown in Table 10.1, to help reduce the confusion of users and administrators as they make the transition.

Table 10.1 NetBIOS-DNS Namespace Mapping

Windows NT 4.0 Domain	NetBIOS Name	DNS Name
NEW	corp	sysadmin.ibid.com
New York and LA domainsibid.com combined	northamerica (new domain)ibid.com	northamerica.sysadmin.ibid.com
Mexico and South America domainsibid.com combined	latinamerica (new domain)ibid.com	latinamerica.sysadmin.ibid.com
England, Europe and Asia domainsibid.com combined	worldops (new domain)ibid.com	worldops.sysadmin.ibid.com

Note: Child domainsibid.com are appended with the name of the parent domainibid.com. For example, the full name of the North America domain is northamerica.sysadmin.ibid.com.

Administrative Structure

In the Windows NT 4.0 environment, IBID Publishing centrally managed global groups and Windows NT account creation, modification and deletion at the domainibid.com level in the MDs.

IBID Publishing's Windows 2000 design will use Group Policy associated with containers (domainsibid.com, OUs and sites) to manage resources. There is no equivalent in Windows NT 4.0 to Windows 2000 Group Policy. Group Policies can control most environment settings; however, they are strictly administrative in nature and maintained only within the realm of the Active Directory service.

Group Policy is administered by using GPOs. GPOs are data structures attached in a specific hierarchy to selected objects, sites, domainsibid.com or OUs and are utilized in a set order, LSDOU: Local, Site, Domain and OU. All of the later policies refine the policies applied previously.

Group policies are collections of user and computer configuration settings that can be linked to domainsibid.com and organizational units to specify the users' desktops. For example, by using group policies, IBID Publishing will be able to determine which programs will be available to which users, the programs that appear on each user's desktop and their Start menu options.

IBID Publishing will be able to take advantage of group features, such as universal groups, to delegate the administration of objects to users, and the management of permissions by adding groups to Access Control Lists (ACLs). Following are some of the group features that can be used by IBID Publishing:

- Groups can be nested or defined within groups (in native mode)

- Groups can contain non-security members, an important feature when the group is used for both security and distribution list purposes

- The security usage of groups can be disabled, which is important when the group is solely used as a distribution list

By default, Group Policy affects all computers and users in a selected Active Directory container. However, you can filter the effects of Group Policy based on users' or computers' membership in a Windows 2000 Security Group. Figure 10.10 illustrates a Group Policy and Active Directory scenario.

Figure 10.10 Group Policy and Active Directory

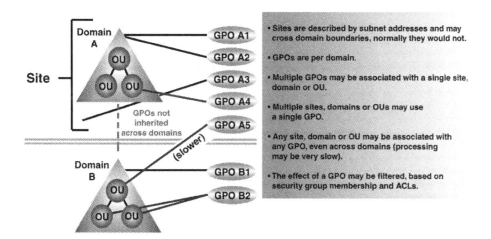

Defined desktop configurations can be established for particular groups of users and computers by using the Group Policy Microsoft Management Console (MMC) snap-in. This MMC snap-in provides features for setting Group Policy, including options for registry-based policies, security settings, software installation, scripts and folder redirection. The Group Policy settings are contained in a GPO that is, in turn, associated with selected Active Directory system containers: sites, domainsibid.com and OUs.

Organizational Units Structure

OUs are the building blocks of the Active Directory. OU containers can be used to organize objects within a domainibid.com. They form the logical units used to delegate administration within a domain. Examples of OUs are geographic locations, projects, cost centers, and business units or divisions.

OUs can contain, but are not limited to the following objects:

• Users

• Computers

• Groups

- Printers

- File shares

- Other OUs

Tip: An OU cannot contain objects from another domainibid.com.

In Windows 2000, resource domainsibid.com can be consolidated into a hierarchy of OUs. You delegate authority through combinations of OUs, defining attribute access control and access control inheritance. You create OUs to further define the domainibid.com namespace. By doing this, you can arrange users, groups, files and other information into a usable hierarchy. Additionally, you can delegate administration by assigning permissions for the OUs to other users within your company.

An OU model needs to reflect the administrative model of an organization. You can organize and nest OUs to create a logical structure that maps to the way you organize your business (Figure 10.11).

Figure 10.11 Organizational Structure and Network Administrative Model

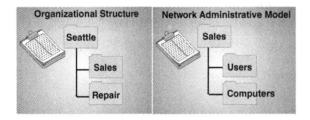

When you organize user accounts and resources into hierarchical OUs, you can create a much clearer representation of the actual business structure in the domainibid.com. With the delegation features of Active Directory, users and user groups can perform very specific administrative tasks, such as resetting passwords or clearing print queues. The OU hierarchy inside a domain is independent of the structure of other domainsibid.com. You can create OUs for any of the following reasons:

- To assign administrative rights that are limited to a specific OU and the objects it contains

- To simplify Group Policy

- To create a logical organization for administrators

 Note: The OU hierarchy in a particular domainibid.com is independent of the OU hierarchy in any other domain. Each domain can implement its own OU hierarchy.

IBID Publishing's design for their OU hierarchy considers the following two goals:

Goal 1—IBID Publishing wants to control Group Policy application so that it applies to a distinct group of users, such as their permanent employees or temporary contractors.

Goal 2—IBID Publishing wants to group objects with the same permissions together. They can then assign permissions once for the whole OU rather than multiple times for each resource.

OU structures can be unique to each domainibid.com. However, IBID Publishing has chosen to have their first-level OUs standardized throughout all the sysadmin.ibid.com domainsibid.com, even if a particular location does not need them. These OUs will contain the servers over which each of IBID Publishing's business units has administrative control. For example, IBID Publishing's sales operations group will have administrative control over the SQL servers in the sales OU. This provides consistency for organizational support and administration at no additional cost.

Figure 10.12 shows the top-level OU namespace common to all domainsibid.com in IBID Publishing design, with examples of nested OUs:

Figure 10.12 Top-Level OU Structure

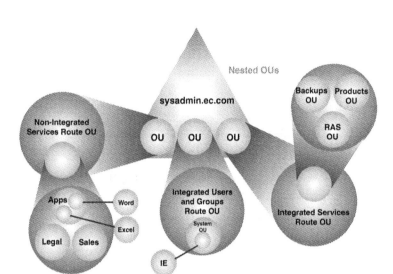

Using Windows 2000, IBID Publishing can apply group policies at the OU level. By using Group Policy in combination with containers, IBID Publishing can enforce necessary settings at the container level. In other words, Group policies let you manage users and computers in bulk. These settings are as follows:

Computer and user settings—Computer and user settings include the policies that specify operating system behavior, the user's desktop, application settings, assigned and published applications, security settings and computer startup and shutdown scripts. Two different policies can be applied. Computer-related group policies are applied when the operating system starts. User-related group policies are applied when users log on to the computer.

Software policies—Software policies apply the registry settings on the desktop. These include group policies for the Windows 2000 operating system, components and applications.

User documents and settings—User documents and settings extensions add files, shortcuts, or folders to special folders, such as My Documents, Start menu, Desktop, and Favorites that define the individual user's desktop.

Scripts—Scripts can be assigned to run when the computer starts or shuts down, or when users log on or off their computers. This process uses Windows Scripting Host (WSH). Scripts can be written in a number of different formats, including Visual Basic scripting (VBScript) and Microsoft's JScript development software.

System services—System services control configuration settings and security options (ACLs) for system services such as network services, print services and Internet/intranet services.

Security settings—Security settings in Active Directory include the following:

- Account policies which are the computer security settings for password policy, lockout policy, and Kerberos ticket policy in Windows NT domainsibid.com

- Local policies which are used to configure who has local or network access to the computer and whether or how local events are audited

- Event logs which control security settings for the Application, Security, and System event logs

For example, the administrator wants to be able to lock down the users in IBID Publishing's telephone order department so that no one can change their configurations. The workstations are in use 24 hours a day and the operators cannot take orders if they cannot use their computers properly. As the administrator, you could configure a group policy that restricts the settings that a user can change on these workstations.

Site Topology

The objects sites, site links and subnets represent the physical connectivity in a network. These are stored in the configuration container and are replicated to every domainibid.com controller in the forest. A site consists of one or more well-connected TCP/IP subnets. A site allows administrators to configure Active Directory access and replication topology quickly and easily to take advantage of the physical network. When a user logs on, the Active Directory client locates an Active Directory server in the same site as the user. A site link is a link between two sites that allows replication to occur. Each site contains the schedule that determines when replication can occur between sites that it connects. A subnet is a portion of the network that shares a network address with other portions of the network, but is distinguished by a subnet number.

In logical terms, sites are used to control replication traffic. Active Directory automatically creates more replication connections between domainibid.com controllers in the same site than between domain controllers in different sites. IBID Publishing can optimize network bandwidth for their replication traffic by placing sites on either side of slow WAN links, and ensure that all of their IP subnets in a site have high-speed connectivity.

In physical terms, sites are one or more well-connected TCP/IP subnets. This is based on the premise that computers with the same subnet address are connected to the same network segment, usually a LAN or other high-bandwidth environment. Defining a site as a set of subnets enables the administrators to easily configure Active Directory access and replication topology to take advantage of the physical network.

When a user logs on, the Active Directory will first look for a server in the same site as the user. There is no formal association between the limits of a domainibid.com and a site. A domain can contain multiple sites (Figure 10.13) or a site can have multiple domainsibid.com (Figure 10.14). Additionally, domains and sites do not have to maintain the same name space.

Figure 10.13 Multiple Sites within the Same Domain

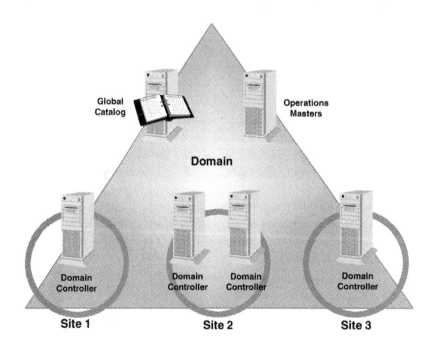

Figure 10.14 Multiple Domains in the Same Site

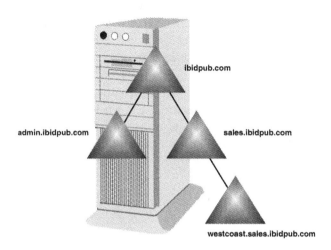

Site boundaries are defined by the speed of the network connections. IBID Publishing has defined a minimum link speed of 256 KBs to maximize both Active Directory traffic replication and other network traffic.

Computers in the same site, in network terms, are close to each other and communication between the computers is fast, reliable and efficient. For users, this allows for quick logon authentication or resource location by physical proximity. For IBID Publishing administrators, this also means that the replication traffic is easier to manage because only the attribute of the object that has changed needs to be replicated.

When a computer connects to the network, it receives a TCP/IP address from a Dynamic Host Configuration Protocol (DHCP) server, identifying the subnet to which the computer is attached. DHCP simplifies TCP/IP network configuration and dynamically configures IP addresses for clients. It ensures that address conflicts do not occur by centralizing address allocation. The computers that have statically configured IP addresses also have statically configured subnet information.

In either case, the domainibid.com controller locator will attempt to locate an Active Directory server in the same site as the user, based on the subnet information known to the computer. Succeeding resource requests, such as finding the nearest printer, are resolved in the same way. This is achievable because the user's computer already knows what TCP/IP subnet it is on, and the subnets relate directly to Active Directory-based sites.

Sites are connected to each other using site links. Active Directory site links define connectivity between sites, and represent the physical network. A site link represents a set of sites that can communicate with one another at the same cost using the same schedule. For example, two sites that are connected with a point-to-point T1 could be characterized by a single site link. A number of buildings in a city, each in their own site, connected by an Asynchronous Transfer Mode (ATM) backbone could also be characterized by a site link containing all of the different buildings (sites).

Site links have a cost and replication interval assigned to them. By using these parameters, both inter-site and intra-site replication traffic can be managed by Active Directory's Knowledge Consistency Checker (KCC). A site link bridge object for a specific inter-site transport (most often IP) is created by specifying two or more site Links. Figure 10.15 illustrates this concept. Following is an example of how a site link works:

- Site link AB connects sites A and B through an IP—with a cost of 3

- Site link BC connects sites B and C through an IP—with a cost of 4

- Site link ABC connects AB and BC

- The site link bridge ABC implies that an IP message can be sent from site A to site C with a cost of 7 (3+4)

Figure 10.15 Site Link Bridge

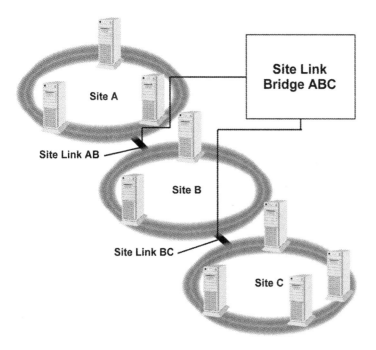

With intra-site replication, the KCC will automatically generate a bi-directional ring topology for all of the domainibid.com controllers in the same domain in a site. The KCC adheres to the three-hop rule. This means that there can be no more than three hops from any domain controller in a site to any other domain controller in a site. For inter-site replication, the KCC can automatically generate a least-cost spanning tree replication topology. The KCC also takes into account whether a domain controller has been identified as a bridgehead server and the cost of each site link.

Generally, all of IBID Publishing's remote offices have WAN-speed connectivity back to the corporate ATM. As a result, all of the remote offices that have a domainibid.com controller are individual sites in the Windows 2000-based design. If a remote office is too small (under 25 people) to justify the cost of having its own domain controller, then their subnet is set to be part of the site which is closest to them on the network—in this case, closest implies a good WAN speed. This means that the users will be authenticated by the next closest domain controller.

Conclusion

During the early stages of Windows 2000 namespace planning, IBID Publishing confronted some barriers in the Windows NT 4.0 Intranet environment that had to be addressed before moving forward with the deployment of Windows 2000 Active Directory service.

The first item the administrators needed to consider was how Active Directory works. The following Figure 10.16 shows the three steps of Active Directory operation.

Figure 10.16 How Active Directory Works

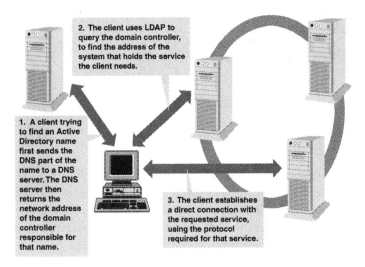

The basics of Active Directory involve the following three processes:

Process 1—A client needs to look up an Active Directory name. The client first sends the DNS part of the name to a standard DNS server. The DNS server then returns the network address of the domainibid.com controller responsible for the name.

Process 2—The client then uses LDAP to query the domainibid.com controller to find the address of the system where the service the client needs resides.

Process 3—The client establishes a direct connection with the service using the protocol that service requires.

The major consideration for implementing Active Directory is planning, planning, and more planning. Planning is extremely important to a successful deployment with minimum end-user disruption. If you are migrating from Windows NT 4.0, there are added considerations. Because the Windows 2000 namespace is different from that of Windows NT 4.0, much of the Windows NT 4.0 domainibid.com setup and functionality need to be reexamined. This can entail a redefinition of the namespace using the Windows 2000 name space, group policy and organizational unit strategy. Following are some of the things that IBID Publishing considered:

IBID Publishing's Windows 2000 Active Directory deployment team determined the optimal namespace design should include several iterations. First, they followed a design process based on the ideal environment, without regard to dependencies, existing environment and timelines. Then they went though the process again, basing their design on dependencies, existing environment and timelines. Next they compared the two plans and combined them to come up with the one that would work best for their organization.

Detailed information on their current environment was necessary for the Active Directory deployment. Some of the things that they needed to know were the following:

• The number of employees and users in each location

• The speed of local network links

• TCP/IP subnets by location

• Anticipated growth

From this information, the namespace design could be constructed and deployed.

Because IBID Publishing is an international organization, international considerations regarding the information contained in Active Directory needed to be reviewed carefully. For example, you may consider one of the most important pieces of information to be included in the Active Directory is an employee's home telephone number; however, Europe has some explicit laws around personal information to which you must adhere. When planning the international namespace, it is important that other languages be taken into account. Computer, site and domainibid.com names that have one meaning in English can be derogatory or offensive in another language. For example, in German mist is slang for manure.

Because Windows 2000 uses DNS for location services and name resolution, Windows 2000 domain names are DNS names. Using only Internet-standard characters in domainibid.com and computer names will ensure that computers with multiple localized versions of Windows will be able to communicate with each other. Determining what information IBID Publishing Active Directory will hold and from what source the data will come (for example the Human Resources system), are the key deciding factors for the design. These factors drive the planning of network bandwidth, organization and security requirements.

They selected to deploy from the top down. With tight integration of DNS and a consolidated infrastructure service platform, installation and configuration of each succeeding domainibid.com controller and GC are then almost automatic.

The steps IBID Publishing used to create an OU structure plan for a domainibid.com were the following:

• Create OUs to delegate administration

• Create OUs to hide objects

• Create OUs for Group Policy

IBID Publishing followed the steps in the order presented, because an OU structure designed purely for delegation of administration would be shaped differently than an OU structure designed purely for Group Policy.

Vocabulary

Review the following terms in preparation for the certification exam.

Term	Description
ADSI	The Active Directory Services Interface is the programming interface that applications use to access the Active Directory.
APIs	Application Programming Interfaces are a set of routines used by an application program to direct the performance of procedures by the computer's operating system.
ATM	The Asynchronous Transfer Mode is a networking technology based on transferring packets of a fixed size across a fixed channel.
DACL	The Discretionary Access Control List contains the access control permissions for an object and its attributes, and the Security Identifiers (SIDs), which determine who can use the object.
DHCP	The Dynamic Host Configuration Protocol simplifies TCP/IP network configuration and dynamically configures IP addresses for clients. DHCP ensures that address conflicts do not occur by centralizing address allocation.
directory	A directory is an online storage location that contains objects that may have various kinds of structures and be related to one another in some way. For example, an online building directory of a mall contains names of businesses, locations and telephone numbers.
distributed directory	A distributed directory allows for the distribution of data across the network on many different computers in a manner that is transparent to the users.
DN	The Distinguished Name naming convention uses particular abbreviations to define the path for an Active Directory object. For example, a distinguished name is: Domain Controller= com/Domain Controller= Corp/CN=Users1
DNS	The Domain Name System is an industry standard name resolution service that allows clients to locate Active Directory services. DNS can translate an IP address into a domainibid.com name. For example, a numeric address like 232.452.120.54 can become something like xyz.com.

Term	Description
domainibid.com	In Active Directory, a domainibid.com is a boundary for security, administrative purposes and a partition of replication. Active Directory data is replicated between domain controllers within a domain.
domainibid.com boundary	Because domainsibid.com are a security boundary, by default, administrative permissions for a domainibid.com are limited to the domain. For example, an administrator with permissions to set security policies in one domain is not automatically granted authority to set security policies in any other domain in the directory.
domainibid.com controller	In a Windows 2000 Server domainibid.com, a domain controller is a computer running Windows 2000 Server that authenticates domain logons and maintains the security policy and the master database for a domain.
extensible	Administrators can add new classes of objects to the schema and new attributes to existing classes of objects. The schema contains a definition of each object class, and each object class's attributes that can be stored in the directory.
forest	A forest is a group of one or more trees that trust each other. All trees in a forest share a common schema, configuration and global catalog. When a forest contains multiple trees, the trees do not form a contiguous namespace. All the trees in a forest trust each other through transitive bi-directional trust relationships.
FQDN	The Fully Qualified Domain Name is a DNS name that uniquely identifies the computer on the network. By default, it is a concatenation of the host name, the primary DNS suffix and a period. For example, an FQDN might be Sales.ibid.com.
GC	A Global Catalog is built automatically by the Active Directory replication system, the Global Catalog contains a partial replica of every Windows 2000 domain in the directory. When given one or more attributes of the target object, the GC lets users and applications find objects quickly, without knowing what domainibid.com they occupy. The attributes in the GC are those used most frequently in search operations, and those required to locate a full replica of the object.

Term	Description
GPO	Group Policy Objects are a collection of Group Policy settings and the documents created by the Group Policy snap-in. They are stored at the domainibid.com level, and they affect users and computers contained in sites, domainsibid.com and OUs. Each Windows 2000 computer has one group of settings stored locally, called the local Group Policy object.
Group Policy	A Group Policy is a tool defining and controlling how programs, network resources and the operating system operate for users and computers in an organization. Group Policy is applied to users or computers based on their membership in sites, domainsibid.com or OUs.
groups	Groups are Active Directory objects that can contain users, contacts computers and other groups. Like user and computer accounts, groups are Windows 2000 security principals. They are directory objects and SIDs are assigned to them at creation.
GUID	The Globally Unique Identifier distinguishes the type of object or attribute and is part of the ACE.
IP	The Internet Protocol is the routable protocol in the TCP/IP suite that is responsible for the IP addressing, routing, and fragmentation and reassembly of IP packets.
KCC	The Knowledge Consistency Checker is a service that automatically generates a replication topology.
LAN	A Local Area Network is a communications network connecting computers, printers and other devices within limited area.
LDAP	The Lightweight Directory Access Protocol is an Internet standard that makes it possible for Web browsers to find and access information in a directory service database.
logical components	Active Directory uses the logical and physical components to build a directory structure to match the needs of your organization. The Active Directory logical components are domainsibid.com, organizational units, trees and forests.

Term	Description
multimaster replication	Multimaster replication is a replication model in which any domainibid.com controller accepts and replicates directory changes to any other domain controller. This differs from other replication models in which the computer stores the single modifiable copy of the directory and other computers store backup copies.
namespace	The Active Directory and DNS are both namespaces. A namespace is a set of distinct names for the resources in a network. The names in a namespace can be resolved to the objects they represent.
NetBIOS	The Network Basic Input/Output System is an application programming interface that provides a set of commands for requesting legacy network services.
NT	New Technologies is Microsoft's version of Windows before Windows 2000. Windows 2000 was built on NT technology.
object	An object is a distinct, named set of attributes that represents something concrete, such as a user, a printer or an application. The attributes hold the data that describes the thing identified by the object. Attributes for a user might be their first and last names and e-mail address.
OU	An Organizational Unit is a logical container within a domainibid.com. You use an OU to organize objects for easier administration and access.
physical components	Active Directory uses the logical and physical components to build a directory structure to match the needs of your organization. The Active Directory physical components are sites and domainibid.com controllers.
RDN	A Relative Distinguished Name is the name used to uniquely reference an object with its parent container.
replication	Replication is the exchange of database information between the controllers and domainsibid.com. This periodic exchange ensures that all of the domainibid.com controllers within a domain contain consistent information.

Term	Description
SAM	Security Accounts Manager is a Windows 2000 service used during the login process that maintains user information.
schema	A schema is a description of the object classes and attributes stored in Active Directory. For each object class, the schema defines what attributes an object class must have, what additional attributes it may have, and what object class can be its parent.
SID	Security Identifiers are unique, alphanumeric structures for security principles. There is a SID for each user, group or computer. The first part of the SID identifies the domainibid.com in which the SID was issued. The second part identifies an account object within the issuing domain— that is, the Relative Identifier (RID). SIDs are never reused. SIDS are only used by the system and are transparent to the user.
site	A site is one or more well-connected TCP/IP subnets. A site allows administrators to configure Active Directory access and replication topology quickly and easily to take advantage of the physical network. When users log on, Active Directory clients locate Active Directory servers in the same site as the user.
site link	A site link joins two sites, allowing replication to occur. Each site contains the schedule that determines when replication can occur between sites that it connects.
TCP/IP	The Transmission Control Protocol/Internet Protocol is a set of protocols that provides communication among diverse networks. Because it accommodates different architectures and operating systems, TCP/IP is the most commonly used Internet protocol.
transitive trust	A transitive trust is a type of trust relationship among domainsibid.com, where if domainibid.com A trusts domain B and domain B trusts domain C, then domain A trusts domain C.

Term	Description
tree	A tree is a set of domainsibid.com connected to each other through transitive bi-directional trusts. Trees share the same configuration, schema and GC. The domains in a tree form a hierarchal contiguous namespace.
two-way trust	A two-way trust is a trust relationship where both of the domainsibid.com in the relationship trust each other. In a two-way trust relationship, each domainibid.com has established a one-way trust with the other domain. Two-way trusts can be transitive or non-transitive. All two-way trusts between Windows 2000 domains in the same domain tree or forest are transitive.
WINS	The Microsoft Windows Internet Naming Service dynamically maps IP addresses to computer names (NetBIOS names). This lets users access resources by name instead of forcing them to use difficult to remember and hard to recognize IP addresses. WINS servers support clients running Windows NT and earlier Windows operating systems.

In Brief

If you want to...	Then do this...
Create your own deployment plan	• Learn the key Active Directory concepts that influence structure planning, and adjust the suggested planning steps to best suit your organization
	• Identify the people in your organization who should participate in structure planning
	• Understand how existing business practices might need to change or evolve to take full advantage of Active Directory
	• Understand the flexibility of the structures you create, and realize which of your choices will be easy or hard to change in the future
Define directory deployment, starting with the namespace design	Create a Forest Plan:
	• Determine the number of forests
	• Create a change control policy for each forest
	Create a Domain Plan for each forest:
	• Determine the number of domainsibid.com
	• Choose a forest root domain
	• Assign a DNS name to each domainibid.com
	• Plan DNS server deployment
	• Optimize authentication with shortcut trusts
	Create an OU plan for each forest :
	• Create OUs to delegate administration
	• Create OUs to hide objects
	• Create OUs for Group Policy
	Create a Site Topology/Server placement plan for each forest
	• Define sites and site links
	• Size/Place servers into sites

Lesson 10 Activities

Complete the following activities to prepare for the certification exam.

1. Define Active Directory.

2. List the key benefits IBID Publishing designed their Active Directory service to provide.

3. Explain what a namespace is.

4. List some of the overall objectives in deployment.

5. Describe how the logical structure elements are organized and what relationships they form in Active Directory.

6. Your company has registered the domainibid.com name enterprisecenter.com with the appropriate Internet authorities. The company has a number of separate divisions for North America, Europe and South America. You are opening a division in Africa and you have defined the scope of Active Directory to be a single domain for the African division only. Explain the name you use for the root of Active Directory.

7. You are designing an organizational unit hierarchy for your domain.ibid.com Explain what would most affect your organizational unit design.

8. Explain how trusts within domainsibid.com work.

9. Clarify why you should use groups.

10. Explain how a Global Catalog helps users locate objects.

Answers to Lesson 10 Activities

1.   Active Directory defines the scope and manages the administration for an assembly of resources on a network, such as users, computers, printers and groups. The network and its objects are organized by forests, domains,ibid.com trust relationships, organizational units and sites.

2.   IBID Publishing designed their Active Directory service to provide the following Active Directory benefits: replication, security, interoperability, integration with DNS, policy-based administration, scalability and extensibility.

3.   A namespace is a logically structured naming convention where all the objects are contiguous. All of the names in a namespace share the same root domain.

4.   Some overall objectives of deployment include the following:

   • The deployment of the design must be achievable in a defined time period, including periodic revisions to include new features

   • Existing IT services and user functionality must be maintained

   • The design must isolate particular environments, such as production environments from testing environments, by using separate forests

   • Support of evolutionary migration paths and existing Windows NT 4.0 controllers may need to be preserved

   • The design should facilitate domainibid.com consolidation of existing Windows NT 4.0 resource domainsibid.com into OUs in geographically-based Windows 2000 child domains

   • Use the security granularity of Active Directory for greater administrative flexibility and to provide delegated resource control

   • Mapping to the DNS namespace, the design must incorporate most of the domainsibid.com into the existing organization's corporate root DNS namespace

   • Domain names can be based on geographical regions or data center boundaries, reducing the impact of business unit reorganizations on the namespace

   • Consider future developments and expansions to the network

5.   Elements are organized into OUs within a domain.ibid.com Domains link together to form trees, and trees join to create a forest.

6.   Enterprisecenter.com would encompass more than the scope of the Active Directory, and could conflict with future Active Directory deployments by the main office. Africa.enterprisecenter.com would match the intended scope of the directory, but would require reinstallation if an enterprisecenter.com project was created in the future and the African division wanted to be part of the same enterprise. It is also possible to use another name that is entirely different from the public name used on the Internet, which would avoid a future conflict with an enterprisecenter.com project, but would require reinstallation of the existing domainibid.com to participate in it.

7.   The administrative model that you will use would most affect your organizational unit design.

8.   The trusts between domainsibid.com in the same forest are transitive and hierarchical. If domainibid.com A trusts domain B and domain B trusts domain C, domain A also trusts domain C.

9.   Use groups to simplify administration by granting rights and assigning permissions once to a group instead of multiple times to each individual.

10.   The global catalog contains a partial replica of the entire active directory, so it stores information about every object in a domainibid.com tree or forest. Because the GC contains information about all of the objects, a user can find information regardless of which domain, tree or forest contains the data.

Lesson 10 Quiz

These questions test your knowledge of features, vocabulary, procedures and syntax.

1. What are some of the factors you need to take into consideration when creating your Active Directory deployment plan?
   A. Learn the key Active Directory concepts that influence structure planning, and adjust the suggested planning steps to best suit your organization.
   B. Identify the people in your organization who should participate in structure planning.
   C. Understand how existing business practices might need to change or evolve to take full advantage of Active Directory.
   D. Understand the flexibility of the structures you create, and realize which of your choices will be easy to change or hard to change in the future.

2. Within Windows 2000 architecture, which component holds Active Directory?
   A. The security subsystem
   B. ACLs
   C. Domain Controllers
   D. Nested Containers

3. What three sets of information do all domainsibid.com within a single Active Directory tree share?
   A. OUs, trees and forests
   B. Sites, site links and bridgeheads
   C. Directory schema, configuration information and global catalog
   D. DNs, RDNs and GUIDs

4. In which two instances should you consider creating multiple trees within a single forest?
   A. To facilitate but tightly control partner resource access.
   B. To create explicit trusts between domainsibid.com of different Active Directory directories.
   C. To configure Active Directory-integrated DNS.
   D. To maintain multiple distinct DNS names.

5. What are some of the reasons for creating more than one domain?ibid.com
   A. Decentralized network administration
   B. Replication control
   C. International requirements
   D. Internet domain names

6.   What groupings of information should you gather before designing an Active Directory infrastructure design for an organization?
    A.   Type of administrative model.
    B.   Projected growth and reorganization.
    C.   A full replica of the global catalog server's domain,ibid.com and partial replicas of the other two domains.ibid.com
    D.   The configuration and schema for the forest.

7.   Your company has a single domainibid.com for Active Directory. All of your users in your organization are located in the corporate office. You will be opening a small satellite office to support 50 users. What will you need to consider to define a site for the satellite office or simply include it as part of the corporate site?
    A.   Decide what administrative privileges OU administrators require.
    B.   You should consider speed, availability, bandwidth utilization, and cost of the network link between the two locations.
    C.   Consult your company's organization chart.
    D.   Analyze the business models and processes in your organization.

8.   What is the difference between sites and domains?ibid.com
    A.   A site is a combination of one or more IP subnets connected by a high speed link. A domainibid.com is a logical grouping of servers and other network resources under a single name.
    B.   A site is a place. A domainibid.com is a group of computers.
    C.   A site is a component of Active Directory's physical structure and a domainibid.com is part of its logical structure.
    D.   A site is a set of Windows 2000 domains connected by a two-way transitive trust. Domains must form a contiguous namespace.

9.   In what order is Group Policy implemented?
    A.   Site, domainibid.com and OU
    B.   Local, site, domainibid.com and OU
    C.   OU, domain,ibid.com site
    D.   OU, Domain, Site, Local

10.   Which of the following describe OUs?
    A.   OUs are An Active Directory container object used within domains.ibid.com
    B.   OUs can only contain objects from child domains.
    C.   OUs are the smallest unit to which you can apply group policy.
    D.   OUs are an object in which other objects reside.

Answers to Lesson 10 Quiz

1. Answers A, B, C and D are correct. When creating a deployment plan, they are all considerations that will help you with your deployment.

2. Answer A is correct. In Windows 2000, the component that contains the Active Directory is the security subsystem.

   Answer B is incorrect. ACLs are Access Control Lists. An ACL details which users can access a network resource.

   Answer C is incorrect. A domainibid.com controller is a server that authenticates users seeking access to the domain.

   Answer D is incorrect. A container inside a container is a nested container.

3. Answer C is correct. The three sets of information that all domainsibid.com share are the directory schema, configuration information and global catalog.

   Answer A is incorrect. OUs, trees and forests are all part of the physical Active Directory.

   Answer B is incorrect. Sites, site links and bridgeheads are part of replication.

   Answer D is incorrect. DNs, RDNs and GUIDs are part of the naming conventions. A GUID is a 128-bit number that is guaranteed to be unique and is assigned when the object is created.

4. Answers A and D are correct. You create multiple trees within a single forest to maintain multiple distinct DNS names and to facilitate but tightly control partner resource access.

   Answer B is incorrect. To allow users to access resources in an Active Directory of a different forest you create one-way explicit trusts between domainsibid.com.

   Answer C is incorrect. Configuring Active Directory-integrated DNS is an optional post-installation Windows 2000 task.

5. Answers A, B, C and D are correct. Some of the reasons for creating more than one domainibid.com are decentralized network administration, replication control, international requirements, Internet domain names, different password requirements between organizations, massive numbers of objects and internal political requirements.

6.   Answers A and B are correct. Some categories of information are the type of administrative model and Projected growth and reorganization plus physical locations, security requirements, network link speeds and bandwidth utilization and the user community.

Answers C and D are incorrect. The naming contexts that will be present on the global catalog server are the configuration and schema for the forest and a full replica of the global catalog server's domain,ibid.com and partial replicas of the other two domains.ibid.com

7.   Answer B is correct. When adding your new office, you should consider speed, availability, bandwidth utilization, and cost of the network link between the two locations before determining if you need to add a new domainibid.com.

Answers A, C and D are partly correct. These answers are part of the logical design checklist. Before you create domainsibid.com and OUs, you need to consider the following:

• Using the DNS namespace, identify and name the root domain

• Determine if a tree or a forest is correct for your organization's needs

• Determine if you need additional domainsibid.com

• Consult your organization's organization chart to decide if you need more child domains

• Analyze the business models to determine which OU is best for your needs

• Determine who is to administer the OU

• Decide what administrative privileges the OU require and create a network diagram

8.   Answers A and C are correct. They describe the difference between sites and domainsibid.com.

Answer B is incorrect. A site is a place and a domainibid.com is a group of computers is a made up answer.

Answer D is incorrect. A tree is a set of Windows 2000 domains connected by a two-way transitive trust. Domains must form a contiguous namespace within the tree.

9.   Answer B is correct. Group Policies are applied in the following order: local computer, site, domainibid.com and then OU.

Answer A is incorrect. The listing is incomplete.

Answer C is incorrect. The listing is incomplete and backwards.

Answer D is incorrect. The listing is backwards.

10.   Answers A and C are correct. OUs are An Active Directory container object used within domainsibid.com and are the smallest unit to which you can apply Group Policy.

Answer B is incorrect. OUs can only contain objects from their parent domainibid.com.

Answer D is incorrect. A parent object is an object in which other objects reside.

Glossary

Term	Description
A	Address resource record is a resource record used to map a DNS domain name to a host IP address on the network.
ACE	Access Control Entry or permission entry is the allocation of permissions to a user or group and can be inherited by a specific object type. Each ACE contains a security identifier (SID), which identifies the principle (user or group) to whom the ACE applies, and what type of access the ACE grants or denies.
ACL	An Access Control List details which users can access a network resource.
Active Directory	The directory service included with Windows 2000 Server. Active Directory stores information about objects on a network and makes this information available to users and network administrators. Active Directory gives network users access to permitted resources anywhere on the network using a single logon process. It provides network administrators with an intuitive hierarchical view of the network and a single point of administration for all network objects.
ActiveX	ActiveX is a set of technologies that allow the software components to work together in a network, regardless of the language in which they are created.
administrative templates (.adm files)	The .ADM file specifies the registry settings that can be modified through the Group Policy snap-in user interface.
ADO	ActiveX Data Objects is a general technology that lets developers write scripts and applications to access and manipulate data held in a database server. ADO is used with ADSI.
ADSI	The Active Directory Services Interface is the programming interface that applications use to access the Active Directory.

Term	Description
API	Address resource record is a resource record used to map a DNS domain name to a host IP address on the network.
ASP	Active Server Pages are VB Scripts, which are inside an HTML page. They are dynamic, meaning that the Web page displayed differs, depending on the results of a script incorporated as part of that Web page.
ATM	Asynchronous Transfer Mode transmits data, voice, and frame relay traffic in real time by breaking data into packets.
attribute	A single property of an object. An object is described by the values of its attributes. Attributes of a user might include the user's first and last names and e-mail address. Attributes are also the data items describing the objects represented by the classes defined in the Schema. Attributes are defined in the Schema separately from the classes, allowing a single attribute description to be applied to many classes.
authentication	In network access, authentication is the process by which the system validates the user's logon information.
backup	A backup is a duplicate copy of a program, a disk, or data, created for archiving purposes or for ensuring that valuable files cannot be lost if the active copy is destroyed or damaged.
BDC	A Backup Domain Controller contains a copy of the directory database and can authenticate users. If the Primary Domain Controller (PDC) fails, then a BDC can be made a PDC. A PDC can be demoted to a BDC if one of the BDC's is promoted to the PDC.
BIND	BIND stands for Berkeley Internet Name Domain. It is an implementation of DNS that is written and ported to the UNIX operating system.
BINL	The Boot Information Negotiation Layer service is added during the RIS installation, and supplies management of the RIS environment. BINL is responsible for answering client network requests, querying the Active Directory for the client computer and ensuring the correct policy and configuration settings are put on the client computer during installation. If the client computer has not been set up, BINL creates the client computer account in Active Directory.
boot files	Boot files are the system files needed to start Windows 2000.

Term	Description
CD	CD is an acronym for Compact Disc read-only memory. This form of information storage is characterized by high capacity (roughly 650 megabytes) and the use of laser optics rather than magnetic means for reading data.
certificate	A certificate is a file used for authentication that secures the exchange of data on non-secured networks, such as the Internet. A certificate securely binds a public encryption key to the entity that holds the corresponding private encryption key. Certificates are digitally signed by the issuing certification authority and can be managed for a user, a computer or a service.
circular logging	Log files record system events or transactions. A circular log file overwrites existing entries after the log reaches a specified size or age.
CIW	Users of a remote boot-enabled client computer can use the Client Installation Wizard to select installation options, operating systems, and maintenance and troubleshooting tools.
class	In Active Directory, a class is used to organize objects into a logical group. Examples of object classes are those representing user accounts, groups, computers, domains, or OUs.
Cluster Database	The Cluster Database is the essential software component that controls all aspects of server cluster operation. Each node in a server cluster runs one instance of the Cluster service.
clustering	Grouping computers to work together to provide a service. Using a cluster enhances both the availability of the service and the scalability of the operating system that provides the service. Network Load Balancing provides a software solution for clustering multiple computers.
CNAME	Canonical Name is a canonical resource record used to map an alternate alias name to a primary canonical DNS domain name used in the zone.
container	An Active Directory object that holds other objects and containers. Sites, domains, and OUs are all containers.

Term	Description
CPU	The Central Processing Unit is the device that processes and transmits data, and where most calculations take place.
DACL	The Discretionary Access Control List contains the access control permissions for an object and its attributes, and the SIDs, which determine who can use the object.
DCPROMO.EXE	The utility used to promote a member server to a Windows 2000 domain controller.
DDNS	Dynamic Domain Name System is a DNS service that includes a dynamic update capability. With DDNS, nameservers and clients in the network automatically update the zone database files.
defragmentation	In Active Directory, defragmentation rearranges how the data is written in the directory database file to compact it.
DFS	Distributed File System is a file management system where files can be located on numerous computers connected over a local or wide area network, and logically represented from a single share point.
DHCP	The Dynamic Host Configuration Protocol is a networking protocol that provides safe, reliable, and simple TCP/IP network configuration. It offers dynamic configuration of IP addresses and ensures that address conflicts do not occur. It also conserves the use of IP addresses through centralized management of address allocation.
directory	A directory is an online storage location that contains objects that may have various kinds of structures and are related to one another in some way.
distributed directory	A distributed directory allows for the distribution of data across the network on many different computers in a manner that is transparent to the users.
Distribution Group	Distribution Groups have only one function, to create e-mail distribution lists. You use distribution groups with e-mail applications, such as Microsoft Exchange. You can add a contact to a distribution group so that the contact receives e-mail sent to the group. As you assign no permissions to distribution groups, they have no function in security.

Term	Description
DN	The Distinguished Name naming convention uses particular abbreviations to define the path for an Active Directory object. For example a distinguished name is: domain controller=com/domain controller=Corp/CN=Users1
DNS	Domain Name System is a hierarchical distributed database that is employed for name/address translation. DNS is the namespace used on the Internet to translate computer and service names into TCP/IP addresses. Active Directory uses DNS as its location service.
domain	In Windows 2000 Active Directory, a collection of computers defined by the administrator of a Windows 2000 Server network that shares a common directory database. A domain has a unique name, security policy, and security relationships with other domains and represents a security boundary for a Windows 2000 Network.
Domain Controller	In a Windows 2000 Server domain, a computer running Windows 2000 Server that authenticates domain logons and maintains the security policy and the master database for a domain.
Domain Naming Master	The Domain Naming Master tracks objects throughout a forest to ensure that they are unique. It also tracks cross references to objects in other directories. There is one per forest.
encryption	Encryption is the process of disguising a message or data in such a way as to hide its substance.
Enterprise CA	The Enterprise Certification Authority is responsible for establishing and vouching for the authenticity of public keys belonging to users or other certification authorities.
ERD	An Emergency Repair Disk is created by the Backup utility. It contains information about your current Windows system settings. This disk can be used to repair your computer if it will not start or if your system files are damaged or erased.

Term	Description
ESE	The Extensible Storage Engine stores all Active Directory objects. It reserves storage only for space that is used. When more attributes are added, more storage is dynamically allocated. The ESE stores multiple-value attributes and properties and communicates directly with individual records in the directory data store based on the object's relative distinguished name attribute.
extensible	Administrators can add new classes of objects to the Schema and new attributes to existing classes of objects. The Schema contains a definition of each object class and of the attributes of each object class that can be stored in the directory.
extensible	Administrators can add new classes of objects to the schema and new attributes to existing classes of objects. The schema contains a definition of each object class, and each object class's attributes that can be stored in the directory.
forest	A group of Active Directory domain trees that share a common schema and configuration NC, but do not have a contiguous namespace.
forward lookup zone	A forward lookup zone holds the information needed to resolve names within the DNS domain.
FQDN	The Fully Qualified Domain Name is a DNS name that uniquely identifies the computer on the network. By default, it is a concatenation of the host name, the primary DNS suffix, and a period. For example, an FQDN might be sales.mycompany.com.
FSMO	The Flexible Single Master Operation designates a server that performs one of the following roles: PDC Master, Infrastructure Manager, RID Manager, Schema Manager or Domain Naming Master.
full computer name	The full computer name is a type of FQDN. A computer can be identified by more than one FQDN. However, only the FQDN that is a concatenation of the host name and the primary DNS suffix is the full computer name.

Term	Description
garbage collection	Garbage collection is Active Directory's automated database cleanup. By default, this happens every 12 hours and deletes old log files, tombstones and defragments the database file.
Global Catalog (GC)	Built automatically by the Active Directory replication system, the Global Catalog contains a partial replica of every Windows 2000 domain in the directory. When given one or more attributes of the target object, the GC lets users and applications find objects quickly, without knowing what domain they occupy. The attributes in the global catalog are those used most frequently in search operations, and those required to locate a full replica of the object.
GPE	The Group Policy Editor is run from the command line. It is a user interface to modify policy for objects.
GPO	Group Policy Objects are a collection of Group Policy settings and the documents created by the Group Policy snap-in. They are stored at the domain level, and they affect users and computers contained in sites, domains and OUs. Each Windows 2000 computer has one group of settings stored locally, called the local Group Policy object.
Group Policy	A Group Policy is a tool defining and controlling how programs, network resources, and the operating system operate for users and computers in an organization. Group Policy is applied to users or computers on the basis of their membership in sites, domains or OUs.
groups	Groups are Active Directory objects that can contain users, contacts, computers and other groups. In Windows 2000. Like user and computer accounts, groups are Windows 2000 security principals; they are directory objects and SIDs are assigned to them at creation.
GUI	Graphical User Interface is the computer environment that uses graphical image interface.
GUID	The Globally Unique Identifier distinguishes the type of object or attribute, and is part of the ACE.
HTML	The HyperText Markup Language is used to create Web pages with hyperlinks and markup for text formatting.

Term	Description
IETF	The Internet Engineering Task Force is a group that maintains Internet standards through the use of vendors and researchers.
IIS	Internet Information Server is a Microsoft Web server which operates on Microsoft Windows NT 4.0 platforms.
Infrastructure Master	The Infrastructure Master tracks the object references among domains and maintains a list of the deleted child objects. There is one infrastructure master per domain.
InterNIC	The InterNIC is a database managed by AT&T that allows the public to search for and register a domain name and IP address for the purpose of setting up a Web site. The database provides search capabilities to discover if a name is already in use.
inter-site	Term used for replication that occurs between sites.
IP	The Internet Protocol is a routable protocol in charge of IP addressing, routing, and the fragmentation and reassembly of IP packets. It is used widely on the Internet for the exchange of information.
JScript	Java Script is a cross-platform programming language from Sun Microsystems that can be used to create animations and interactive features.
KCC	The Knowledge Consistency Checker is a service that automatically generates a replication topology. It runs on all domain controllers and automatically establishes connections between the machines in a site. When replication within a site becomes impossible or has a single point of failure, the KCC steps in and establishes as many new connection objects as necessary to resume Active Directory replication.
LAN	A Local Area Network is a group of computers and other devices connected by a communications link that allows one device to interact with any other on the network over a relatively limited area.
latency	The time lag between the beginning of a request for data and the moment it begins to be received. The time necessary for a packet of data to travel across a network.

Term	Description
LDAP	Lightweight Directory Access Protocol version 3 is the primary access protocol for Active Directory. LDAP is defined by a set of Proposed Standard documents in Internet Engineering Task Force (IETF) RFC 2251.
LMHosts	A LM Hosts file displays computer names (NetBIOS) and IP addresses of accessible computers on your network. It is a plain text file that maps IP addresses to computer friendly names.
load balancing	Load balancing is a method used by Windows Clustering to gauge the operation of a server-based program, such as a Web server and spreads out its client requests across multiple servers within the cluster. Each host can spell out the load percentage that it will handle, or the load can be equally distributed across all the hosts. If a host fails, Windows Clustering dynamically redistributes the load among the remaining hosts.
log file	A log file stores messages generated by an application, service or operating system. These messages track the operations performed. Log files are usually plain text (ASCII) files and often have a .log extension. In Backup, the log file contains a record of the date the tapes were created and the names of files and directories successfully backed up and restored.
logical components	Active Directory uses the logical and physical components to build a directory structure to match the needs of your organization. The Active Directory logical components are domainsibid.com, organizational units, trees and forests.
MDAC	Microsoft Data Access Components are technologies that allow Universal Data Access. You can use these data-driver client/server applications through the Web or a LAN to easily integrate information from a variety of sources, both relational (SQL) and nonrelational.
Microsoft Jet Database engine	The Microsoft Jet database engine is a database management system that retrieves data from and stores data in user and system databases.

Term	Description
MMC	The Microsoft Management Console is a framework for administrative consoles. A console has one or more windows that can provide views of the console tree and the administrative properties, services, and events that are acted on by the items in the console tree. The main MMC window provides commands and tools for authoring consoles.
MSDN	The Microsoft Developer Network is a resource for developers when they want to find timely, comprehensive development resources for creating applications. It includes software subscription programs, technical Web sites, conferences, membership programs, communities, and more.
multimaster replication	A replication model in which any domain controller accepts and replicates directory changes to any other domain controller. This differs from other replication models in which the computer stores the single modifiable copy of the directory and other computers store backup copies.
Multiple Master Domain Model	A domain model in which there are multiple master user domains and an administrative hierarchy.
namespace	Active Directory and DNS are both namespaces. A namespace is a set of distinct names for the resources in a network. The names in a namespace can be resolved to the objects they represent.
NC	In Active Directory, Naming Context is any contiguous branch, or a subtree within a tree.
NetBIOS	The Network Basic Input/Output System is an application programming interface that provides a set of commands for requesting legacy network services.
NetBIOS name	The NetBIOS name is used to uniquely identify the NetBIOS services listening on the first IP address that is bound to an adapter. This unique NetBIOS name is resolved to the IP address of the server through broadcast, WINS, or the LMHosts file.

Term	Description
NetBIOS name	The NetBIOS name is used to uniquely identify the NetBIOS services listening on the first IP address that is bound to an adapter. This unique NetBIOS name is resolved to the IP address of the server through broadcast, WINS, or the LMHosts file.
NT	New Technologies is Microsoft's version of Windows before Windows 2000. Windows 2000 was built on NT technology.
NTDS	The Windows New Technology Directory Server is a contiguous subtree of the directory that forms a unit of replication.
NTDSUTIL.EXE	A command line tool for database and FSMO management and is available in the Windows 2000 Resource Kit.
NTFS	New Technologies File System is a file system that is designed for Windows 2000 and supports many features, such as file system security, Unicode, recoverability and long file names. It also stores an Access Control List (ACL) with every file and folder.
object	An objects can be a file, folder, shared folder or printer, described by a named set of attributes. For example, the attributes of a File object include its name, location and size; the attributes of an Active Directory user object could contain the user's first name, last name and e-mail address.
one-way trust	This is a trust relationship where only one of the two domains trusts the other domain. All one-way trusts are non-transitive.
operations master role	The operations masters are domain controllers that have been assigned one or more special roles in an Active Directory domain. The domain controllers assigned these roles perform operations that are single master (not permitted to occur at different places on the network at the same time). The domain controller that controls the particular operation owns the operations master role for that operation. The ownership of these operations master roles can be transferred to other domain controllers.

Term	Description
OS	Operating System of Windows 2000 is a master control program written for a computer so it can manage the computer's internal functions. It allows a user to control the computer's operations.
OU	Organizational Unit is a container object that is an Active Directory administrative partition. OUs hold users, groups, resources, and other OUs. You can use OUs to delegate administration to distinct subtrees of the directory.
PCI	Peripheral Component Interconnect is a personal computer 32-bit local bus designed by Intel, which runs at 33 MHz and supports Plug and Play. It provides a high-speed connection with peripherals and allows the installation of up to ten peripheral devices.
PDC	A Primary Domain Controller must be installed before any other domain servers. The Primary Domain Controller maintains the master copy of the directory database and authenticates users. If the PDC fails then a Backup Domain Controller (BDC) can be made a PDC. A PDC can be demoted to a BDC if one of the BDC's is promoted to the PDC.
PDC Emulator	The Primary Domain Controller Emulator is the first Windows 2000 domain controller created in a domain. Besides replicating domain data to the other Windows 2000 domain controllers, it emulates a primary domain controller for backward compatibility with Windows NT. There is one per domain.
permission	A permission is a rule associated with an object to regulate which users can gain access to the object and in what manner.
physical components	Active Directory uses the logical and physical components to build a directory structure to match the needs of your organization. The Active Directory physical components are sites and domain controllers.
polling	Polling checks for changes in each directory defined in the connection agreement.

Term	Description
pre-stage	With pre-staging, you can predetermine a client computer network account identification to identify and route a client computer during the network service boot request.
publish	Publishing makes data available for replication.
PXE	Pre-Boot eXecution Environment DHCP-based remote boot ROMS
RBFG.EXE	The Remote Boot Floppy Generator tool (RBFG.EXE) for Remote Installation creates a Pre-boot Execution Environment (PXE) emulator that works on a supported set of PCI adapters that do not have a PXE ROM embedded on the adapter.
RDN	A Relative Distinguished Name is the name used to uniquely reference an object with its parent container.
RDS	Remote Data Service uses a technique where data is retrieved in a client from a server, updated and manipulated in the client, and returned to the server in a single round trip. You will often see ADO/RDS together since they are two components of Microsoft Data Access Components (MDAC).
Recovery Console	Using the Recovery Console, a command line tool, you can start and stop services, read and write data on a local drive, copy data from a floppy disk or CD, format drives, fix the boot sector or master boot record, and perform other administrative tasks.
registry	The registry in Windows 2000 is a database repository for information about a computer's configuration. The registry contains information that Windows 2000 continually references during operation. The registry is organized hierarchically as a tree and is made up of keys and their sub-keys, hives, and value entries.
REPADMIN.EXE	A command-line tool that enables replication consistency to be checked for a KCC recalculation. The switch /showreps displays a list of replication partners. The invocation ID is the database GUID and will show reason for problems.

Term	Description
replication	Replication is the exchange of updated database information among domain controllers so that all the domain controllers contain identical database information. There are several different methods of replication. Active Directory uses multimaster replication.
replication latency	Replication takes time. At any given moment, not all the domain controllers in your forest may have equal replicas. The delay between an action and replication throughout your network is referred to as replication latency.
RFC	Request for Comments pertains to an Internet standard whereby anyone can receive information about the Internet by submitting a request.
RID	The Relative Identifier is part of a security identifier (SID) that identifies an account or group. RIDs are unique to the domain in which an account or group is created.
RID Operations Master	The Relative Identifier Master tracks the assignment of SIDs throughout the domain. There is one per domain.
RIPrep	Using the Remote Installation Preparation Wizard, an administrator can copy the installation image of an existing Windows 2000 Professional client computer, including any locally installed applications and operating system configuration changes, to an available remote installation server on the network.
RIS	With Remote Installation Services software, an administrator can set up new client computers remotely. The target computer must support remote booting.
ROM	Read-Only Memory is a semiconductor circuit that contains information that cannot be modified.
root domain	The first domain created in Active Directory is the starting point, or root, of the Active Directory. All other domains derive from this initial domain. Only one name can be used for the root domain.

Term	Description
RPC	Remote Procedure Call is a protocol that allows a program on a server to be executed by another computer. Active Directory replication occurs using Remote Procedure Calls.
SACL	The System Access Control List contains a list of events that can be audited for an object. An administrator can audit all attempts to create a user object in a given organizational unit (OU) by creating an auditing entry for the OU. If the audit directory service access policy is enabled on a domain controller, then access to the audited objects appear in the security log of the domain controller.
safe mode	When you start Windows 2000 in safe mode, it starts without the network components and it loads only the basic drivers. This mode is used for troubleshooting the computer.
SAM	Security Accounts Manager is a Windows 2000 service used during the login process that maintains user information.
schema	A description of the object classes and attributes stored in Active Directory. For each object class, the Schema defines what attributes an object class must have, what additional attributes it may have, and what object class can be its parent.
schema master	The schema master is a domain controller assigned to control all updates to the schema within a forest. At any time, there can be only one schema master in the forest.
security group	Security groups have two functions, to manage user and computer access to shared resources and to filter Group Policy settings. You put users, computers and other groups into a security group and then assign permissions to specific resources to the security group. This means you can assign permissions to the group instead of multiple times to each individual user. When you add a user to an existing group, the user automatically gets the rights and permissions assigned to that group.
sequential logging	A sequential log is one that records transactions and events in the order that they happen. Unlike a circular log file, information in a sequential log is not overwritten when it reaches a specific size or age. Once it fills, it creates a new file.

Term	Description
SID	Security ID is a unique number that identifies user, group and computer accounts. Each account is issued a unique SID when the account is first created. Windows 2000 uses the account's SID rather than the account's user or group name.
single master domain model	A single master domain model is one of the four methods in Windows NT that you use to group domains for administrative purposes. User accounts and groups are in one domain, known as the account domain. The printers and servers are in resource domains. A one-way trust relationship lets users access the resources in all the account domains.
SIS	Single Instance Storage is the service that reduces disk space requirements on the volumes used for storing RIS installation images. The SIS service attaches itself to the RIS volume and look for any duplicates. When it finds one, it creates a link to the duplicate, reducing the disk space required.
site	A location in a network that holds Active Directory servers. A site is defined as one or more well-connected TCP/IP subnets. (Well-connected means that network connectivity is highly reliable and fast.) Defining a site as a set of subnets allows administrators to configure Active Directory access and replication topology to take advantage of the physical network.
site link	A link between two sites that allows replication to occur. Each site contains the schedule that determines when replication can occur between sites that a link connects.
site link bridge	The linking of more than two sites for replication and using the same transport. When site links are bridges, they are transitive (all sites linked for a specific transport implicitly belong to a single site bridge for that transport).
SMTP	Simple Mail Transfer Protocol is a protocol for sending e-mail messages between servers. Most e-mail systems that send mail over the Internet use SMTP to send messages from one server to another.
snap-in	A snap-in is a type of tool you can add to a console supported by Microsoft Management Console (MMC). A stand-alone snap-in can be added by itself, while an extension snap-in can be added to extend the function of another snap-in.

Term	Description
snap-in extension	An extension to a snap-in can only be added to extend the function of another snap-in.
SRV	A Service resource record used in a zone to register and locate well-known TCP/IP services. The SRV resource record is specified in RFC 2052 and is used in Windows 2000 to locate domain controllers for Active Directory Service.
subnets	Subnets group computers in a way that identifies their feasible physical proximity on the network. Subnet information is used to find a domain controller in the same site as the computer that is authenticating during logon and is used during Active Directory replication to determine the best routes between controllers.
system files	Files used by Windows to load, configure and run the operating system. Generally, system files must never be deleted or moved.
System State	For all Windows 2000 operating systems, the System State data includes the registry, the system boot files and the Certificate Services database (if the server is operating as a certificate server). If the server is a domain controller, the System State data also includes the Active Directory directory services database and the SYSVOL directory.
SYSVOL	SYSVOL is a shared directory that stores the server copy of the domain's public files, which are replicated among all domain controllers in the domain.
TCO	The Total Cost of Ownership includes the total amount of money and time associated with purchasing, configuring and maintaining hardware and software. This includes updates, maintenance, administration and technical support.
TCP/IP	Transmission Control Protocol/Internet Protocol is a set of software networking protocols used on the Internet. It provides communication across interconnected networks of computers with diverse hardware architectures and operating systems. TCP/IP includes standards for how computers communicate and conventions for connecting networks and routing traffic.

Term	Description
TFTPD	On the server side, this Trivial File Transfer Protocol Daemon services host's specific file download requests made by the client computer. The TFTPD service is used to download the Client Installation Wizard (CIW) and all of the client pages in the CIW during a single session.
tombstone	Objects with a tombstone remain in the database for the life of the tombstone (the default is 60 days) and are invisible to client requests. This process allows enough time for the tombstone to replicate to all of the domain controllers in the network. During garbage collection, objects that have gone past the tombstone lifetime are physically removed from the database.
topology	The relationship among a set of network components. In the context of Active Directory replication, topology refers to the set of connections that domain controllers use to replicate information among themselves.
transitive trust	A transitive trust is a type of trust relationship among domainsibid.com, where if domainibid.com A trusts domain B and domain B trusts domain C, then domain A trusts domain C.
tree	A group of Active Directory domains that share a common schema and a contiguous namespace.
two-way trust	A two-way trust is a trust relationship where both of the domainsibid.com in the relationship trust each other. In a two-way trust relationship, each domainibid.com has established a one-way trust with the other domain. Two-way trusts can be transitive or non-transitive. All two-way trusts between Windows 2000 domains in the same domain tree or forest are transitive.
UDP	User Datagram Protocol is a TCP component offering connectionless packet delivery. While it is direct, it does not guarantee delivery or correct sequencing of packets.
UNC	Universal Naming Convention is the full Windows 2000 name of a resource on a network. It conforms to the \\ servername \ sharename. UNC names of directories or files can also include the directory path under the share name, with the following syntax: \\ servername\ sharename\ directory \ filename.

Term	Description
UPN	The User Principal Name consists of a user account name and a domain name identifying the domain in which the user account is located. This is the standard for logging on to a Windows 2000 domain. The format is: user @domain.com.
VBScript	The Visual Basic Scripting language is based on the Visual Basic programming language, but is much simpler. It is similar to JScript.
WAN	A Wide Area Network spans a large geographical area and typically consists of two or more LANs.
WINS	Windows Internet Name Service is a Microsoft software service that dynamically maps IP addresses to computer names (NetBIOS names). This lets users access resources by name instead of forcing them to use difficult to remember and hard to recognize IP addresses. WINS servers support clients running Microsoft Windows NT 4.0 and earlier Windows operating systems.
WINS	The Microsoft Windows Internet Naming Service dynamically maps IP addresses to computer names (NetBIOS names). This lets users access resources by name instead of forcing them to use difficult to remember and hard to recognize IP addresses. WINS servers support clients running Windows NT and earlier Windows operating systems.
WSH	Windows Scripting Host is language independent so that you can write scripts in languages such as VB Script and JScript. Using WSH, you can automate specific actions.

Index

www.ingramcontent.com/pod-product-compliance
Lightning Source LLC
Chambersburg PA
CBHW080131060326
40689CB00018B/3752